The Director's Craft

The process of directing a play stretches from the first script reading to the last night of the run, and anyone planning to make this journey will find *The Director's Craft* an invaluable guide.

This book explains the key practical tools that one of the UK's most respected directors uses to approach her work with not only actors and production teams, but also the text itself. Katie Mitchell addresses topics as diverse as:

> **The ideas that underpin a play's text**
> **Preparing improvisations**
> **Twelve golden rules for working with actors**
> **Managing the transition from rehearsal room to theatre**
> **Analysing your work after a run has ended**

Each chapter concludes with a summary of its key points, making this an ideal reference point for those wishing to improve specific areas of their craft, as well as complete novices in search of a step-by-step map of a director's role.

Katie Mitchell has directed plays for the Royal Shakespeare Company, the Royal National Theatre, the Royal Court, the Young Vic and the Donmar Warehouse. Outside the UK she has directed at the Royal Dramatic Theatre in Sweden, the Cologne Schauspielhaus in Germany and the Piccolo Theatre in Italy. Her opera work includes productions for Welsh National Opera, Glyndebourne Festival Opera and English National Opera. She has received two *Time Out* Awards and one *Evening Standard* Award for Best Director.

The Director's Craft

A Handbook for the Theatre

Katie Mitchell

Routledge
Taylor & Francis Group

LONDON AND NEW YORK

First published 2009 by Routledge
2 Park Square, Milton Park, Abingdon, Oxon OX14 4RN
Simultaneously published in the USA and Canada
by Routledge
711 Third Avenue, New York, NY 10017 (8th Floor)

Routledge is an imprint of the Taylor & Francis Group, an informa business

Designed and typeset in Albertina by Libanus Press Ltd, Marlborough

Printed and bound in Great Britain by T J International Ltd, Padstow, Cornwall

British Library Cataloguing in Publication Data
A catalogue record for this book is available from the British Library
Library of Congress Cataloging in Publication Data
A catalog record for this book has been applied for.

ISBN 10: 0-415-40438-X (hbk)
ISBN 10: 0-415-40439-8 (pbk)

ISBN 13: 978-0-415-40438-9 (hbk)
ISBN 13: 978-0-415-40439-6 (pbk)

CONTENTS

PART TWO
REHEARSALS   113

PART THREE
GETTING INTO THE THEATRE
AND THE PUBLIC PERFORMANCES

PART FOUR
CONTEXT AND SOURCES

For Edie

ACKNOWLEDGEMENTS

With thanks to Ulla Aberg, Sebastian Born, Elen Bowman, Paul Clark, Will Cohu, Paule Constable, Stephen Cummiskey, Gareth Fry, Anastasia Hille, Nicola Irvine, Erland Josephson, Alena Kyncl, Ivan Kyncl, Clare Lizzimore, Struan Leslie, Michael Mitchell, Sally Mitchell, Vicki Mortimer, The National Endowment for Science and the Arts, Tatiana Olear, Vicky Paul, Sunita Pandya, Robin Tebbut and Talia Rodgers. Thanks also to all the actors I have worked with and all the directors I have taught. With special thanks to Lyndsey Turner.

The photographs in this book were taken by Ivan Kyncl, a photographer of genius with whom I worked for nearly 20 years. Ivan died suddenly in 2004 and therefore did not take any photographs of the production of *The Seagull* that I directed in the same year. The images you will see are a homage to his artistry and vision; I hope they will also inspire the reader with the possibilities of theatre photography.

FOREWORD
Nicholas Hytner

It is still the case that in the British theatre, most directors become directors by saying 'I am a director!' and hoping that someone will believe them. Some have been actors, a few have been stage managers, but most nowadays emerge from university bursting with ideas, but otherwise more or less clueless. If they are lucky, they are given the opportunities to discover how clueless they are; if they are wise, they start to piece together a version of how the theatre actually works; if they are talented, it's a mixed blessing, as they find themselves in the spotlight long before they've worked out how to deploy their talents usefully. They are encouraged to think of themselves as artists, but they've yet to learn the director's craft.

Here at last, is the book that lays it all out, from the moment the director starts to think about a play until the night it closes. There are many marvellous books about acting (some of the best by directors) and many inspirational books about the purpose of theatre. There are books about verse speaking, manuals about lighting and sound, and histories of costume. I have never before come across a book that so clearly and so rigorously insists on the practical necessities of a job that requires its taker to lead a team all of whom are more expert in their particular craft than their leader is.

When I was appointed Director of the National Theatre, it was one of my first priorities to make it a home to Katie Mitchell. Her productions had always struck me as marrying a seriousness of purpose and emotional intensity to a peerless theatrical know-how. I've not always agreed with her about a play, but I've never been less than gripped by the way she has gone about bringing it to life. Over the years, I've watched her continuing journey with unbounded admiration; and it hasn't surprised me that my admiration is shared particularly by young directors starting their lives in the theatre. They cite her as their guiding light more than anyone else (rather as my generation cited Peter Brook), and that's not just because she devotes more of her time to teaching than any other comparable director. Her productions never leave you in any doubt that what you're seeing is the consequence both of profound thought and ferocious attention to detail. Her creative life is marked by a passionate attachment to the boundless expressive possibilities of the theatre. It is wonderfully encouraging that so many young directors want to be like her.

Her book will help them, as it will enlighten anyone who wants to know something about the process of bringing a play to the stage. She covers more or less everything. It is detailed and provocative about her discoveries about how to inspire and guide actors. It is uncompromising about how all-encompassing a director's preparatory work must be, severe in its demands on those who want to undertake it. It offers advice on everything from the provision of tea and coffee in the rehearsal room to the conduct of technical rehearsals, and it insists on the necessity of merciless self-analysis at the end of every run of every play. Above all, it reveals that there are essential skills that every director has to learn. Ideas are easy to come by; everyone has them. Her emphasis is on what's needed to make them live on the stage. Katie uses Chekhov's *Seagull* as her test case, and it's a mark of the thoroughness of her approach that you could apply her processes to your own production of that play and come up with a production completely different from hers at the National in 2007. Where it wouldn't differ is in the integrity with which she insists you approach the job of directing it.

This book should become an essential guide for directors in the English speaking theatre.

Nicholas Hytner
National Theatre, June 2008

Endgame by Samuel Beckett

INTRODUCTION

Early attempts at directing can flounder because directors do not have certain simple tools. Without these tools, directing becomes a process based on chance rather than skill. The tools in this book will help you to make work that is closer to what you want to see – or what you have imagined in your head. It will also encourage you to think about directing as a craft, with skills that can be learnt and built up over time.

There are two broad schools of thought about the training of directors. Some think that directing is an inherent talent that can only evolve on the rehearsal room floor, during the process of making shows. Others think that it is a skill that can be learnt over time in an educational context. I am of the latter opinion and I find it strange that most actors, at least in the UK, undergo a structured training, whilst directors do not. I regret not having been taught myself and feel that the craft of directing, like acting, can only benefit from a preliminary training period. Many directors at the early stages of their career are overwhelmed by the expectation that they are somehow supposed to stand and deliver brilliant directing. A few basic skills might make all the difference to their confidence and ability to direct coherently. When selecting the exercises and advice contained in this book, I have tried to think back to the tools that I needed when I was starting out. However, it is important to differentiate between the productions I make and the tools this book describes. If ten different directors were to use these tools, the outcomes would be radically different. Nonetheless, there are certain basic skills that have to be put into practice in any production, whatever the vision, voice or interpretation of the director. It is these skills that I am attempting to isolate and describe.

The book outlines the essential practical skills needed at each stage of the production process, from choosing a text through to the final performance. The main emphasis is on work with actors. However, the book also includes the key steps in building a production with the members of the creative team. This includes work on set, costumes, lighting, sound, movement, voice and music. The only relationship that is not covered is the one with a living writer. I work mainly on plays by dead writers, and therefore have very little experience of working with playwrights on new plays. There are directors, like Max Stafford Clark and James Macdonald, who are specialists in this field and whose thinking and writing on new plays is expert.

Most of the tools described in this book come from Konstantin Stanislavsky's teachings, mediated by a secondary interpreter, and then test-run in my own work. Others come from my recent research into the biology of emotions. The rest are the result of common sense and hard lessons learnt on the rehearsal room floor. I have used a specific play – *The Seagull* by Anton Chekhov – to illustrate and describe the process I undergo when making a production. The play is translated by Michael Frayn and published by Methuen (1998) in a collection of four Chekhov plays (*The Seagull* is about the loves and losses of a group of close friends and family living on a rural estate in Russia). However, the tasks in the book can be applied to any material – be it Chekhovian realism, abstract texts by writers like Beckett and Pinter, or new plays – or even highly stylised work, such as eighteenth-century operas.

You can dip in and out of this book to solve immediate problems in your rehearsals or you can study it in greater detail in relationship to *The Seagull* – and thereby extract a more comprehensive view of the process. Alternatively, you could pick and mix elements from the book with ingredients of your own – possibly using ideas in the book to guide you through new challenges or strengthen weak points in your own process. Depending on what stage you have reached in your evolution as a director, it might help if you were to jot down a list of the strengths and weaknesses of your work before you start reading. That may give you a sense of purpose in reading the book. Also, try test-running the preparation tasks on plays that you are working on or thinking of directing to see if the tasks help deepen your understanding of the material. Nor do you need to subscribe to every aspect of the process I outline. If an exercise doesn't make sense to you, it might be better not to take it into a rehearsal room. If you use an exercise that is only half digested or understood, there's a real chance that it will end up confusing or frustrating the actors. This could undermine your confidence and their respect for you.

The book assumes that you are interested in building an imaginary world for the actors to inhabit, using ingredients from real life and circumstances suggested by the text itself. It also assumes that directing is a job that requires considered and careful preparation before rehearsals begin. The rehearsals themselves are critical, but you can save a great deal of time by preparing efficiently. Detailed preparation will ensure that you use the rehearsal process much more economically. Thorough preparation does not work against the creativity or input of the actors in rehearsals; instead it feeds, focuses and inspires the actors' work. Preparation also makes you more confident as a director and, in turn, gives the actors confidence in you.

Part I of this book covers the work that you do on your own before you start rehearsing, including advice on building the relationships with everyone involved in making the production other than the actors. Part II describes the rehearsal process, and Part III takes you through technical rehearsals, dress rehearsals and the way in which you might work on the performance during its run. Part IV describes the evolution of my relationship with the work and legacy of Stanislavsky.

First, here are some suggestions on how you should go about reading a play either when you are considering directing it or when you are starting to work on it. Before you can interpret a play you should find out exactly what it is made of. Resist the desire to rush at the material with your own ideas and step back in order to assess the ideas of the writer and what is actually on the page in front of you.

When reading a text you want to direct, you will often find that your heartbeat increases and your body temperature rises. It is a feeling akin to falling in love. You may feel excited and, as a result, you will not always read the text very carefully or slowly. Instead, your eye slides and skids over the words, every now and again concentrating on a section you particularly like. You jump over the sections that don't immediately interest you. 'I'll sort them out later,' you say to yourself. If you were to direct the play on the basis of these early readings, the performance would reflect your unsteady excitement and be uneven.

When I was directing Aeschylus' *The Oresteia*, I was particularly interested in the story of the sacrifice of Iphigenia. *The Oresteia* is a trilogy of plays and the story of Iphigenia's sacrifice is the engine of the first play. It is not the engine of the second play and barely features in the third. Other than Iphigenia's story, my interest in the text was sporadic and this lack of interest was finally legible in the production. The production became less focused as the evening progressed, the audience grew more restless and the characters who had no direct relationship to Iphigenia's story were neglected. My inclusion of a ghost who represented Iphigenia and wandered through the action of the trilogy was, ultimately, confusing for the audience. The production was an accurate reflection of my first over-excited and uneven reading of the text, but not a very accurate representation of the play that Aeschylus had written.

It is therefore important to read the text carefully and slowly in order to check that you are actually reading all its scenes and not just a few of them. Learning to do this with a clear head will also help you to make a decision about whether you actually want to direct the play.

Another obstacle to reading a play clearly is an affinity that can get in the way of your understanding of the text, much like the radio static that interferes with the reception of a programme you are listening to. Affinities are the things that you are drawn to in the play because they relate to your own life or how you look at the world. An affinity can be both useful and somewhat limiting. It is useful in that it could give you added insight into an aspect of the text or a character that you would not otherwise have. For example, you may decide to direct a play set in a doctor's surgery. If your father is also a doctor in real life then you will know quite a lot about the profession, both in public and in private, and this may help you to direct the play. But the same affinity that gives you a special insight into the life of a doctor could encourage you to make the action too close to that of your father's surgery or could stop you seeing other aspects of the play.

You may see this same problem interfering with an actor's work. For example, the actor playing Arkadina (who is herself an actor) in *The Seagull* might be drawn to the character because that actor has an obvious affinity with the character's profession and the emotions associated with it. However, that is not all that Chekhov requires the actor to play. Arkadina is also a mother who finds herself in a relationship with a younger man. Much of the action in the play relates to these roles as much as – if not more so than – her profession. The same is true of a director. A director might have an affinity with the theatrical aspects of the play, again for the obvious reason that it is their profession. This would mean that the other themes of the play – unrequited love, destroyed dreams and family – would be neglected. The production would be unbalanced.

When you are imagining a play in your head or reading it through, it is possible that you are only really imagining what the speaking characters will be doing or where they might be standing. In a play with a large number of characters, this means that you won't have imagined everyone on stage. Therefore, when the time comes to direct the scene, you won't know what to do with the non-speaking characters. This lack of attention to the non-speaking characters will be legible to the audience. So, you need to prepare the text by imagining every character at every moment, regardless of how much they have to say. Even if it is a smaller role without any text, like a maid or a waiter, the characters will be present on stage and what they are doing must be clear. In the first scene of *The Seagull*, for instance, you may forget that there are also workmen present with Masha and Medvedenko. They are behind the curtain of the improvised stage, working. When you prepare the scene, you may only work on what Masha and Medvedenko are playing. You will then turn up to rehearsals and the three actors who are playing the workmen will be ready to work and you will just look at them blankly. You will then have to come up with solutions on the hoof that may not be as thorough as your prepared work.

Learning to hold the whole picture of what the audience will see in your head as you read the text is critical. Do this by running the action of the play in your head as if it were a slice of naturalistic cinema. Imagine what the audience will be looking at frame by frame. Do not invent a complex sequence of pictures; instead, make the simplest sequence possible. Remember, this exercise is not about working out exactly how you will direct each scene – that is a task you will approach much later on in the process. Rather, it is about having a firm grasp on all the elements you need to attend to when you direct the play.

Visualising the action like this will also remind you to hold a consistent picture of place in your mind. When you read a play you can easily forget that a piece of furniture, or a location, like a lake, is permanently present and visible in a scene. You imagine these objects and geographical details when someone talks about them, but you might forget them when the subject of the conversation changes. Subsequently, you might not direct the actors to respond precisely and consistently to their environment. In one section of a scene a character may mention that it is hot, so everyone in that section starts to play the heat. Five minutes later the text will no longer be discussing the heat, and everyone will stop playing it – even though they are in exactly the same place and there is no change in the weather. This will confuse an audience.

Finally, remember that you are reading the play in order to come up with concrete tasks for the actors. So you need to practise translating your intellectual understanding of the material into specific tasks for the actors to execute. If you talk to the actors using the language of literary criticism or abstract ideas they will struggle to respond to your instructions precisely and, as a result, their work will be vague. Of course, most actors are perfectly capable of holding an intellectual conversation about a play, but that is not what they are in the rehearsal room to do. Their job is to slip inside the skin of a character and enact credible emotions, thoughts and actions. Your job is to get them inside that skin. Consider how you might give someone directions for a car journey. If you give woolly instructions of the landscape they are to look for, forget to tell them about a T-junction in the road, or talk to them about the purpose of their journey, they will get lost. The driver needs precise information with clear points of reference about roads, signs and landmarks. The clearer the instructions are, the quicker the driver will arrive at their destination. It is the same with actors. Part I of this book will show you how to extract information from the text that will help you to shape concrete tasks for the actors to do.

Easter by August Strindberg

PART ONE

PREPARING FOR REHEARSALS

Endgame by Samuel Beckett

Preparing for rehearsals

This section of the book describes everything you need to do to prepare for rehearsals. The goal of your preparation should be extracting information from the text that will help the actors to perform the characters and situations in the play.

When you look at a situation in life, you will notice that the behaviour of the individuals involved is determined by a complex set of factors. Think back to the last time you observed a couple in a room having an argument. Did you notice whether the room they were standing in was hot or cold, airy or stuffy? Did you notice whether it was a room in a house or a flat? Did you notice whether there were people near who could overhear or not? Did you notice the time of day? Did you have any future pictures about what the people were going to do next? Did you have any past pictures of events in the relationship that were determining the present action? Were you able to notice any of these things, even if the words the two people were saying to each other did not touch on any of these subjects directly? Did you notice what each of them wanted from the other person? Did they want to be forgiven or to be understood?

A lot of this information will be legible in what the couple do physically – you will be able to read information by how they sit, how they move, how they spread the butter on their toast or put their coat on as they are leaving. For example, if it is cold the two people will make involuntary and voluntary gestures to keep warm. If one person is late, their actions will be faster than those of the other person. Other information will emerge from how they talk to each other, whether quickly or slowly, quietly or loudly. The information this couple communicate about themselves and their relationship is therefore both verbal and physical. And if it is verbal, the tone of how they speak is as significant as the content of what they are saying.

When you read a play, it is a good idea to search for information about all the factors that create or affect the behaviour of the characters in the action of the play (or the factors that determine the changes in their behaviour). If these factors are not explicitly stated, you might need to read the scenes carefully to infer the precise circumstances in which the characters find themselves. The factors you need to search for come under the following headings:

Place: The environment the characters are in.

Character biographies: The events in the past that shape the characters.

Immediate circumstances: The 24 hours preceding the action of each scene or act.

Time: The year, or season, or hour the action takes place in, or the effect of the passage of time between acts or scenes.

Events: The changes that affect the behaviour of the characters.

Intentions: The pictures of the future that drive the present action of the characters.

Relationships: The thoughts about others that calibrate the behaviour of the characters.

There are, of course, other preparations that you need to make before directing the play and these preparations will be investigated in the chapters that follow. But identifying the factors that determine the behaviour and the actions of the characters should lie at the heart of your preparatory work.

The Maids by Jean Genet

CHAPTER 1

Organising your early responses to the text

This chapter is about organising your early responses to the text and building the world that exists before the action of the play begins. It has six steps:

Using lists of facts and questions
Organising information about what exists before the action of
    the play begins
Research
Answering difficult questions about the text
Place
Character biographies

Undertaking these steps will ensure that you have an objective relationship to the play. Your objectivity will help you to build a world that is specific and, later on, it will help you talk about the play in a way that actors will find useful.

Using lists of facts and questions

When you first start working on a play, you need a simple way of organising your discoveries and responses. Listing information in the form of facts and questions will help you to do this. Facts are the non-negotiable elements of the text. They are the main clues that the writer gives you about the play. In *The Seagull* they include things like 'Arkadina has a son called Konstantin' or 'Medvedenko is a school teacher' or 'It is Russia'. Questions are a way of notating the areas of the text that are less clear or that you are simply not sure of. Ask a question about anything that is not simple or clear. Questions might include things such as 'What happened to Konstantin's father?', or 'What season is it?', or 'Where is Sorin's estate in Russia?' Always write facts and questions down in simple and objective sentences. As a rule of thumb, if you are not immediately sure that what you have identified is a fact, turn it into a question.

Organising information in this way encourages you to hold an objective relationship to the material and inhibits premature attempts to interpret the play. Lists of facts and questions will be used in the exercises outlined in this chapter and in Chapter 2, when working on the action of the play.

Summary
Use lists of facts and questions to organise your responses to the text.

Organising information about what exists before the action of the play begins

Organising information from the text about what exists before the action of the play begins will help you to map the physical, geographical and temporal certainties of the play – and create a picture of each character's past. No rehearsal process occurs without the actors asking questions about what has happened before the action of the play begins, and it is therefore enormously advantageous to have a firm grasp of this information. This will enable you to address simple questions about place like, 'Where have I just come from?', or more complex questions about past events in characters' lives like, 'When did I first meet Trigorin?'

Use the facts and questions format to collect information about everything that exists or has happened before the action of the play. Make two lists: one of facts and one of questions. I call these lists the 'back history' lists. Facts include things like 'Arkadina married Gavril Treplev' or 'It is Russia' or 'Nina's mother is dead'. Every fact must be written down – however tiny. It might just be a brief and apparently irrelevant event like Sorin's description of how one of his deputy prosecutors told him his voice was disagreeable, or the fact that Trigorin's writing is translated into other languages, but each one matters when it comes to building a past life for the character. Questions include things like 'What happened to Konstantin's father?', or 'Where is Sorin's estate in Russia?', or 'When and where did Arkadina play La Dame aux Camélias?'

Remember, if you are uncertain about whether something is a fact or a question, put it down as a question. For example, you may want to put 'Arkadina played Gertrude in *Hamlet*' as a fact because she quotes from the Shakespeare play in Act One, but there is no direct evidence that she played Gertrude so it is best to write the question 'Did Arkadina ever act Gertrude in *Hamlet*?' Sometimes you will find that questions you ask at the beginning of the task are answered later on in the action. When this happens, cross out the question and add the answer to the list of facts. Remember, however, not to list any information about events in between scenes or anything that happens during the action of the play.

Here are the first few facts established by reading Act One of *The Seagull*.

It is Russia.

There is an estate, which belongs to Sorin.

There is a park.

There is a broad avenue of trees leading to the park.

There is a lake.

There is a platform, which blocks the view of the lake.

There is some shrubbery.

There are a few chairs and a garden table.

There is a curtain and it is lowered.

Masha has worn black for as long as Medvedenko has known her.

Medvedenko earns 23 roubles a month, less deductions for his pension.

Masha's father is an estate manager.

There are beggars.

Medvedenko has a sick mother, two sisters and a little brother. He supports his family financially.

Konstantin is in love with Nina.

Medvedenko lives three miles away from the estate.

Medvedenko has declared his love to Masha.

Medvedenko is a school teacher.

Snuff exists.

Masha has a snuff box containing snuff.

It is close.

It is evening.

Here are the first few questions established by reading from Act One.

What year is it?

Where is Sorin's estate in Russia? (Is it based on a real place that the writer knew?)

How large is the estate?

What was the normal size of an estate at the time in Russia?

What type of trees line the avenue?

What size is the lake?

What type of shrubbery is it?

Why does Masha wear black?

How much is 23 roubles worth in pounds today?

What was a teacher's pension at the time?

What would an estate manager earn at the time?

Does Masha have a job?

What is the illness that Medvedenko's mother has?

What are the names and ages of all Medvedenko's family?
What has happened to Medvedenko's father?
Where do Medvedenko and his family live?
Where does Medvedenko teach?
What was a teacher's life like in the Russian countryside at the time?
When did Medvedenko declare his love to Masha and what was her response?
How common was snuff taking at the time, for women and men? (How would you take it? What effect would it have on you? What size and type of tin would it be stored in?)

Listing these facts and questions will help you with any kind of text, be it modern or old. Here is an example of the first few facts and questions from Samuel Beckett's *Not I*.

There is a woman.
There is someone listening to the woman.
The woman was born prematurely by one month.
She was brought up in a religious orphanage.
What year is it? 1972?
Who is listening to the woman?
How long has this person been listening to the woman?
What is their purpose in listening to the woman?
What is the gender of the person listening?
What is a djellaba?
Who wears djellabas and in which countries are they worn?
Why did her parents abandon the woman after she was born?
How old is the woman now?
When did she wander in the field looking for cowslips? Recently or in the distant past?
What religious denomination was the orphanage?

You may be daunted by the number of facts and questions that emerge from the first few scenes or acts. Do not panic. The list will get shorter as you go through the play (unless your play operates outsides a linear time pattern). If your play is not written in linear order, it can help to cut and paste the scenes together in linear order before embarking on this exercise.

At the end of this process you have two long lists: one of facts and one of questions. Read each of the lists back to yourself and consider how your picture of the play has altered as a result. The list of facts will make you feel secure and confident about the certainties preceding the action of the play. It will give you a picture of the world in which the action of the play occurs. The questions will make you concerned about the amount of work you have to do to answer them all. Instead of worrying about this, try to see the questions as a means of deepening your understanding of the material and anticipating the concerns the actors will have about their characters or the world of the play. If something in the text causes you to ask a question, you can be sure that an actor will ask the same question in rehearsals. See this process, therefore, as one that enables you to think about a possible answer before the actor poses the question, or as a way of saving time in rehearsals.

By the end of your preparation, you will have answered all the questions on this master back history list. The different tasks you encounter throughout the next few chapters will help you to answer these questions.

Summary

Make two lists – one of facts and one of questions – about everything that exists or happens before the action of the play begins. These are the 'back history' lists.

Do not list any information about what happens in between scenes or acts or during the action of the play.

Read the lists back to yourself and see how your picture of the play has altered.

Do not worry about the length of the list of questions. See it as a way of usefully anticipating questions that will arise in the rehearsal room and deepening your understanding of the material.

Research

Research helps you know the play better, clarifies the world you will be building and makes you feel more secure as a director. It is a lengthy process but really worth doing. It will root your understanding of the text in a strong sense of the historical period in which the play is set – be that nineteenth-century Russia or twenty-first-century London. You will feel more comfortable about many tiny details in the script that were opaque when you first came across them. Good research will help you to answer a substantial proportion of the questions in your back history list. Remember, however, that you are not doing research to present a historical reconstruction of a period (like those stale period room displays in museums, with plastic dummies representing people). Rather, you are collecting information that will help the actors to say and do everything they have to say and do in the action of the play.

First, read through all the questions on your master back history list and highlight all the questions that need researching. Here is an example of the type of questions you should be highlighting:

What year is it?

Where is Sorin's estate in Russia? (Is it based on a real place that the writer knew?)

What was the normal size of an estate at the time in Russia?

How much is 23 roubles worth in pounds today?

What was a teacher's pension at the time?

What would an estate manager earn at the time?

What was a teacher's life like in the Russian countryside at the time?

How common was snuff taking at the time, for women and men? (How would you take it? What effect would it have on you? What size and type of tin would it be stored in?)

Now undertake the research necessary to answer each question. That way you will only research what is essential for a proper understanding of the play. If you do have a tendency to lose yourself in research, catch yourself at the moment when you are about to take a diversion and remind yourself to answer the question in front of you. Ideally, use libraries or books to answer all your questions. If you use the Internet make sure you check any facts from reliable printed sources. Always use at least two sources and make sure one is not copied from the other.

Here are some examples of answers to a few of the research questions.

What year is it? *Chekhov wrote the play in 1895 and the action covers two years. Given the fact that he did not stipulate the action takes place in the future, the simplest reading is that Acts One, Two and Three take place in summer 1893 and Act Four takes place in autumn 1895.*

Where is Sorin's estate in Russia? *In July 1895 Chekhov travelled to see his friend, the painter Levitan, who was staying on his mistress's remote estate, called Gorki. This estate was on the shores of a lake 50 miles from Bologoe and halfway between Moscow and St Petersburg. This seems to have been the setting that Chekhov decided on for* The Seagull. *Bologoe is about 200 miles from Moscow.*

How much is 23 roubles worth in pounds today? *In the 1890s 1 rouble was worth 3 shillings and 2 pence in the UK at the time and was worth approximately £11.01 in 2002. This means that Medvedenko would be earning £253.23 a month, Arkadina has about £770,000 in the bank and Dorn spends £22,000 on the Italian holiday he takes in between Acts Three and Four.*

At the end of this process you will have quite a few dates when specific historical events occurred. Put these events in chronological order. This will be useful later when you are working on your characters' biographies. It will allow you to see the relationship between historical events and the events in a character's life. Here is an example of some of the historical event facts for *The Seagull*.

1812: Defeat of Napoleon's army

1820–1880: Golden Age of Literature in Russia

1840: Zola born

1850: Maupassant born

1852: First performance of La Dame aux Camélias

1859: Eleonora Duse born

1861: Emancipation of the serfs

1865–1869: Tolstoy wrote War and Peace

1875–1877: Tolstoy wrote Anna Karenina

1879: Electric light was introduced into theatres, replacing gaslight and candles

1880s: Beginning of collapse of estates of landed gentry

1881: Assassination of reforming Tsar, Alexander II, and succession of autocratic Alexander III

1888: Tolstoy celebrated his 60th birthday

1889: Eiffel Tower finished

1890s: French company developed a monopoly on sulphur production and sales
Switzerland world leader in watch production
Rise of the Decadent School

1892: Maupassant attempted suicide

1893: Maupassant died

1894: Succession of Tsar Nicholas II, aged 26

Take a note of the research tasks that you think are particularly useful for certain actors to do and books that might be helpful to read. In *The Seagull*, the actor playing Masha can research snuff, the actor playing Konstantin can research Maupassant's response to the Eiffel Tower, and the actors playing Arkadina and Nina can read the book *Women in Russian Theatre: The Actress in the Silver Age* by Catherine Schuler, which describes how women worked in the theatre at the time. If you have a short rehearsal period, select one key piece of research for each character to ask the actors to do.

You will also come across photographs, paintings and sometimes references to films. Collect all this material to show to the actors. Still or moving images can be a very efficient way of communicating a sense of place, period or atmosphere. Many actors think visually and may respond more to images than words. This is also material which can help fuel the process of working with a designer.

Even if you are doing a new play, you will find that there are research tasks to do. In 2000, I directed Martin Crimp's play *The Country*, which was set in the same year. One of the characters was a doctor who regularly took heroin. Research questions that emerged included things like 'What is heroin made of?', 'What effect does it have on you?' and 'How would a doctor get hold of it without anyone noticing?' There were also references to the Roman ruins in the area where the characters were living. This gave rise to questions such as 'When did the Romans occupy northern England?' and 'Why did they build straight roads?' All these questions needed thorough research.

Even if you intend to change the setting of a play from the time the writer intended to another period, it is important to conduct research into the period the writer had in mind when writing the play. The research you undertake into that period will help you know what the pitfalls or problems are in making the transition from one era to another. Then you will have to do new research into the period you are going to set the play in. When I directed *Women of Troy*, written in the fifth century BC, I set the action in a contemporary warehouse. Before making this decision, however, I undertook detailed historical research into three specific time periods. This meant reading about the actual historical events in Troy, descriptions of the same events in Homer's book *The Iliad* and, finally, information about Euripides' own period. Supported by this research, I was able to navigate the actors through the sections of the text where there was the greatest tension between a historical truth and the modern setting – and we drew from all three historical periods to create a coherent imaginary world.

If possible, make field trips to places where the action is set. These trips offer a sensory experience of the world of the play that you cannot get from reading books or surfing the net. In 1993 I went on a field trip to Norway with the designer Vicki Mortimer in preparation for directing Ibsen's play, *Ghosts*. We visited Oslo, Bergen and Skien, where Ibsen was born. We took photographs, collected flowers and leaves, and even made recordings of bird song. The impressions we had of light, colour and the weather informed how the show was lit, designed and directed. It also provided useful visual material to share with the actors so that they could imagine where the characters lived.

At the end of these tasks you will have answered many of the questions on your back history list. Now you will be ready to answer the remaining questions about place but, before moving on, you need to work out how to answer difficult questions about the play.

Summary
Write down all the questions from your master back history list which need researching.
Use libraries or books to answer the questions. Be cautious about using the Internet and double-check all information from that source.

Put any historical dates you uncover into chronological order.

List research tasks which are useful for specific characters.

Collect all visual or film material you come across whilst doing the research.

If possible, make field trips to any of the places mentioned in the text that you can.

Answering difficult questions about the text

When you answer research questions you will always be satisfied by a clear factual answer. However, the remaining questions on your back history list will not be so easy to answer, especially events in the characters' past that the text does not give any precise information about. How, when and where, for example, did Trigorin and Arkadina meet? When and where did Nina and Konstantin fall in love? The text does not describe these events. In these cases you will have to rely on your impressions of the text to infer factual material about past events.

The process of inferring factual information from conversations containing no facts is what we do in life. Apparently banal human dialogue can contain a great deal of information if it is read correctly. Even if we are listening to two people in a cafe exchange a series of banalities about shopping or the weather, gradually information about their past crystallises in our mind. We might realise that they have been friends for several years or that they have only just met.

Use your impression of the text to answer the outstanding questions on your back history list. These questions need to be answered so that the actors have clear pictures of what happened in the past from which to build their character and relationships. A relationship in real life is a result of several events shared between two people over a period of time. Actors need to build the relationships between characters in a play in a similar way, by inventing shared pictures of past events that determine the relationship they have in the play.

An 'impression' is the term I use to refer to information that I derive from a reading of a line or a section of a play that contains no obvious facts. You might use these 'impressions' to piece together information about the characters and the world they inhabit. Reading the text carefully for the simplest or clearest impression of what the writer intends is an important skill to develop as a director. When you first try this it can be like looking through thick fog for a landmark. Your eyes can mislead you and you can see landmarks where there are none or discover that they were right in front of you all along. Try to take your time with this task and do not rush to solve things. Keep reading the relevant bits of the text until the fog clears and the possible meaning or meanings are revealed. Crucially, you should look for the simplest or most logical reading of the text rather than the most complex. This is because the simplest or most logical meaning is often what the writer intended and therefore the one the audience are most likely to hear when the line is spoken. For instance, there is no point deciding that Nina knows what Trigorin looks like and finds him attractive before the action begins, because in Act One she asks Konstantin 'Is he young?' and the simplest thing the line will make the audience hear is that she does not know what age Trigorin is or what he looks like.

Summary
Practise reading the text to infer factual information that is not directly stated by the writer.

Place

Place, like time, affects how we behave. There is a difference between having a conversation when we are standing in an open field and having a conversation standing in a stuffy office in a tower block. Building a complete picture of the place or places in which the action of the play occurs helps the actor enter and believe in the world in which their character exists. Organising your own pictures of place before rehearsals will make you feel as if you are constructing an environment that is solid and real, and will therefore prepare you to help the actors fully imagine the world of the play. This will give you confidence in handling the offstage world during rehearsals and help you to overcome any problems you may have when blocking the scene. 'Blocking' is the term used to describe how you make the action clear for the audience. I write more about this in Chapter 11.

When we talk about place we often use the phrase 'the fourth wall'. If you were to do a traditional design of a room in a proscenium theatre there would be three walls visible to the audience. The phrase 'fourth wall' refers to the imaginary wall that makes up the rest of the room but is not physically present. The phrase implies that the actor only needs to imagine what is on or beyond the plane that separates the action from the audience. The actor needs to imagine what is surrounding them on all sides. If the actor were to stand in the middle of the stage and turn 360 degrees, they should be able to tell you what their character can see all around them, like a view through a window, where a particular door leads or what that the attic is like above them. If the actor were to do this in Act One of *The Seagull*, their character would see the lake, the farm buildings, the house and the park (including the croquet lawn) and the sky above. The audience will see only a fragment of these views manifest in the design. Perhaps they will see a bit of the lake, the side of the house and a slice of the park. The only way they can see all the other things is through the actors. If a character behaves as if the things were actually there, it will allow the audience's imagination to see those places too.

Sometimes when you are watching a production you may suspect that the actors only have a partial picture of the place in which the scene is taking place. Characters enter a room and you can see they have a picture of where they have come from by the way they hold their bodies or dust down their trousers or rub their hands. But then they will look out of the window in the room and they will seem to have no picture of what they are looking at. These gaps in their picture of the immediate surroundings take the actors out of the imaginary world of the play for a few seconds, or even minutes. They may then betray themselves, and the production, by filling in the gaps with artificial or self-conscious actions or gestures.

Prepare the geography of the production by putting all the facts about place from your back history list onto a separate sheet of paper. In *The Seagull* these include the following.

> *It is Russia.*
> *There is an estate, which belongs to Sorin.*
> *There is a house; there is a dining room.*
> *There is a park.*
> *There is a broad avenue of trees leading to the park.*
> *There is a lake.*
> *There is some shrubbery.*
> *Medvedenko lives three miles away from the estate.*
> *There are five derelict estates around the lake.*
> *There is Paris.*
> *There is Odessa.*
> *There is Kiev.*
> *There is Moscow.*

Having completed your research, this list will now include new facts such as the average size of an estate in Russia at the time. Next, transfer the remaining questions about place onto another list. The 'place' questions in *The Seagull* include things such as the following.

> *How large is the estate?*
> *What type of trees line the avenue?*
> *What is the size of the lake?*
> *What type of shrubbery is it?*
> *Where do Medvedenko and his family live?*

Where does Medvedenko teach?
How far is the town from the estate?
Why are the five estates around the lake derelict?
Where is Odessa?
Where did Konstantin go to university?

Next, answer all the questions by undertaking further research or by reading the text for the simplest impression the words give you. At the end of this process, you will have one long list of facts about place. It will combine old facts with new.

The estate is about 24 square acres.
Lime trees line the avenue.
The lake is ten miles long and one mile wide.
The shrubbery is pampas grass.
Medvedenko and his family live three miles away in a village where Medvedenko also teaches.
The town is five miles from the estate.
The five other estates around the lake are derelict because of bankruptcy due to economic problems experienced by the landed gentry from the 1880s onwards.
Odessa is 200 miles to the south.
Konstantin went to university in Moscow.

You will see that there are ever increasing circles of place, like the ripples made by a pebble thrown into a pool. In *The Seagull* the circles of place are as follows.

The house itself.
The immediate surroundings of the house and the estate, including the lake.
The county, including the town, the railway station, and Medvedenko's school and home.
The Russian Empire, including the places mentioned in the play such as Kharkov, Moscow, St Petersburg and Poltava.
The world outside Russia, which includes countries such as Italy and France, which are referred to in the play.

Every play you read will have a series of circles of place like this.

Draw a series of rough maps of each of these circles of place. These maps should be drawn without the audience in mind – as if they were plans of real places that existed in real time. For example, draw the ground plan of Sorin's house by combining facts in the text with research into estate houses of the time. Or draw a map of the estate that the house is on. Or find a modern-day map of Russia and mark on it all the places mentioned in the text. Then find pictures of these places. If the places referred to are imaginary, then find images that could represent those places. For instance, with *The Tempest*, you might want to find some pictures of a real island that has all the geographic elements the text of the play describes. The maps and images of the nearest circles of place, like the house or estate in *The Seagull*, will provide the basis for the design process. The maps of the wider circles of place, like the Russian Empire, will provide the actors with a picture of places they talk about in the action but which the audience do not see.

In life, when we mention a town or place we know, a picture appears in our mind. If I say 'Birmingham', I have a picture of Spaghetti Junction, or if I say 'Moscow', I have a picture of snow on an onion church dome. When you observe someone talk about a place you will notice that they are seeing the picture they have of it as they talk. This is evident in their tone of voice, their eye line, the angle of their head and the way they hold their body. This is the case whatever attitude they have to the place. Similarly, characters in a play have pictures in their heads when they mention places like Kharkov or their own granary. The actor must have a picture in their head for every place that their character talks about or listens to – both near and far. If they see the place in their mind, then they will adjust their tone of voice and bodies accordingly. The audience will then have the impression that they are referring to real places.

Working on place is not just useful for old plays. New plays will also benefit enormously. If you are working on a new play, ask the writer questions about place to clarify where every scene occurs, or discuss the places referred to in the action but not seen. In *The Country*, Martin Crimp did not specify in the text where the play took place or the city the characters had come from. When I asked him about it he said he imagined the couple as living in North London originally and moving to Northumberland. I subsequently researched both places and his research helped me to guide the actors into the world of the play.

You need to do work on place for all plays, whether they are realist or symbolist in style. Even if you are working on a surreal play, like Strindberg's *Dream Play*, you will still need to build concrete pictures of place. In dreams, places are often made up of fragments of several real locations put together in an unexpected combination – we experience place as clearly in a dream as we do in life. Even on an imaginary island, like in *The Tempest*, the characters experience where they are as a real environment.

Now you have a clear sense of where the action occurs and the places talked about in the text, you are ready to study who is in the action and how they were shaped by past events.

Summary

Take all the facts and questions about place and put them on a separate sheet.

Answer all the questions by further research or by reading the text for the simplest
    impression it gives.

Draw maps or plans of all the 'circles of place'.

Find images or pictures for each circle of place.

Character biographies

Directors often avoid preparing information about the characters in a play, as they
feel that this is the territory of the actor and therefore an aspect of the text that
cannot be explored before rehearsals begin. However, careful preparation of character biographies will ensure you guide the actors in the right direction for the play
and avoid both of you wasting time going up blind alleys. Always measure your
suppositions about the past against what the character does and says in the present
action of the play. There is no point building an extraordinary past for a character,
then discovering that this colourful person cannot credibly say and do all that they
have to in the action of the play. Preparing a biography with this in mind will help
you to stop an actor from inventing a tuba-playing, ex-ice-skating manic depressive
from scratch in order to make their performance 'interesting'. The work you do on
your own is not written in stone. Details will change in response to needs or
insights from the actors in rehearsals. But you will have somewhere to start from.
Working through every character's biography also allows you to see the play as
each actor does – through the eyes of one person. This perspective prepares you for
the concerns and interests of all the actors in the rehearsal room. It also puts you
in the shoes of each character and stops you from making simplistic value judgements. Similarly, it helps you to see the logic between how characters interact in
the past and how they relate to each other in the present action of the play. If
you get the picture of what happened in the past right, it will make what the characters do in the play more accurate. For example, in *The Seagull*, if the actors playing
Trigorin and Arkadina have a clear and shared picture of how they met and started
their relationship, it will help them act their scenes together. If they do not have
a shared picture, or if they have different pictures in their heads, the relationship
and the interaction in the play itself will be, at best, confused and, at worst,
unbelievable. Working out what has happened in the past is therefore the first
step you take towards directing the action of the play.

Work on the characters in the order in which they are listed in the dramatis
personae. That way, your affinities will not draw you to analyse your favourite

character first and neglect other characters you are less interested in. Make sure you study all the characters in detail, even those with few details such as a maid or waiter. Make sure that you go for the simplest and most logical impressions of what happened in each character's past.

Start with the first character and return to your back history list of facts and questions. Put all the facts about that character on a separate sheet. Here is the list of facts about Arkadina.

> Arkadina's son is called Konstantin and her brother is called Sorin.
> Arkadina is an actress and has been in a play called La Dame aux Camélias.
> People write about Arkadina and Trigorin in the papers.
> Arkadina has 70,000 roubles in a bank in Odessa.
> Arkadina is 43 years old.
> Arkadina was 18 years old when she gave birth to Konstantin.
> Arkadina is in a relationship with a writer called Trigorin.
> Arkadina was married to a well-known actor from a shopkeeping family in Kiev.
> In 1873 at the fair in Poltava, Arkadina gave a performance. She was 23 years old and her son was five years old.
> Arkadina used to work for the State Theatre and lived at that time in a block of flats with a courtyard. There was also a washerwoman living in the block. One day the washerwoman got so badly beaten that they found her unconscious. Arkadina kept going to see her, took her medicine and bathed her children in the washtub. There were also two ballerinas living in the block of flats who used to come and have coffee with Arkadina. They were religious.
> Arkadina and Trigorin live in Moscow.
> Arkadina used to play the card game Lotto with her brother and mother when she was a child on the estate in the autumn.

Next, put these facts into rough chronological order. There will be very little straightforward information about dates and timescales, except things like ages, which will give you dates of birth. For example, Act One of The Seagull takes place in 1893 when Arkadina is 43 and Konstantin is 25. From this you can calculate that Arkadina had Konstantin in 1868 when she was 18 years old. There might be the odd mention of actual dates, but this is rare (although in The Seagull there is the mention of Arkadina's performance at the fair at Poltava in 1873). Your research will give you some clues. By establishing the age at which young men went to university and the average length of a degree course, you will be able to work out that Konstantin went to university in 1886 when he was 18 years old. However, there will still be areas where you have to rely on reading the impressions in the text. At this stage it will help enormously if you decide on the simplest version of events. For example, you might have to decide when the relationship between Trigorin and Arkadina began even though no date is mentioned in the text. This is Trigorin's first visit to the estate, so the simplest conclusion I reached was that their relationship was relatively new (starting under a year ago in 1892) and that this was their first summer holiday as a proper couple.

Here is an example of a simple ordering of events.

1850   *Arkadina born. She has an older brother, called Pyotr.*
Plays card game, Lotto, with mother and brother in the autumn evenings.
Meets Gavril Treplev, a well-known actor, who originally came from a shopkeeping family in Kiev.
Marries Gavril Treplev.

1852   *Premiere of* La Dame aux Camélias *in France.*

1859   *Eleonora Duse born.*

1868   *Konstantin born.*

1873   *Performs at fair in Poltava, aged 23. Her son is five years old.*
Works in State Theatre and lives in block of flats near washerwoman and ballet dancers.
Performs in La Dame aux Camélias.
Opens a bank account in Odessa and starts saving money.

1886   *Konstantin goes to Moscow University.*

1890   *Konstantin leaves Moscow University without finishing his degree.*

1891   *Konstantin goes to live with her brother on the estate.*

1892   *She meets Trigorin and begins an affair. She starts to live with Trigorin. The papers write about their relationship.*

1893   *Takes Trigorin on holiday for summer to her family estate.*

You will notice that I have also added in some facts that I came across in my research, such as the premiere of *La Dame aux Camélias* and the birth of the Italian actress Eleonora Duse.

Now jot down all the questions about the character from your back history list. Below is an example of my list of questions for Arkadina in *The Seagull*.

Why did Arkadina put her money in a bank in Odessa? Is it a tax haven?
Why does Arkadina not want to share her money?
What do people write about Arkadina in the papers?
How well known is Arkadina and what is she known for?
When did Trigorin and Arkadina meet?

When did the relationship end with Gavril Treplev? Is he alive or dead in 1893?

What kind of celebrities visit Arkadina's home?

How did Arkadina meet Gavril Treplev and where did they meet?

How did Arkadina become an actress?

Did Arkadina have an affair with Dorn?

Has Arkadina played Gertrude in Hamlet?

When did Arkadina start smoking?

Was Arkadina brought up on the estate?

How often does Arkadina go on tour and stay in hotels? Where does she tour to? Does Trigorin go with her?

How often does Arkadina come to the estate? Only in the summer holidays? What events is she referring to when she claims that she is insulted every summer?

How much does Arkadina pay for her outfits?

Where was the State Theatre that Arkadina worked in when she was living in the block of flats?

How old was Arkadina and her brother when they played Lotto with their mother?

When did Arkadina's mother and father die?

Next, answer all the questions. Sometimes you will not be able to pinpoint precise dates, so put down the earliest and latest dates between which the event could have occurred.

For example, the text that describes Arkadina playing Lotto with her mother gives the impression that she was a little girl but does not tell us precisely how old she was. I chose to date this event as happening when Arkadina was between five and twelve years old. You can decide on a precise date for the Lotto-playing with the actors later on in rehearsals. You might sometimes have to invent the dates or years when certain events occurred. Read the text carefully to ensure that your decisions chime with the impressions the text gives and always go for the simplest answer. Remember that it is impossible to make decisions about a single character without referring to the biographies of other characters. Make sure you cross-reference facts between the biographies of the various characters so that you make decisions that will work for everyone. Use these answers to flesh out your first sketch of the character's biography. Here is a first sketch of Arkadina's biography after this process has been completed.

1850 *Arkadina born on an estate by a lake. She has an elder brother, called Pyotr.*

1852 *(Premiere of* La Dame aux Camélias *in France.)*

1855–1862 *Played Lotto with her mother and brother in the autumn evenings.*

1859 *Eleonora Duse born.*

1866 Her mother dies.

1867 She meets Gavril Treplev (aged 45) a well-known actor who came originally from a shopkeeper's family in Kiev. She sees him perform in a play at the theatre in the town Bologoe, near the estate. She runs away from her family.

1868 Aged 18, marries Gavril and her family disinherits her. Konstantin is born.
Gavril helps her to start her acting career, playing minor roles in productions he is starring in.

1872 Gavril dies, leaving her with nothing.

1873 Aged 23, performs at the agricultural fair at Poltava. Konstantin is five.

1874/5 Aged 24/25, works in State Theatre in Moscow. Lives in tenement block; cares for a beaten-up washerwoman. Two ballet dancers come round regularly for tea. She is poor.

1877 Her father, Nikolay, dies and her brother Sorin inherits the estate. There is a reconciliation between her and her brother.

1878 Konstantin and Arkadina start to visit the estate every year for their summer holidays. She meets Dr Dorn and has a brief fling with him.

1880 Her career starts to take off with a performance of La Dame aux Camélias and she starts to save money in a bank account in Odessa. It is a tax haven. She gets a nice flat in Moscow and starts to have fellow theatre artists, musicians and painters round. She takes up smoking. She has to pay between 300 and 400 roubles for each costume.

1880s Beginning of the collapse of many estates belonging to the landed gentry.

1886 Konstantin goes to university in Moscow.

1890 Konstantin leaves Moscow University without finishing his degree.

1890s Rise of Decadent School.

1891 Konstantin moves back to the estate where he lives permanently. Arkadina has refused to look after him in Moscow because he failed to complete the university course she had paid for.

1892 She meets Trigorin (aged 30) after a performance of Hamlet in which she has been playing Gertrude. He is looking for a new actress for his play. They begin an affair. She stars successfully in the performance of Trigorin's new play in Moscow. The papers start to write gossipy articles about her and Trigorin's relationship.

Autumn 1892 Trigorin moves into live with Arkadina in her apartment, thereby cementing their relationship.

1893 Arkadina invites Trigorin to stay with her on her family estate for the summer holidays.

This is the sketch biography that will be the basis of your work with actors in the rehearsal room. Repeat the same exercise for each character in the play.

Characters about whom there is very little past information need careful thought. If there are blank sections in their biographies, there is a danger that the director or the actor will invent information that will not help the actor act the play. Instead, you could try to find the simplest way of filling in the gaps. The character of Trigorin in *The Seagull* is particularly difficult to write a biography for. There is no information in the text about his family background, his education or how he became successful as a writer. Make some simple decisions. Assume that he is educated and has a university degree. Find out some basic information about nineteenth-century Russian education such as the age that children started primary school or began a university course, and add this to Trigorin's biography. Then read about how Chekhov's career as a writer developed and give Trigorin the same basic steps. Finally, give him a slightly different class background to the *milieu* in which we see him. One of the simplest reasons for people withholding information about their background is that they come from a different class. Chekhov came from the shopkeeping class, so make the same decision about Trigorin.

You also need to work on characters who do not appear in the action of the play but are strongly present in the minds of all or some of the on-stage characters. These characters are called indirect characters and their existence affects what the character says or does in the action of the play. There are people mentioned in *The Seagull* (listed below) who feature strongly in certain characters' lives; it is important to build a clear picture of them.

> *Nikolay Sorin*
> *Mrs Sorin*
> *Gavril Treplev*
> *Nina's mother*
> *Nina's father*
> *Nina's stepmother*
> *Medvedenko's father*
> *Medvedenko's mother*
> *Medvedenko's two sisters*
> *Medvedenko's brother*

As you are working through each of the characters in the play, take a note of facts and questions about the indirect characters. Once you have finished building a biography for the on-stage characters, start to build the biographies for the indirect characters using the same process. After you have gone through all the seen and indirect characters, make one master date sheet that combines all the characters' back histories. This will provide you with an overview of their lives.

Constructing a biography for each character before rehearsals begin will also help you when you are preparing to direct a new play. If the writer is willing, you can work alongside them to build these biographies together. You can also work on character in the same way for plays that are more abstract or stylised, such as those written by Beckett or Pinter. When I directed Beckett's *Not I*, I constructed the biography for the character Mouth in just the same way as I would have done for a character in a Chekhov play. I also use this process when working with singers on operas. Even though an opera is a highly stylised form, with repetitive musical structures, character biographies can really help root the singers.

By the end of this process, you will have a separate sketch biography for each of the characters in the play. You will also have answered most of the questions on your back history list of facts and questions. The outstanding questions will be answered in your work on immediate circumstances in Chapter 2. Chapter 5 describes how to deepen the work on character, by looking at relationships and planning improvisations.

Summary

List all the facts about each character on separate sheets and put each of them in rough chronological order.
List all the questions about each character on separate sheets and answer them.
Transfer the answers to your questions to the individual character biographies.
Work on the biographies of all the indirect characters.
Combine all the biographies into one master list.

A checklist of all the work done in this chapter

A master list of back history facts and questions: the back history list
A list of answers to all the research questions
A chronology of relevant historical events
A list of all the research tasks for specific characters
A collection of visual or film material
Documentation of any field trips
A list of facts about place
A series of rough maps of each 'circle of place'
A series of images or pictures of each 'circle of place'
A sketch biography for each on-stage character
A sketch biography for the indirect characters
A master list that combines all the biographies

CHAPTER 2

Organising information about each scene

This chapter looks at how to organise information about each scene so that you have some simple starting points for rehearsals. The conclusions you make can be jotted down on A4 sheets of paper and slipped into your script before the relevant scene. It has three steps:

> Immediate circumstances
> What happens between scenes or acts
> Time

Immediate circumstances

'Immediate circumstances' are the events that happen in the 24 hours or so leading up to the action of a scene. They might include what happened a couple of minutes before the scene begins or something that occurs on the previous evening. These events have a direct impact on the action of the scene and immediately give the actors something concrete to play.

When you write your initial back history list of facts and questions about *The Seagull*, you will notice there is a difference between the things that have been there for a long time, like a lake, and recent additions such as the hurriedly improvised stage. You will also notice the difference between events in the distant past that shaped the characters (like Arkadina's marriage to Gavril Treplev) and recent events that have just occurred to the characters (like the walk from which Masha and Medvedenko have just returned in Act One). Recent events or additions to the landscape, such as the improvised stage and the walk, constitute the immediate circumstances of the first act.

Because you have already answered the majority of questions on your initial back history list through careful research or by receiving simple impressions from the text, your list will now contain only the immediate circumstances for the first scene or act. Here is a list of the immediate circumstances for Act One of *The Seagull*.

There is a stage that has been hurriedly run up.

There is a platform blocking the view of the lake.

There is a curtain and it is lowered.

Masha and Medvedenko have been for a walk.

It is close.

It is damp.

It is dusk.

Last night Sorin went to bed at 10pm and woke up this morning at 9am.

There has been dinner.

Sorin fell asleep at lunchtime.

The performance of the play starts at 8.30pm and will last no longer than half an hour.

There are wings at the side of the platform.

There is no scenery.

The dog was howling last night and the night before. Arkadina complained to Sorin about it.

Nina has to leave after half an hour, at 9pm.

Nina's father and stepmother have gone out.

The sky is red.

Last night Dorn sat on the veranda talking with Arkadina.

Eight people have been invited to watch the play.

There is a large stone on the platform.

Here is a list of the questions related to these facts.

When was the platform put up and by whom? Why was it hurriedly done?

Where are the workmen from and what do they normally do on the estate?

What is the curtain like and how does it operate?

What day of the week is it?

Why did Masha and Medvedenko go for a walk and how long have they been walking?

What time was dinner and who was eating it? What did they eat?

Who invited everyone to see the play and when were they invited? What did Konstantin say to Arkadina about the play?

When did Trigorin arrive at the estate?

How has Konstantin been attacking Arkadina since she arrived?

When did Arkadina tell Sorin about the dog howling?

What season is it?

Has the dog kept anyone else awake in the night?

Why was the dog howling?

Does Konstantin know that Nina has to leave by 9pm before she tells him?

Were Nina's father and stepmother late leaving and is this the reason for her lateness?

Or is there another reason?

Where have Nina's parents gone?

Has Yakov rehearsed the technical effects with Konstantin? If so, when?

What were Dorn and Arkadina talking about last night on the veranda? Where was everyone else?

What time did Dorn leave last night? When did he arrive this evening?

What is Nina wearing to perform the play? Who made it or put it together? Is she bringing the costume with her or is it waiting for her at the house?

When was the white stone put on the platform? By whom? How big is it?

Next, use your impressions of the text to infer factual information with which to answer the questions. Then draw up a draft chronology of what happened before the scene or act begins. Here is my first draft of that chronology for Act One.

Mid-August
Friday
Late afternoon: *Konstantin and Nina did their final rehearsal of the play. Nina let him know that she would be free to do the performance tomorrow from between 8pm and 9pm. The play runs at just under half an hour.*

The night before: *Dorn and Medvedenko came for supper. At the table Konstantin invited Sorin, Arkadina, Dorn, Shamrayev, Polina, Masha and Medvedenko to see the play the next evening. He said that it was a bit of light entertainment lasting under an hour. Sorin went to bed at 10pm. Arkadina teased him about this and Konstantin told her rather sharply not to be mean. Dorn stayed with Arkadina on the veranda, talking until late, observed by Polina who was overseeing the clearing up of the meal and the preparations for breakfast. Everyone else had gone to bed or home. They caught up on each other's lives since they saw each other last summer and, in particular, Dorn updated Arkadina on how Nina's father had remarried and written her out of the will. Dorn left just after midnight. After supper Konstantin and Yakov worked on the special effects for the first time. They got the sulphur and spirits from Shamrayev and Dorn. The red spots are created by Yakov holding lanterns with red paper shades on the boat that he has rowed silently out onto the lake. The dog woke Arkadina up again.*

Saturday
6am: *Shamrayev and workers got up to start work in the fields.*

9am: *Sorin woke up.*

At breakfast: *Arkadina complained to Sorin about the howling dog for the second night running. Konstantin told her not to make a fuss. The dog guards the millet because there are* *thieves (as a result of the famine). No one else was kept awake by the dog because they are all so used to it.*

All day: Everyone in the household was busy preparing for Trigorin's arrival at tea time.

After lunch: Sorin fell asleep.

3pm: The workmen started to build the platform and put up the mechanism for the curtain that operates on a simple pulley system. They include Yakov, who is a household servant, and two serfs who had been doing the harvest. They were released late because the weather changed for the worst and everyone had to work longer to get as much of the harvest in before the rain arrived.

Late afternoon: The weather has got closer and closer with the odd rumble of thunder in the distance. Polina finishes Nina's costume and gives it to Konstantin. The white stone was levered onto the platform.

4pm: Shamrayev and Arkadina went to fetch Trigorin from the station.

5pm: Trigorin arrived on the estate.

6pm: Dorn arrived and they had lamb stew for dinner. Sorin, Konstantin, Trigorin, Arkadina, Dorn, Polina, Masha and Shamrayev ate it. It is close and damp. A thunderstorm is approaching. Nina's father and stepmother were late leaving for their visit to a neighbour for drinks.

7.30pm: Masha and Medvedenko went for a walk. Medvedenko wasn't invited to supper and he arrived early, so Masha had to get up from the dinner table and take him for a walk.

When you have finished your chronology for the first scene or act, work on the immediate circumstances of each scene or act that follows. There won't be any information from your back history list to draw on for the immediate circumstances of the subsequent scenes. This is because that back history list did not contain information about what happened between scenes; it was only looking at what existed before the action of the play began. So for the subsequent scenes you will have to read each scene and draw up two fresh lists about the immediate circumstances: one list of facts and one of questions. Then answer the questions and draw up a sketch chronology of the 24 hours leading up to the action of each scene. Make sure that affinities do not creep into this process – meaning that you only concentrate on what happens to key characters instead of all the people involved in the action.

At the end of this process you will have an immediate circumstances chronology for each scene or act. Jot down your first drafts for each scene on separate sheets of A4 paper and slip them into your script before the relevant action. That way, when you come to work on the scene, you can easily find your notes. Adding this information to your script will also help you to understand the material more precisely when you read the play again as a whole. The immediate circumstances – and later, your work on the events that happen in between scenes – will help you to understand the action of the play as a series of links in a longer chain of events. Some of these events will be seen by the audience in the scenes of the play and some will not be seen (because they happen off-stage or before the action of the play begins). However, for the play to function all the events must be fully imagined.

The chronologies can be changed later in response to observations made by the actors in rehearsals. If they disagree with anything, then you can easily make alterations – as long as the list of questions relating to the immediate circumstances of each scene is answered, agreed and played by the end of rehearsals.

Giving notes to actors about the way in which they are playing the immediate circumstances is one of the most efficient ways of altering what they do in the action of the scene. Learning to affect the action of a scene indirectly like this is one of the finer skills of directing – and can be easily overlooked. Directors can tend to repeatedly note the present action of the scene without these notes having any impact on what the actors are doing – or without creating credible behaviour or action. But an apparently tiny note about time of day or what the characters have been doing immediately before the action begins can alter the tempo, temperature and tone of the entire scene, and make the scene suddenly spring to life. Noting actors indirectly like this also leads to acting choices that last over a longer period of time. If, for example, you tell an actor to speed up what they are doing, the new speed will last for a couple of performances and then you will probably have to give the note again. If, on the other hand, you give a concrete instruction about the immediate circumstances (such as 'remember that Nina needs to leave at 9pm'), it will speed up the scene and last over more performances. This might be because it is more interesting to play an immediate circumstance than it is to play an anchorless note about pace. Try to become more aware of the relationship between immediate circumstances and how the scene will unfold. Check that your first draft of the immediate circumstances chronology will take the scene in the direction you want it to go on. If you give Nina, Konstantin and Yakov several rehearsals of Konstantin's play in the few days before Act One, then the performance that happens in the action of the play will be smooth and the characters will look confident. If, on the other hand, you give them only one rehearsal, then the performance will be jagged and they will all be more tense about it. Notice how these decisions help you to take the first small steps towards interpreting the material.

Finally, take a note of the events in the immediate circumstances that would be useful to improvise before you rehearse the scene.

Summary
Write a list of all the facts and questions about immediate circumstances relating to each act or scene.
Answer the questions for each scene or act, then put all the immediate circumstances for each act or scene in chronological order.
Put your proposal for the immediate circumstances of each act or scene on separate sheets of A4 paper. Slip the sheets into your script at the relevant point before each scene or act.
Note the immediate circumstances you plan to improvise.

What happens between scenes or acts

We all know how the passage of time etches itself onto our bodies and changes our behaviour. We may think we look the same as we did two years ago but, when we meet someone who hasn't seen us for a while, they might point out a lot of subtle differences in our tone of voice or how we hold ourselves. If we have experienced a difficult event during those two years (like Nina's loss of her child in the two years between Acts Three and Four) we find ourselves altered both physically and emotionally. The effect of these changes can be neglected by actors and some productions, subsequently, give the impression that scenes scripted as taking place over several years are all happening on the same day. This is because the actors do not have concrete pictures of the events that have taken place in between the scenes and how these events have changed their characters.

The immediate circumstances only cover the 24 hours leading up to a scene or act. In many plays more than 24 hours passes between the scenes and you will therefore need to draw up another list to cover these events. This list will contain the events that reshape the characters over a longer period of time, such as the two years that pass between Acts Three and Four in *The Seagull*. The actors will need to have clear pictures of these events and how they have affected them before they can start to play the immediate circumstances leading up to the scene. Notate these events using the tool of facts and questions. Here, for instance, is a list of information about what has happened between Acts Three and Four.

> *Two years have passed.*
> *The drawing room has been turned into a study for Konstantin to work in.*
> *Konstantin has a key to one of the doors.*

No one has taken down the temporary platform built for Konstantin's play two years earlier.

Masha and Medvedenko have married and had a baby boy. Masha is living with Medvedenko and they have employed a wet nurse called Matryona.

Konstantin has published his work in literary magazines. He writes under a pseudonym. His mother has not read his work.

Medvedenko has been promised a transfer to teach in another district.

Dorn has spent all his savings on his holiday in Italy. His favourite city was Genoa and he stayed in a hotel there.

Nina ran away from home to Moscow where she had an affair with Trigorin. Nina's father and stepmother disowned her. She became pregnant and had a little boy, who died.

Trigorin went back to Arkadina.

Nina made her debut as an actress at a summer theatre outside Moscow. She then went to the provinces. Konstantin followed her, watching her work. Nina took on big parts but played them crudely and vulgarly with a lot of large gestures and noisy speaking of words. Nina refused to see Konstantin whenever he went backstage at the end of the performances. The maid did not let him in. After a while, Konstantin stopped seeing her work and returned home.

Nina started sending Konstantin letters which she signed 'The Seagull'.

Shamrayev has had the dead seagull stuffed.

Sorin's health has gradually declined.

Here is the list of questions about the events that occur between Acts Three and Four of *The Seagull*.

What month is it? And therefore precisely how long has passed since the end of Act Three?

When was the drawing room turned into a study for Konstantin? What has changed? What has been added and what subtracted?

Why has no one taken down the platform on which the play was performed?

Where is the key to one of the doors kept? Why does he only have one key to one door?

When did Masha and Medvedenko get married? When did they have their baby boy?

When was Konstantin published in literary magazines? Which magazines was he published in? What is he paid? What is his pen name? Why does he write under a pen name?

When did Medvedenko get his transfer and where is he going? Who initiated the move? Has Medvedenko become aware of Masha's feelings for Konstantin? If so, how?

> When did Dorn go to Genoa? How long for? Why did he blow all his savings on this
>   holiday? Has his illness worsened?
> When did Nina run away from her family home? When and why did her family disown
>   her?
> When did the affair with Trigorin begin? When did she get pregnant? When did she have
>   the baby? When and how did the baby die? When did Trigorin go back to Arkadina?
> When did Nina make her acting debut in the summer theatre outside Moscow? When,
>   and for how long, did she tour the provinces? How long did Konstantin follow her?
>   When did he stop it? When and why did she write to him? What did her letters contain?
> When did Shamrayev have the seagull stuffed?
> What were the stages of Sorin's decline or were there none?

When you have answered these questions you can draw up a sketch chronology
of the events. Here is the chronology of the events that occur between Acts Three
and Four.

1893

September: Nina went to Moscow the day after Arkadina and Trigorin left Sorin's estate. She
went to the hotel that Trigorin suggested and booked into a room. She brought some of her
mother's jewellery, which she pawned to get some cash to tide her over. Trigorin then footed the
bills. Trigorin came and stayed with her on the second night and the affair began. Konstantin
followed Nina to Moscow. From now on Trigorin split his time between Nina and Arkadina,
trying to hide this from both women. Nina's father and stepmother disowned her.

Early autumn: Trigorin got Nina a small role in a production in a theatre outside Moscow.
Konstantin went to see the production. He went backstage afterwards but Nina refused to see
him. Shamrayev had the seagull stuffed.

October: Masha and Medvedenko married. Masha moved into Medvedenko's house with his ill
mother, two sisters and baby brother.

November: Nina conceived a baby.

Winter season: Nina went to work in the provinces. She took some large roles. Konstantin
followed her there. Trigorin repeatedly criticised her acting making her lose confidence in what
she was doing.

1894

June: Nina stopped work now that she was seven months pregnant. Konstantin found out about
the pregnancy and stopped following her. He started to write seriously – short stories. He writes
under a pseudonym.

August: Nina had a baby boy.

September: *Nina resumed work and a wet nurse looked after the child at Trigorin's expense. Konstantin had his first story published in a magazine in Moscow.*

October: *Masha conceived a baby.*

December: *Nina's baby died of dysentery aged four months. Trigorin left Nina and returned to Arkadina. Nina had a breakdown.*

1895
January: *Nina started work again in the provinces. Konstantin's writing career began to take off. Nina started to send Konstantin letters, in which she signed herself 'The Seagull'.*

July: *Masha's baby was born and they employed a wet nurse.*

August: *Dorn went on holiday to Italy for two and a half months. He visited cities like Genoa. Konstantin took over the dining room as his study. It meant he could easily go out into the garden. Arkadina's acting career began to slide downhill.*

September: *Sorin's health seriously began to deteriorate.*

Winter season: *Arkadina toured the provinces playing to student audiences in cities like Kharkov. Nina was due to start work in a provincial theatre in Yeletz.*

November: *The action of the play begins.*

Write a chronology for the action between each scene or act. Then put each chronology on a separate sheet of A4 paper and slip it into your script before the relevant scene. After you have done this, read back over the chronologies and choose the events that might be useful to improvise during the rehearsal period. For instance, it may be helpful to the actors to do an improvisation between Nina and Trigorin set immediately after their child was born to give both actors a clear picture of what went wrong with their relationship and why it went wrong. Similarly, it may be useful to do the improvisation of the reconciliation between Trigorin and Arkadina so that both characters have a clear picture of how and why they got back together.

Summary
Write a list of all the events that occur between each act or scene.
Write a list of questions about those events.
Answer the questions and draw up a chronology of what has happened between each scene or act.
Put each chronology on a separate sheet of A4 and slip it into your script at the relevant place.
Draw up a list of events to improvise.

Time

Time has a powerful influence on our behaviour. There is, for example, a difference between doing your ironing at midday compared to doing it at 3am. At midday you will be somewhat fresher and more focused than at 3am when you may well be suffering from lack of sleep. Similarly, there is a difference between walking by a lake in the autumn rain compared to sitting by it in the summer sun. You may walk faster and look at the view less in the rain compared to the leisurely pace of a walk on a summer's afternoon when there is also lots of time to stand and look at the view. There is also a difference between sitting and chatting when you have all the time in the world and when you have a train to catch in half an hour. These differences affect how we feel emotionally, mentally and physically. The playing of time is often neglected. You see scenes in some productions in which the writer intends that the characters are talking whilst operating under a time pressure where one actor is playing it and the other is not, or no one is playing it at all. This gives conflicting information to the audience, who might become confused about why one character seems to be hurrying while the other looks as if they have all the time in the world. Deciding on the time at which each scene is set helps you to avoid this sort of problem. It also binds all the actors together in the same world and gives the audience a clear grasp of what it going on.

Your work on immediate circumstances will include discoveries about time. Time includes specifics about year, month, day of the week, time of day and season in which a scene is played. Time information provides the director with some simple starting points for the actors and, in turn, gives the actors concrete things to do. This can be because the weather has a physical impact on them. Or because they have something to do by a particular time so that the time pressure affects how they behave. For example, in Act One of The Seagull the combination of the fact that it is evening, August, that the weather is close and that a thunderstorm is approaching immediately provides the actors with something to do during the action. They can fan themselves, swat mosquitoes or discreetly wipe away sweat. The degree to which they do this will depend on their health, clothing and insect resistance. In Act Three the action begins at midday. The horses are ordered for 1pm to transport Trigorin and Arkadina to the station where they will catch the 1.55pm train to Moscow. Time would be felt strongly throughout the act and would affect the characters more intensely as the action advances. The characters would start to check their watches frequently, speed up what they were saying, or look out of the window for the approaching carriage. A decision about time also affects the overall musical tempo of the production and is therefore another small step towards shaping the final outcome the audience will see. In Act One of *The Seagull* we know that the performance of Konstantin's play starts at 8.30pm. If you choose to begin the action at 8.10pm, the tempo of the scene will be slow. If you start it at 8.20, it will be fast. As you make decisions about time, start to think about their impact on the speed of scenes or sections of the show.

Put together a plan of time for the whole play by combining facts from the writer (we know that the performance of Konstantin's play starts at 8.30pm) with things you surmise or invent from the text, such as the decision that Trigorin's train arrives at 6pm in Act Four or that the action of Act One starts at 8.10pm. As you do this, remember that decisions about time will help you to influence both the pacing of individual scenes and the overall tempo and rhythm of the show. Noting time is another indirect way of determining the action of the scene – as you discovered with immediate circumstances.

Here is my time plan for the four acts of *The Seagull*. I have put everything I invented within these acts in a bold typeface.

Act One
It is 1893.
It is August.
It is Friday.
It is dusk.
The action starts just after 8.10pm.
The performance starts at 8.30pm.
Nina has to leave by 9pm. **Her parents are due back at 9.30pm. It takes 15 minutes to ride from her estate to Sorin's.**
It is close.
It is damp.
There is a thunderstorm coming.

Act One to Act Two
A week has passed.

Act Two
It is August.
It is a Friday.
The action starts at midday.
Lunch will be at 12.30pm.
Lunch is late. Normally it is served at 12.
It is very hot.

Act Two to Act Three
A week has passed.

Act Three
It is September.
It is Friday.
The action starts at midday.
The train leaves at 1.55pm. It is just under an hour's ride to the station. Sorin has
ordered the horses for 1pm. **The stone laying for the new government building is**
taking place at 2.30pm in town.
It is raining and overcast. Sometimes it gets so dark that you have to turn on the
lights inside.
The doctor was supposed to arrive at 10am.

Act Three to Act Four
Two years and two months have passed.

Act Four
It is 1895.
It is November.
It is Sunday.
It is twilight.
There is a storm outside, with driving wind and rain. The wind is so strong that it is
making waves on the lake and noises in the chimneys.
Trigorin's train arrived at 6pm. They will be back from the station at about 7pm.
The action starts at 6.45pm.

This plan anticipates episodes that could be slow, pedestrian or boring in performance. For example, the top of Act Four until the entrance of Arkadina and Trigorin could drag – especially given the amount of exposition it contains. Therefore, in the time plan Trigorin and Arkadina are described as due in 15 minutes. This decision will add edge and pace to what the actors do and therefore keep the audience engaged.

A writer like Chekhov pays great attention to time. This is not the case for all writers or all plays. If your play does not have any references to time, then make decisions about when the scenes take place before you start rehearsing.

Now put all the information about the time of each scene on a separate sheet of paper and slip it into your script before each relevant scene.

Summary

List all the facts that relate to time for each act or scene.

List all the facts that relate to time between each act or scene.

Answer all your questions that relate to time by making simple deductions about the text.

Map out all the decisions about time scene by scene.

A checklist of all the work done in this chapter

Immediate circumstances sketch chronologies for each scene or act

List of immediate circumstances to improvise

Sketch chronologies for the events between each act or scene (if the time that has passed is more than 24 hours)

List of improvisations of events that occur between the acts or scenes

Time plan for each scene

Three Sisters by Anton Chekhov

CHAPTER 3

Investigating the big ideas of the play

This chapter look at the bigger picture of the writer's relationship to the material, what the play is about and how to identify the genre. It has three steps:

> The writer and the play
> The ideas that underpin the text
> The genre or style of the play

The writer and the play

If you are working with an older play, written by an author who is now dead, first find out the basic facts about the author and ask: 'How do these facts shed light on the play?' For example, here are some key facts about Chekhov.

> He was doctor.
> He was a short story writer.
> He was a playwright.
> He owned an estate called Melikhovo.
> He had tuberculosis from his late 20s.

Here is how you might use these facts to shed light on *The Seagull*.

One of the characters in the play, Dorn, is a doctor, so you can assume that everything in the play relating to his profession is accurate. Similarly, you can assume that all the references to medicine, illness and the sciences are correct. For example, the physical symptoms of Dorn and Sorin's conditions will be precisely drawn, as will the psychological causes of Masha's alcoholism and possible depression. Of course, any writer who wants to include a specific illness in a play will research that condition well, but there will always be a difference between research and actual experience. The actor playing Dorn can read details about how, where and for how long Chekhov trained and worked to help build his pre-play biography. The writer's biography will also give this actor a clear idea of what it was like to work as a doctor at the time.

As a short story writer, Chekhov would have understood the difficulties of writing – both the problems of starting out (as in the case of Konstantin) and maintaining high standards later on in a career (as in the case of Trigorin). By 1895 he was famous, mainly for writing short stories, so he would also understand the impact of fame on people like Arkadina and Trigorin. The actors playing Trigorin and Konstantin can study his biography for information about how you begin a career as a writer, how much you get paid and so on.

As a playwright, Chekhov would be able to talk about theatre authoritatively and understand the difficulties of the search for new forms. Like Konstantin, he experienced an unsuccessful premiere with his first play, *Ivanov*, and it would be useful for the actor playing this part to read about the genesis and reception of that early play.

As the owner of an estate, like Sorin, he was plagued with inefficiency in the management of his farming concerns. However, as a more hands-on owner than Sorin, he could also be sympathetic to Shamrayev's attempts to save money and protect the granary. Both sides of the coin will be accurately drawn in the play. The actors playing Sorin and Shamrayev could study how Chekhov ran his estate to understand more about farming at the time.

As someone with a terminal illness, Chekhov's thinking about death will be higher than other writers. His thinking about death is obviously present during the action of the play in Konstantin's two suicide attempts, Sorin's gradual demise and the death of Nina's baby. However, it is also there in a hidden way in the number of deaths that precede the action and less obvious references to death during the play. Arkadina and Sorin's parents are dead, as is Arkadina's husband. Nina's mother died relatively recently, as did Medvedenko's father. Polina and Shamrayev only have one child which, given the time period and the absence of effective contraception, implies medical complications at the birth of Masha, or later miscarriages or child deaths. During the action, Polina's concern for Dorn's health in damp air implies that he has some sort of condition – possibly tuberculosis – which perhaps explains why he blows all his savings on an Italian holiday. The subject of death itself is also talked about quite a few times. The presence of this subject can be overlooked when you first read the play but, on a second reading, the frequency of references cannot just be put down to high mortality rates at the time. The fact that the writer was coping with a terminal illness should encourage you to read the text with this in mind.

Next, look for any details from the writer's life that talk specifically to the play. This could include real people that characters are based on, or events that happened to the writer which occur in the play. Find them by reading a biography.

In *The Seagull*, for example, several of the characters reference people Chekhov knew. Nina is based on one of his girlfriends (Lika) and Trigorin is based on a friend (Potapenko, who took Lika away from Chekhov). Chekhov was given an inscribed medallion by an actress, while the failed suicide drew on a real attempt by his friend, the painter Levitan.

Then look at what was happening in the writer's life at the time when they wrote the play. This can give you an idea about why the play was written. Finally, take note of everything the writer says about the play, either in books, newspaper articles or recordings. However, it is wise to approach their words with caution, as there will always be a difference between the play the writer claims to have written and the actual material. This difference was brought home to me when I was working with Martin Crimp on his play *Attempts on Her Life*. I listed the images that appeared in the play and counted the number of times each one was used. Unexpectedly, the most recurrent image was children. When I asked Martin what he thought the most common image in the play was, he confidently said war, then ashtrays and, finally, aeroplanes. When I told him it was children, he put his hands over his face and bowed his head. This outcome had never occurred to him consciously but, as soon as it was pointed out, he knew that he had put the experience of children at the heart of the play.

There is obviously a huge difference between undertaking research about a dead writer and working with a living writer, and, as I wrote in the introduction, the relationship with a living writer is not within the scope of this book. In my limited experience, you can ask living writers questions about the relationship between their life and the action of the play, but you should be prepared not to receive a direct answer – or any answer at all. Some writers will not reveal the private or personal motivations behind their work – understandably. Or they might not be conscious of them. Respect their privacy.

Remember that the attempt to create some sort of picture of the person who wrote the play – and why they wrote it – is essential, even if, like Shakespeare, very little factual information is known about the writer. Just spending an hour or so thinking about the tiny fragments of information known about a long-dead writer can shed light on the text. If no information exists at all, imagining the person who could have written the play and where their passions lay, will not be time wasted.

Finally, I would advise against reading any critical literature about the play or writer, unless the person writing has a firm grasp on the process by which theatre is made. Literary criticism may encourage generalisation and vagueness in your thinking about the play. There are always exceptions to this rule and some articles or books can be an invaluable source of information about a play or a writer. I find biographies of dead writers to be useful both in yielding information about the person who wrote the play and in helping actors to build their character biographies.

Summary
List the simplest facts about the writer's life.
Ask yourself how these facts shed light on the play.
Look for any details of the writer's life which talk more specifically to anything in the play.
Find out what was happening in the writer's life at the time the play was written.
Be prepared to receive no direct answers from a living writer about their personal life.
Read with caution any critical literature about the writer or the play.

The ideas that underpin the text

The ideas that underpin the text determine everything that is said and done during the action of the play, so you must have a firm grasp on them. There is, however, a difference between identifying these ideas and arriving at a concept of how you are going to interpret a play. A concept is something that the director imposes on a play. An idea is what the writer focused on whilst writing the play – either consciously or unconsciously. A word of warning though: do not mistake the search for the ideas that underpin the text as a licence to return to literary criticism or engage in discursive abstract debates. The process is simpler.

Most plays contain between three and four major ideas. Search for them by reading the play slowly and repeatedly asking yourself the question: 'What is the play about?' Answer the question with simple sentences such as: 'The play is about the passage of time' or 'The play is about death'. Avoid long-winded and complex answers. Write down all the answers on a piece of paper. By the end of the process you will have between five and ten possible answers. An idea must have a relationship with nearly every character in the play and large chunks of the action must be concerned with investigating this idea. Measure each of your possible ideas against the characters and the action.

When I first read *The Seagull* I was struck by how many characters were unhappy in love. I wanted to see if this was a possible idea and this is how I notated my investigation.

> *Arkadina:* The fact that she and Gavril are no longer together could be a result of unhappiness in their relationship. In the action her love for Trigorin is unhappy because of his affair with Nina.
>
> *Konstantin:* His love for Nina is unrequited.

Sorin: *His love for Nina is unrequited.*

Nina: *Her love for Trigorin is unrequited after the initial affair has ended.*

Shamrayev: *Perhaps his love for Polina is in some way unhappy because of her love for Dorn and the possibility that Masha is not his child. However, there is no evidence in what he says or does to suggest that he thinks like this.*

Polina: *She is unhappy in her relationship with Dorn, whom she loves.*

Masha: *Her love for Konstantin is unrequited.*

Trigorin: *His love for Nina peters out in between Acts Three and Four and you have to ask whether he is happy in his relationship with Arkadina after that.*

Dorn: *There is a possibility that his love for Arkadina is unrequited. Also, at 50 he is still unmarried, which might suggest some unhappiness in that aspect of his life. His affairs which took place when he was in his 40s probably caused some unhappiness for others.*

Medvedenko: *His love for Masha is not met by an equivalent strength of feeling from her, even though she marries him. They are clearly an unhappy couple in Act Four.*

Yakov: *There is no evidence that he is unhappy in love.*

Eight out of 11 characters are unhappy in love and two more (Dorn and Shamrayev) are possibly unhappy – although this is not stated explicitly in the text. In the action of the play we repeatedly see people in love, falling in love and being unhappy in love. Because it affects so many characters, and because it impacts on the action of the play, I decided that unhappiness in love was definitely an idea.

You might test-run the theme of death/illness because of your work on the writer's life.

Arkadina: *She has possibly lost her husband, and her mother and father are dead (although some time ago).*

Konstantin: *He attempts suicide twice, the second time successfully.*

Sorin: *He is ill throughout the play and has had a heart attack by Act Four, suggesting that he is close to death.*

Nina: *Her mother died before the action began and her baby son dies during the action.*

Shamrayev: *He was a soldier and was therefore possibly involved in military action where he saw people die. The absence of a second child may hint at a fertility problem.*

Polina: *She has only one child, which would have been strange at the time. Perhaps she lost other children?*

Masha: *She dresses in black as if she were in mourning.*

Trigorin: *During the action of the play he loses his baby son.*

Dorn: *His work puts him in touch with death and illness.*

Medvedenko: *His father died before the action began.*

Yakov: *There is nothing to link him to the theme of death and illness.*

Konstantin, Sorin, Nina, Trigorin, Dorn and Medvedenko have direct experience of death and illness. The other characters may have direct experiences of death and illness but this is not concrete evidence. Because the idea doesn't affect every character, you can choose to include it or not.

The four ideas I isolated for use in my own rehearsal room were: destroyed dreams, unhappiness in love, family and art. Notice how these descriptions reduce big ideas to simple and concrete phrases that the actors can easily grasp. However, do not think about this process as a reductive one that oversimplifies a more complex picture. Rather, see it as a way of efficiently mapping the intellectual structure behind the action. At the end of the process, ask yourself which of the ideas you have the greatest affinity with. Then for the rest of the process remember to work on all the ideas and not just that one.

Next, select the most important idea that you have identified. This will help you to understand what the play is about. Sometimes the key idea will stand out very clearly from the others. If it does not, return to the play and read it again with all the ideas in mind. Studying the action will normally guide you to the answer. For example, in *The Seagull*, I decided that the most important idea is destroyed dreams. If you have reread the play and are still struggling to select one idea, the title might help. Go through all the references to the title in the play and see whether they all point in the direction of one idea. For example, if you go through all the moments when the seagull is mentioned you will quickly discover that it is not only associated with Nina. It is also a symbol of dreams or ideals and, during the action, as it is shot and stuffed it grows into a symbol of dreams that are destroyed.

If you diagnose the ideas correctly, the process takes you deep inside the writer's head and it is crucial to honour these ideas – however else you may interpret the material. Chapter 10 will help you to use ideas in a practical and concrete way with the actors.

Summary
Jot down the ideas which underpin the text.
Check the accuracy of your choices by seeing that most of the characters have a relationship to these ideas and that large chunks of the action are concerned with exploring them.
Isolate the idea with which you have the greatest affinity.
Select the most important idea of the play in order to find out what it is about.

The genre or style of the play

Style and genre define the world that the audience see and the way in which the characters interact in that world. Working out the genre or style of a play you are about to direct will help you to communicate the material accurately. Each genre – from symbolism to satire, from black comedy to farce – has its own history and its own logic. For example, if the genre is realism (as in John Osborne's *Look Back in Anger*) the characters will obey the logic of real-life behaviour with the accuracy of a film documentary. If the genre is surrealism (such as August Strindberg's *A Dream Play* or Pablo Picasso's *Desire Caught by the Tail*), the characters will obey the logic of dreams, where the banal and the fantastical can co-exist in the same place unchallenged.

Realism and naturalism are the dominant genres in Western European theatre. These terms describe very different things in painting and literature, but in theatre, the words are interchangeable. Remember that actors from the West will automatically apply the rules of realism to a text, unless you guide them in a different direction. Know, however, that actors are more than capable of working with many genres – as long as you are clear about the rules of engagement from the outset.

A decision about genre should not remain as an intellectual cloud floating vaguely above the production or just hovering in your head; it must be translated into concrete action for the audience to watch. Start to think about how to do this. For example, I decided to direct *The Seagull* as symbolism; this decision required delicate handling at every step of the performance. There is, for instance, a stage direction in Act Four that Konstantin opens the window and a gust of wind blows into the room. In a realistic production this would be a slight and unnoticeable moment, but in a symbolist production it is an event that you must present strongly so that all the characters and, in turn, the audience experience the strange, premonitory disturbance that Chekhov intends. If you had to name the event, you could describe it baldly as: 'The writer lets us know that Konstantin will die soon.' I worked on a mechanism for the window so that, after he had opened it, it continued to bang. We put a large wind machine behind the window so that the curtains billowed. A tray with glasses on it fell off the table as a result of the blast of wind and Konstantin's papers flew across the room. If this were realism, you would not present it in this manner; it would be a more discreet moment where a window would open a fraction and perhaps one piece of paper would float to the floor.

You could also consider drawing up a list of concrete guidelines about the genre for the actors. For example, with surrealism you could jot down the following list.

It is like being in a dream. Strange things may happen but people might not comment on them, as they would in real life.

You pursue what you want with intensity.

You are often misunderstood by the people you are talking to.

Objects may take on a significance out of proportion with their import.

The physical laws of the universe may be subject to alteration.

Sometimes, it will not be possible to pinpoint the genre with razor-sharp accuracy. You may, for example, read one scene of *The Seagull* and think it is realism, then read another and have the impression that it is symbolism. What matters is that you read the play with both possibilities in mind and see what concrete evidence in the action of the play there is for either view – and then make a clear decision which you follow through thoroughly in the production.

Remember, also, that you can apply the tasks outlined in the previous and forthcoming chapters to any genre of play. Even if the actor is playing Big Foot in a play by Picasso, he needs to know whose foot he belonged to, how he became detached and what he wants at each stage of the action.

Summary

Work out the genre of the play you are going to direct.

Be careful not to direct every play as if it were realism.

Translate the intellectual idea of the genre into things we can see actors do or that entails a concrete change in the environment.

Draw up a list of concrete guidelines for playing the genre.

A checklist of all the work done in this chapter

A list of the basic facts about the writer and brief notes about how these facts shed light on the play

Documentation of how the life of a dead writer informs the play

A list of the ideas underpinning the text

A note of the genre

A list of concrete guidelines for playing the genre

Ivanov by Anton Chekhov

CHAPTER 4

Analysing the action of the play

This chapter is about preparation of the script and analysis of the action in the play. It has five steps:

> Preparing the layout of your directing script
> Giving a name to each act or scene
> Events
> Intentions
> Getting the text ready for the actors

Preparing the layout of your directing script

So far you will not have written anything into your text. However, at specific points you will have slipped several sheets of paper into your script giving you information about things like immediate circumstances.

As you start to analyse the text, you will begin to write on the pages of your script for the first time. Before you do this, think about how to lay out your script so that you give yourself enough space to write down everything clearly, and so that you can flick your eye across the page and pick up all the information needed quickly and easily in the rehearsal room when you are under pressure. Remember, also, that a clean and carefully laid out script will help you to direct more precisely and will give the actors the impression that you are organised.

If you are working on a classic play, never work with the book in which the text is printed, because there is not enough space to write clear notes. Instead, photocopy the text and blow up the print size a little. Put it in a file. It's best not to photocopy the text onto both sides of each A4 sheet. Instead, keep the back of each sheet blank. You can then use the blank page opposite the photocopied text to write down notes about your analysis of the play. Leave a big enough margin on the right-hand side of the text pages to jot down other notes. New plays will usually be laid out in a well-spaced script with blank pages facing printed pages. If this is not the case, ask the writer if you can change the layout.

Summary

If you are working with a classic published text, photocopy the text and blow up the print size a little. Don't photocopy the text onto both sides of the A4 sheet of paper.

If you are working on a new play, and the text is a little small or tightly laid out, ask the writer if you can change the layout and spacing.

Giving a name to each act or scene

The words 'Act One' or 'Scene One' do not give the actor anything specific to do in a scene; indeed, they underline the fact that the actor is in a play, not in a real situation. Instead, invent a new title for each act or scene that describes what actually happens during the action and that immediately gives the actor something concrete to play.

The titles should relate to what everyone does in the act or scene and should describe what happens throughout the act or scene, not just one moment of it. Try to make sure that the title is written as a simple sentence. Start the sentence with a noun and not a character's name; that way, everyone can have a relationship to the title instead of just one character. Most importantly, the titles should immediately give the actors something to focus on and do. For example, in *The Seagull*, rename Act One 'The Performance of Konstantin's Play'. Everyone knows what it is like to get ready to watch a play, however amateur or improvised. You check your watch, pick up the programme or look at the other audience members. By naming Act Three 'The Preparation for Arkadina and Trigorin's Departure to Moscow' you will ensure that everyone has something to do: they can pick plums for the journey, get books signed, try to find the right moment to say goodbye, help with the packing or moving of suitcases, or check their watches.

Be careful not to name the act by referring only to the event that interests you most. For example, you could name Act Two of *The Seagull* 'Trigorin and Nina Seal their Relationship', but none of the other characters are privy to the scene in which this happens so they cannot play the title. Instead, call it 'The Entertainment of the Celebrity Guests'. This describes what everyone is doing throughout the act, including the action in the scene between Nina and Trigorin. Try not to name the act by describing the effect you want from the action, like 'There is Fragmentation and Disjunction'. This is too abstract for the actors to respond to on a practical level. Similarly, do not use an idea you have isolated to name a scene, like 'Everyone Shows How Unhappy They Are In Love'. This is too vague and general, and will lead to vagueness and generalisation in the acting.

Finding an accurate title for each act is not always straightforward, as it can be difficult to see what is going on. You should always look for the simplest description possible and one that every character can have a relationship to. Be aware that the title will guide the actors to play the act or scenes in a certain way. The choice is therefore like giving a directing note and will have an incremental effect on their work on the scene.

Here are my titles for each act of *The Seagull*:

Act One: 'The Performance of Konstantin's Play'
Act Two: 'The Entertainment of the Celebrity Guests'
Act Three: 'The Preparation for Arkadina and Trigorin's Departure for Moscow'
Act Four: 'The Gathering to say Final Farewells to Sorin'

Once you have chosen the title cross out the words 'Act One' in your script and replace them with the new title. The title is useful for you, as well as the actors, in reminding you of what is going on. It is easy to get lost in the density of detail that a scene or act contains and forget this simple idea.

> **Summary**
> Give a simple name to each act which describes what happens in it.
> In your script replace 'Act One', etc., with your new titles.

Events

An event is the moment in the action when a change occurs and this change affects everyone present. 'Event' is really just a simple word for something that happens regularly in life. We regularly find ourselves trying to achieve one thing when something happens which changes what we want to achieve. It can happen when we are alone or it can happen when we are with other people. For example, a couple are on the sofa happily discussing a film they have just seen. Suddenly the man puts his head in the woman's lap, and says 'I can't go on like this'. The woman freezes for a second and takes a sip of her wine. She then sits up and pushes the man's head off her lap. 'I think you should go,' she says. 'I'm so sorry,' says the man. The event is the moment when the man puts his head in the woman's lap and says 'I can't go on with this' and it radically alters what they both want. Initially they both want to have a nice evening. After the event the woman wants the man to leave and the man wants the woman to forgive him.

Events have a whole variety of different forms: they can be sudden (such as if someone threw a stone through a window during a family meal) or gradual (as when a group of people in a remote building slowly realise there is a stalker outside). This 'gradual' event might start with the barely audible crunch of footsteps on the gravel outside and end with the definite sound of someone trying to unpick the lock of the front door. The responses that people have to these events can be slow or sudden, strong or weak.

On a simple level, a play is a series of changes that take place amongst a group of people. To qualify for 'event' status, a change must affect everyone in the scene in some tangible way. A simple example of an event in *The Seagull* is when Konstantin stops the performance of his play halfway through. Everyone is clearly affected by his action – whether they verbalise their reactions or not.

Analysing a text is about looking for where these changes happen. Go through the whole play and isolate all the events. It is often difficult to find events and it takes time to practise. Be reassured that all entrances and exits are events. This will provide you with a starting point. Do not worry if you cannot see all the events to begin with. The important thing is that you have started to look for the changes in the action. It may help to study events in real life and begin to notice how a change occurs and how it affects what people are doing.

Once located, the events provide you with a way of dividing the text into smaller sections to work on. When I first started directing I wanted to divide the text into small chunks but I did not know how to do it. Arbitrarily I put a line across the script once every two or three pages. I called these sections 'units' or 'beats' and rehearsed them as such. But the place where the line was drawn was not logical or useful to me or to the actors. Sometimes it was a downright hindrance, as it created a false stoppage in the flow of the scene in the actors' minds. It was only when Tatiana Olear taught me about events that I suddenly realised how to divide up the text using events as bookends of each section. For example, my first rehearsal section will begin at Masha and Medvedenko's entrance and last until Konstantin's entrance.

Events don't just alter what the actors play, they also affect what the audience see and often change the tempo of what happens. Using events to structure a play therefore makes things clear for the actor and the audience in equal measure. They are the most essential directing tool in this whole book – determining the variety, shape and life in the overall structure of the performance. When Tatiana introduced me to them in 2000, it was a complete revelation and my ability to structure and shape my work improved hugely. This way of analysing a play has also proved itself to be helpful for actors, because it is based on a simple and readily observable process that happens all the time in life.

Use only pencil when you ringfence an event in the script. Later on in rehearsals, the actors may point out subtle errors you have made and you may need to alter the positioning of an event – or even add a few more.

The text will always contain small and subtle clues that point you towards where the event is located. In the example below you will notice that the first event (Masha tells Medvedenko that she does not love him) is framed by two actions connected with snuff: the first is Masha taking a small fix to get up her courage before delivering the news about not loving Medvedenko; the second is a conciliatory gesture of offering him a pinch of snuff to try to repair the damage she has caused. Then there is the fact that the verbose character, Medvedenko, stops talking altogether immediately after the event. Finally, there is a pause carefully positioned after the event. These clues should help you to identify accurately the location of the event.

This is how your script might look with the first two events marked in it.

Act One

MEDVEDENKO: Why do you always wear black?

MASHA: I'm in mourning for my life. I'm unhappy.

MEDVEDENKO: Why? [*reflectively*] I don't understand. You've got your health. Your father may not be rich, but he's not badly off. I have a much harder time than you. I get 23 roubles a month all told – less deductions for the pension – and I don't go round in mourning.

[*They sit*]

MASHA: It's not a question of money. Even a beggar can be happy.

MEDVEDENKO: Theoretically. In practice it comes down to this: my mother and I, plus my two sisters and my little brother – and only 23 roubles a month coming in. You mean we don't have to eat and drink? There's no need for tea and sugar? No need for tobacco? I don't know how to manage.

MASHA: [*looking round at the improvised stage*] The show will be starting soon.

MEDVEDENKO: Yes. A play written by Konstantin, and his Nina will be acting in it. Two people in love, and today their souls will merge as they strive to create a single artistic impression. Whereas my soul and yours have no point of contact. I love you – I can't stay at home I long to see you so much – I walk three miles here and three miles back every day – and all I get from you is indifference. Well, it's understandable. I've no money – I've a large family … Who wants to marry a man who can't even support himself?

MASHA: Oh, fiddle.

[*Takes a pinch of snuff*]

I'm very touched that you love me, but I can't say the same in return, and that's all there is to it.   EVENT

[*Offers him the snuffbox*] Have a pinch.

MEDVEDENKO: Not for me.

[*Pause*]

MASHA: So close. We'll probably have a storm during the night. If you're not philosophising you're going on about money. You seem to think the worst thing that can happen to anyone is poverty, but I think it's a thousand times easier to go round in rags and beg your bread than it is to … Well, you wouldn't understand …

[*Enter, right,* SORIN *and* KONSTANTIN]   EVENT

Be careful you do not mistake a subject change for an event. For example, when Masha says to Medvedenko, 'The show will be starting soon', you might think that this was an event but I would disagree. It is an intensification of Masha's intention: to get Medvedenko off the subject of his recent proposal. Your work on the character biographies will also stop you from making errors. For example, you could mistake Medvedenko's words, 'I love you' for the event. A clear study of the scene for the events that precede it will help you to realise that Medvedenko has already told Masha that he loves her and asked her to marry him before the action of the play starts. Masha has not responded either to his declaration or to his proposal. Since that proposal he has walked to see her every day, waiting for an answer. Her words, 'I'm very touched that you love me, but I can't say the same in return, and that's all there is to it' – the event – is the first concrete response he has had since the proposal.

Once you have identified an event give it a simple and clean name, like: 'Masha informs Medvedenko that she does not love him'. Use cool words like 'inform' because you do not want to colour or influence how the actor might choose to play this moment – or to prejudge the characters in any way. Notice also that this scene between Masha and Medvedenko has other characters in it – the workmen banging behind the curtain. When you prepare the events and intentions for this scene you will also have to consider what they are playing and doing, and how it will support your analysis of the event. It may help, for example, to decide that they change their activity when the event occurs, perhaps changing from banging to sanding. You will also need to make a simple decision as to who can hear what, as this will affect how everyone plays the scene and the reaction to the event. Write down the name of the event in pencil, just as you drew the line across the page to ringfence the event. Again, the precise syntax of the name may well alter ever so slightly when you go through the script with the actors later on in rehearsals.

Not all events allow you to mark a clean and neat line across the page. Some might begin midway through a line or stage direction and finish midway through another speech. You will have to draw a squiggle around the relevant words in the play script rather than a line. What matters is that the words and actions inside the event are accurately ringfenced.

Here is a list of the events in Act One of *The Seagull*. If you want to practise finding events you can stop reading here and go through the text for yourself before comparing your results with the following list.

> *Masha informs Medvedenko that she does not love him.*
> *Sorin and Konstantin are heard approaching the auditorium.*
> *Konstantin and Sorin see Masha and Medvedenko in the auditorium, and Konstantin sends Masha and Medvedenko back inside. (The seeing of Masha and Medvedenko and telling them to go away happens in a split second, so it is one event.)*
> *Masha and Medvedenko leave the auditorium and go inside.*
> *Yakov informs Konstantin that he and the workmen are off for a swim.*
> *Yakov and the workmen leave to go swimming.*
> *Sorin asks Konstantin why Arkadina is out of sorts.*
> *Konstantin and Sorin hear footsteps.*
> *Konstantin recognises that the footsteps are Nina's.*
> *Nina enters.*
> *Konstantin informs Nina and Sorin that 'It's time to start'.*
> *Sorin goes back inside the house to fetch everyone.*
> *Nina and Konstantin kiss.*
> *They hear footsteps.*
> *Yakov informs Konstantin that he is behind the curtain.*
> *Yakov goes to prepare the special effects for the performance.*
> *Konstantin and Nina hear people approaching (I added this event as a reason for Nina and Konstantin leaving).*
> *Konstantin and Nina leave.*
> *Polina and Dorn come out from the house to watch the play.*
> *Polina challenges Dorn about his feelings for Arkadina.*
> *They hear people approaching.*
> *Arkadina, Sorin, Trigorin, Shamrayev, Medvedenko and Masha arrive.*
> *Konstantin comes out from behind the improvised stage.*
> *A horn sounds behind the improvised stage.*
> *The curtain rises.*
> *Marsh lights appear (these are stage-managed by Yakov and the workmen).*
> *Yakov and the workmen make two red lights appear on the lake to herald the approach of the Devil in the performance, together with releasing the sulphur.*

Konstantin stops the performance (this event is only complete when the curtain is
 lowered).

Konstantin leaves.

They hear someone start singing over the other side of the lake.

Arkadina reminds everyone of Konstantin.

Masha goes to look for Konstantin.

Nina emerges from behind the curtain.

Dorn suggests that the curtain is taken up.

Yakov takes the curtain up.

Shamrayev tells a crass joke.

Nina announces her departure.

Nina leaves.

Sorin suggests they go inside because it is damp.

Everyone except Dorn goes inside.

Konstantin enters.

Konstantin notices that Nina has gone.

Masha enters.

Konstantin tells Masha not to follow him around.

Konstantin goes to look for Nina.

Dorn throws Masha's snuff box in the bushes.

Masha asks Dorn to stay.

Masha discloses her love for Konstantin to Dorn.

Next, work out which event is the most important in each act and designate it as
the 'main event'. Isolating the main events helps you and the actor know how to
measure the value and weight of all the events in each act. Here are the main events
of *The Seagull*.

Act One: The cancellation of the play
Act Two: The refusal of the horses
Act Three: The announcement of the arrival of the horses
Act Four: The arrival of Trigorin with Arkadina from the station

You will notice that I have changed the way I phrased the main event of Act One
from 'Konstantin stops the performance' (the phrasing I used in the long list of Act
One events) to 'The cancellation of the play'. By rephrasing the event so that it starts
with a noun rather than a character's name, everyone can have a relationship to
what you are describing. Crudely put, if the main event was described with a
sentence beginning with the name 'Konstantin', the other ten or so characters
might think that this event was Konstantin's 'moment', and not consider fully what

their character's responses might be. The event only works if all the characters play it fully and clearly.

If you are working on a modern play that is structured as a string of scenes (rather than acts), try to look at the overall movement of the action before selecting the key events. Drawing one event up above the rest in an act or a string of scenes begins to help you sculpt the overall shape of the performance. One of the pitfalls in early attempts to direct is a levelling-out, in which all the moments in the action are given equal value by the performers. Instead, guide both the actors and audience to the most important events in the action.

Finally, every play has an event that takes place before the action begins and which sets off a chain reaction that leads to the events that occur in the play. This is called the 'trigger event'. In *The Seagull*, the trigger event is the announcement of the arrival of Trigorin and Arkadina on the estate. This is the moment when the letter arrives at the estate from Moscow telling everyone the news of the visit. It sets off the following course of events:

> *Konstantin decided to write a play; he asked Nina to be in it; Arkadina arrived; the auditorium was built; Nina met Trigorin, etc., etc.*

If Trigorin and Arkadina had not decided to spend their holidays on the estate, Konstantin might not have written the play, Trigorin wouldn't have met Nina, Konstantin might not have killed the seagull, Nina wouldn't have run away to Moscow and so on.

When you have isolated the trigger event, take a few minutes to document the events that happened as a result and the order in which they happened. Here is an example of that for *The Seagull*.

> **Over a fortnight ago:** *Arkadina persuades Trigorin to go with her on holiday on her family estate.*

> **A fortnight ago:** *Arkadina's letter saying she will be bringing Trigorin with her for her summer break arrives at the estate at breakfast time.*
> *Konstantin starts writing his play.*
> *Medvedenko proposes to Masha.*

> **A week ago:** *Konstantin asks Nina to be in his play.*

> **Three days ago:** *Arkadina arrives on the estate.*
> *Konstantin talks to Shamrayev about the workmen needed to build the platform.*
> *Konstantin's first rehearsal with Nina on the play.*

After you have done this, put a star by the events that you think might be useful to improvise.

Remember that there are no definitive answers and that you are only working with your impressions of the text. You could, for example, argue for a different trigger event, like Konstantin decides to write the play. The question is whether that would create the most dynamic playing of the scenes that follow and whether it makes sense of everyone's actions; that is a judgement you have to make. Choosing the right trigger event helps the actors enter the play through the right door. The trigger event is also an important one to put on your list of improvisations.

Events can be very useful when you are devising a piece of theatre. Instead of thinking in terms of plotting a story, focus on planning the changes that will occur. Organise your material around these landmarks. They also help when you are directing opera. In particular, choosing the main events in each act helps the singers grade what they are doing.

At the end of this task you should have a script with all the events ringfenced and named. These divisions will break down the text into smaller sections for you to rehearse. I describe how to draw up your rehearsal schedule around these sections in Chapter 11.

Now you are ready to start working on intentions.

Summary
Go through the text and isolate all the events or changes that take place.
Write a simple sentence to describe each event.
Select the main events in each act or series of scenes.
Isolate the pre-play event that sets the action of the play in motion.
Highlight the events which may be useful to improvise.

Intentions

'Intention' is the word that describes what a character wants and whom they want it from. In this process, the characters' intentions only change at events and the analysis of intentions will therefore evolve naturally from your study of events. Before rehearsals begin, try to work out exactly what each character wants in between every event in the play – and from whom.

When you are trying to identify the intentions of the characters, try to see through the surface detail of the words into the thoughts or desires that are motivating those words (or actions, in the case of stage directions). Identifying intentions is like taking an X-ray in which you see the bone structure under the skin.

If a character does not speak in a section between events you must still find an intention for them. People can often use silence in a very active way to have a strong impact on others.

I always find the preparation of intentions an enormously difficult task and I often procrastinate about doing it. This is because I know that the ability to diagnose an intention lies at the heart of the work we do with actors. Work on intentions helps directors to answer the most difficult questions an actor can ask: 'Why does my character do this?' and 'Why does my character say this?' If I do not prepare intentions, I know that I will waste valuable time in rehearsals debating character motivation. Of course, preparing intentions will not rule out debate entirely but it will definitely limit it to something more helpful and manageable.

Here are some tips about your work on intentions.

First, be careful not to mistake a subject change for a new intention. Characters can change subject repeatedly in order to achieve one intention. For example, in the opening scene of *The Seagull*, Masha changes the subject when she says 'The show will be starting soon', but this is just another tactic in her overall intention to get Medvedenko off the subject of love.

Second, remember that intentions have to emerge from the logic of the situation. Sometimes a quick reminder of the title of the act or scene can suddenly help you to see the characters' intentions more distinctly.

Third, be aware that scenes work best when they contain a simple conflict. So ensure that the intentions contradict, or interact dynamically, with each other. For example, if you are going to ask the actor playing Masha to play the intention 'to get Medvedenko off the subject of his marriage proposal', then it might be interesting to give Medvedenko the intention 'to get Masha to give him an answer to his marriage proposal'. Do not give everyone in a scene the same intention.

Fourth, if you are struggling to identify an emotion, ask yourself what picture the character has in their head of the desired outcome of the intention. That outcome, or future picture, should always involve a change in what the other character or characters do or say. Does the character, for example, want the person that they are talking to do something particular, such as sit down, to go inside or to stop blushing? When Konstantin stops the performance of his play in Act One, does he want the audience to sit silently and feel awful? Or does he want them to get up and storm about, cursing him? If it is the former, then his intention is: to make everyone feel ashamed. If it is the latter, then his intention is: to make everyone frustrated.

Finally, remember that the character may not always be conscious of what they are playing and this will make the task of diagnosing the intention harder. I write more about this issue in Chapter 11, when I describe how to work with actors on intentions. If you are still finding it hard to find the intentions, it may help to jump forwards in the book now and read the section on the first scene rehearsal in that chapter. Remember that you can practise diagnosing intentions by watching people operate in real life. Observe how they interact and work out what they want behind the words they are saying or try to notice what your intentions are when you interact with others.

When you have isolated an intention, write it down. Do not worry about making beautiful sentences. Use simple words and cool, unemotional language – just like you did when naming events. You will hone the sentence later when you work with the actors. Make sure you write the intentions down in pencil so that you can easily make changes during rehearsals to what you have written. Remember that intentions only change when an event happens: you will need to find an intention for every on-stage character for every section of the play. In *The Seagull*, here are the intentions in the first section between Masha and Medvedenko.

> **Masha:** *To get Medvedenko off the subject of his proposal.*
> **Medvedenko:** *To get Masha to give him an answer to his proposal.*
> **The event:** *Masha informs Medvedenko that she does not love him.*
> **Masha:** *To make Medvedenko feel better.*
> **Medvedenko:** *To convince Masha he is not affected by the rejection.*

Next, look at how each character tries to get what they want. You will notice that characters use a whole range of different tactics. Make sure that you do not get confused between what the character wants – the intention – and how they achieve it – the tactic or means. It is not essential to notate the character's tactics before rehearsals begin, but jot down any particular ones that stand out.

'But how do I work out intentions if there is only one person in the play?', you might ask. First, be aware that it will be very rare for a character to talk directly to 'the audience' who are actually watching the play. So, if you are directing a monologue, simply ask yourself whom the character is talking to. Are they talking to themselves or to another person or people? Are these people or this person imagined or real, dead or alive? Where are these people or this person? Once you have answered these questions, you can ask what the character wants from whom they are talking to. Then, when you rehearse the scene, the actor will need to practise imagining this person or these people.

This way of working has a final refinement that was suggested to me by actors I regularly work with. They said there should be intentions inside many of the events, especially when the events take place over several lines. The actors pointed out that, if the event is a sudden appearance of an armed gunman, there is no time to play an intention during it, but if the event is the gradual disclosure of a secret (such as Masha telling Dorn about her feelings for Konstantin), then the actors do have time to play a separate intention 'inside' the event. The absence of an intention over an event lasting several lines means that the actors have nothing to play and feel that they are just standing around waiting to latch onto their next intention. When you first use this way of working, I suggest that you only prepare intentions between events, but if there are any events that happen over several lines or several seconds, you might like to identify an intention inside the event.

At the end of this exercise your script will now contain events and the intentions that sit between these events (as well as some intentions that happen 'inside' events).

Summary
Go through the text to identify and describe the intentions between the events.
Do not mistake a subject change for a new intention.
Remind yourself of the title of the act or scene if you are struggling to identify an intention.
Ensure that the intentions you select will interact dynamically with each other.
Practise diagnosing intentions by watching people operate in real life.
Write down intentions in unemotional and simple sentences.
Start to notice the 'tactics' each character uses to play their intentions.

Getting the text ready for the actors

Preparing the rehearsal script is about making a document that is easy for the actors to read and use – and includes space to write notes, events and intentions. Remember that a printed published play script is laid out for people to read and not to use as a rehearsal tool. Consider this when you choose which edition of a classic play you will use. If you decide to photocopy a published play script, think about whether you want to blow up the size of the print or leave blank pages for notes.

The other decision you need to make about the script is what you keep in and what you cut out in terms of stage directions and descriptions about how characters should say lines. Some directors cut all stage directions from the text because they can predetermine the moves and actions of the characters. They also remove all adjectives that precede lines, like 'angrily' or 'through tears' because these words might put the actor under pressure to deliver slabs of generalised feelings. Others prefer that every stage direction, comma, full stop and adjective that came from the writer's pen is retained in the text. Alternatively, you might prefer to remove information from the script that is at odds with your interpretation of the play, or your process. For example, I removed the word 'audience' from the first stage direction of *The Seagull* because I did not want the actors to think about an audience – I wanted them to think more about the character they were playing and the situation they were in. I also removed the references to 'stage left' and 'stage right' for similar reasons. Remember, however, that you should only make changes to the script of a living writer with their full agreement.

In the rehearsal process this book describes, the actors will never rehearse a scene holding a script in their hands, so you do not have to worry about making a script that is easy to hold when a person is walking around. However, if you do want the actors to hold their scripts when they rehearse, consider the best way of laying out and binding the script so that they can do this efficiently. Remember, however, that many actors will turn up with their own systems for this.

Make sure that this script is sent to all the actors before rehearsals begin so that they can spend time absorbing the text you want them to work on. Actors will often prepare their scripts for rehearsals by highlighting all their lines or putting notes or questions alongside sections of the text. If you present them with a new script on the first day with changes in the pagination or the layout, they may have to spend time transferring information from one script to the next.

Finally, ensure that everyone in the room has the same script. Sometimes with an old play people bring different versions or translations. If paginations vary from script to script, time will be wasted in rehearsals scrabbling through different documents to find the right page.

Summary
Put together a script for the actors that is easy to read and in which there is space to write things down.

Remove any stage directions from the text that are at odds with your interpretation of the play or your process.

Consider whether you want to remove any stage directions or information from the writer about how lines should be said.

If you want the actors to hold their scripts as they rehearse, consider how you will bind their scripts.

Consult carefully with a living writer about any changes you want to make to the rehearsal script.

Consider different ways of laying out the script so that it can be used as a performance score by actors and send your version of the script to actors before rehearsal begins.

A checklist of all the work done in this chapter

By the end of this chapter your script contains:

a name for each act or scene

lines marking each event and simple sentences describing each event

a notation of the main events of each act

simple sentences describing the characters' intentions between each event

a layout which you are happy with

a decision about whether to keep or cut stage directions and descriptions of how to say lines.

The Mysteries by Edward Kemp

CHAPTER 5

Deepening work on character

This chapter is about deepening the work on the characters and starting to think about improvisations. It has three steps:

> Characters' thoughts about themselves
> Relationships
> Preparing improvisations

Characters' thoughts about themselves

Chapter 1 describes the building of a biography for each character. A biography allows you to stand on the outside of the character and see what they have done in their lives. Now you need to step inside the characters and look out at the world through their eyes. To do this you need to work out their thought structures.

Our thoughts exist as a collection of sentences or pictures in our heads; these sentences and pictures entered our heads at identifiable points in our lives. Some of our thoughts are relatively new, some are old and some are contradictory. They therefore have different holds on our behaviour. Our collection of thoughts is constantly reshaping itself in response to new stimuli or events in our lives. These thoughts determine how we respond to events in our lives. Imagine, for instance, watching the response of two different drivers to being cut up by another driver at a roundabout. The first driver turns to his passenger and says, 'How frustrating. I wish people would learn to drive properly', then starts to drive erratically himself. The second driver experiences exactly the same event and turns to his passenger and says, 'Poor man. I bet he was late for an urgent hospital appointment or he needed to attend to an emergency at home', and his driving is unaffected. The response to the same event reveals the different thought structures that the two drivers have: the first driver has the thought 'Life is frustrating' and the second driver has the thought 'Life is simple'. You can discover the thought structures of characters in plays just as you can observe them in operation in real life. Pinning down the key thoughts will help you to guide the actors to build more accurate characters with consistent responses to events.

The first thoughts to look at are those a character has about themselves before the action of the play begins. Make a list containing everything that character says about themselves. Make sure you quote the text verbatim and put the page number next to each quote, as you may want to double-check something later on. Actions reveal as much about people's thoughts as words, so add any relevant information from the stage directions (if you intend to use them). Avoid any possible affinities that draw you to one character over another by starting at the top of the dramatis personae and working down. At times it will be difficult to know what to include and what to leave out. If you are in doubt about the relevance of a quote, put it down anyway. Here is a list of quotes for Arkadina.

Act One

For the sake of amusement, I'm prepared to sit through even the ravings of delirium. Because I work, I'm alive to the world around me, I'm always busy; whereas you're such a stuck-in-the-mud, you don't know how to live … Also I make it a rule not to look into the future. I never think about old age, I never think about death. What will be, will be.

Act Two

Oh, what could be more boring than this sweet country boredom. Heat, quiet, nothing anyone wants to do, everyone philosophising away. It's nice being with you, my friends, it's a pleasure to listen to you, and yet … to be sitting in a hotel room somewhere learning your lines – could anything be better than that?

Act Three

I suppose I might arrange a little more for clothes [for Konstantin], *but as for going abroad. No, at the moment I can't even manage the clothes.* [Decisively] *I've no money.* [Sorin laughs] *I haven't!*
[On the verge of tears] *I've no money! All right, I have money, but I happen to be in the theatrical profession – my outfits alone have nearly ruined me …*
I haven't any money. I'm an actress, not a bank manager.
I'm a woman like any other – you can't speak to me so.
Am I really so old and ugly that you can talk to me about other women without so much as batting an eyelid? [Embraces and kisses him] *That last page of my life!* [Kneels] *My joy, my pride, my delight …* [Embraces his knees] *Leave me for a single hour and I'll not survive it, I'll go mad, my amazing man, my magnificent man, my sovereign lord …*

Act Four *Three baskets of flowers, two garlands and this.* [Takes a brooch off her breast and throws it on the table] *I was wearing an amazing outfit. Whatever else, I know how to dress.*

[She is alarmed by the sound of the shot] *Oh, it frightened me! It reminded me of the time when* … [Puts her hands over her face] *I thought for a moment I was going to faint* …

Now distil these quotes into a series of nouns and adjectives that can be added to the sentence, 'I am …' Do this by asking the question: 'What are the simplest thoughts that someone who says this has about themselves?' Ask this question of each quote you have written down and then find an accurate word as an answer. For example, on page 42 of the play, you may look at Arkadina's trembling when Trigorin says he wants to go off with Nina and get the impression that 'I am ageing' is one of Arkadina's thoughts about herself. You should end up with a list of four or five key 'thoughts' for each character. Arkadina's thoughts might be: I am a bad mother, a survivor, ageing, a great artist, worthless, poor. Try to avoid thoughts that are value judgements that someone outside the person might make about them. Instead, try to get inside the person's head and think from their point of view. Start to use the sorts of words that they would use.

If you are having difficulties identifying the character's thoughts about themselves, look back over the sketch biography and search for events in the characters' lives that may have generated those thoughts. For example, by focusing on the hardship Arkadina experienced early on in her career performing at the agricultural fair in Poltava in 1873 and, later, when she lived in a tenement in Moscow, it becomes evident that the thought 'I am poor' must figure quite strongly in how that character understands herself.

Summary
List everything that a character says about themselves during the action of the play.
Boil down the list of quotes to some simple nouns and adjectives to finish the sentence 'I am …'
If you are having difficulties identifying the characters' thoughts about themselves, look back over the sketch biography and search for events in the characters' lives that may have generated those thoughts.

Relationships

Before you begin rehearsals, it is worth finding out what the character thinks of each of the other characters prior to the action of the play. This task helps you look at the text as a web of interrelated relationships between characters and stops you directing it from one character's point of view.

Start from the top of the dramatis personae and work through each character, writing down everything they say about all the other characters in turn. Transfer the lists of quotes to different pages and organise them under separate headings like this:

> Arkadina's thoughts about Konstantin
> Arkadina's thoughts about Sorin
> Arkadina's thoughts about Nina … and so on.

Remember to add the page references next to each quote. Make sure that you look at all the relationships, including relationships between the main characters and the minor characters such as servants. If the character says nothing or very little about another character, study the scenes in which they are on stage together and see if you can tease out any additional information. Alternatively you could jot down the simplest impression the text gives you of the relationship, before adding it to your list. Again, remember that there is not a definitive set of quotes for each relationship that you should be aiming at; this list will always vary from director to director.

When you have finished this process, boil everything down to simple adjectives or nouns and add them to the sentences: 'Konstantin is…', 'Sorin is …', 'Nina is …' and so on. This way of notating thoughts helps you stay inside the character's head. Do this for each character in turn. Here are Arkadina's thoughts about two other characters.

> Sorin is my brother, mean, dying, a failure.
> Konstantin is a burden, a nonentity, unemployed, a parasite, my own dear child.

Notice that characters, like people in life, have contradictions in their heads about each other; this is certainly the case with Arkadina's thoughts about her son. Try not to iron out these contradictions as they can help an actor with, for example, their character's inconsistent behaviour.

Sometimes the interaction of characters in a play is brief or non-existent. In these cases it is difficult to diagnose what the characters think about each other. Be simple and list the most obvious things they might think. For example, in *The Seagull* Polina and Arkadina barely interact and yet Arkadina must have thoughts in her head about Polina. At the very least she would think that Polina is the housekeeper, Shamrayev's wife and her contemporary. In the action Arkadina goes into town with Polina in Act Two and forgets to pick up the plums that Polina gives her for the journey in Act Three. Here is an example of how you can boil all this down into a simple sentence:

> Polina is a servant, a bad mother, an old friend, old, bullied, dull.

Summary
Compile a list of what each character thinks of every other character.
Boil down the list of quotes into simple adjectives and nouns.

Preparing improvisations

The aim of improvisations is to build pictures of the past that will support what the characters do and say in the present action of the play. In *The Seagull*, Masha and Medvedenko need a shared picture of Medvedenko's recent proposal of marriage before they can play the first scene and, behind this, they need a picture of how they first met. In the same scene, Medvedenko needs a clear picture of the family life he talks about as well as a picture of the circumstances of his father's death or disappearance. Similarly, Konstantin needs past pictures of his mother to underpin his long chat about her with Sorin in Act One. He needs a picture of her reciting Nekrasov, ministering to the sick and acting. The improvisations you do should reconstruct these events and thereby lodge a lasting and concrete picture of what happened in the actors' minds – almost as if it were an actual memory. These pictures will then determine how their relationships are played in the action of the play or how the characters talk about the past. You can use improvisations of the action that occurs in between scenes to fuel subsequent scenes.

Your work on character biographies, the trigger event, immediate circumstances and events in between scenes will provide you with a list of all the things you can usefully improvise. In an ideal world, you would have a long rehearsal period and you would be able to improvise everything on your list. In a shorter rehearsal period, you may have to select key events; this is the moment to make that selection. If you have very little time, focusing solely on the trigger event can often provide you with lots of material for improvisations. If you were working on the trigger event of *The Seagull*, you could improvise the following events (or a selection of these events).

> In Moscow, Arkadina asks Trigorin if he would like to come on holiday with her in the summer.
> Arkadina's letter announcing her and Trigorin's arrival on the estate is delivered and discussed by Polina, Sorin, Shamrayev, Konstantin and Masha at breakfast.
> Konstantin sits in the study and begins some sketches for a play to perform when Trigorin and Arkadina arrive.
> Konstantin asks Nina to be in his play and they do a read-through.
> Polina, Masha and the servants plan the jobs they need to do before the arrival of

> Trigorin and Arkadina.
> Konstantin asks Shamrayev for help building the set for his performance.
> Arkadina arrives on the estate.

Even if you only have time to do three of these improvisations, it will help the actors enormously in their work on the scenes.

The best way to direct an improvisation is to structure it well. When I first started directing I gave very few instructions. Consequently, the improvisations were very long: nothing much happened in them and the actors regularly slipped in and out of character. Avoid this sort of outcome by planning improvisations as if they were scenes from a play, giving the actors immediate circumstances, events, intentions, and a clear sense of place and time. The more concrete the information you can provide for each improvisation, the better – and remember that actors can cope with more information than you might imagine. If you structure your improvisations clearly, you will also reduce the gap between doing improvisations and working on scenes in the play. When you come to rehearse the scenes themselves, they will feel like improvisations.

Here is the plan for the improvisation of Medvedenko's proposal to Masha.

Place: *The library on Sorin's estate.*

Time: *1893, August. Sunday. 11am. It is very hot.*

Immediate circumstances: *Medvedenko is returning a book he borrowed from Masha yesterday. It is Shakespeare's* Hamlet. *Medvedenko has walked three miles in his best suit from home. He is a little hot and sweaty. His family expect him back for lunch. This morning he had an argument with his mother about the weekly housekeeping. She was particularly angry because of his expenditure on cigarettes. Masha is reading Schopenhauer in the library in order to impress Konstantin with her knowledge – he brought up this philosopher the evening before. She has the window open because of the heat. She has an hour off before she will have to help her mother with the lunch. Konstantin is away shooting all morning, Shamrayev is working in the fields preparing the harvest, Polina is in the kitchen and Sorin is writing letters in his study.*

Masha's first intention: *To get Medvedenko to entertain her.*

Medvedenko's intention: *To prepare Masha for the proposal.*

The event: *Medvedenko proposes to Masha.*

Masha's second intention: *To get Medvedenko to give her time to think about the proposal.*

Medvedenko's second intention: *To get Masha to give him a clear answer immediately.*

You can also plan very simple improvisations such as one that will help Nina with her relationship with Trigorin.

Place: *Nina's bedroom.*

Time: *1892, March, 4.30pm.*

Immediate circumstances: *Her stepmother and father have just left to go shopping in town which gives her an opportunity to work on her Trigorin scrapbook. This morning she received a monthly literary magazine from Moscow with a new story by Trigorin called 'In the Summer Moonlight', about a hopeless love affair in the Russian steppes. She read it over breakfast and now she is cutting it out of the magazine and pasting it into her Trigorin scrapbook. The room is quite chilly.*

Nina's first intention: *To entertain herself.*

The event: *The paste spills over the scrapbook.*

Nina's second intention: *To stop herself from panicking.*

This planned improvisation is not as dynamic as a scene from a play (and may even be a little dull to watch) but it will give the actor a clear picture of what Trigorin writes, his status and how important he is to her. As a result it will help her when she says lines in Act One, such as 'Such wonderful stories he writes' and 'I don't mind your mother, I'm not afraid of her, but you've got Trigorin here …' It will also help her play the scene where she meets him for the first time.

Prepare all the improvisations you have decided to do in exactly the same way. Remember that a well-organised improvisation can take ten minutes to do, whereas a conversation in rehearsals about the same event can take half an hour. Bear this in mind when you are deciding how many events to improvise. Put each planned improvisation on a separate sheet of A4 paper and arrange them in chronological order.

Summary
Select the improvisations you are able to do in the time you have to rehearse.
Prepare the content of all the improvisations and structure them as if they
were scenes from a play.
Put the plans for each improvisation on separate sheets of A4 paper so you can
find them easily when you are in rehearsals.

A checklist of all the work done in this chapter
A list of words describing each character's thoughts about themselves
A list of each character's thoughts about all the other characters
A list of all the events you plan to improvise
A series of plans for each improvisation arranged in chronological order

CHAPTER 6

Building relationships with your production team

This chapter describes how to build all relationships with everyone involved in making the production other than the actors. It has seven steps:

> **Design**
> **Lighting**
> **Sound**
> **Music**
> **Video**
> **Voice**
> **Movement**

Do not be daunted if your own creative team is smaller than that described, or if you don't have the money or time to build the relationships as I describe them. There are always ways of keeping standards high, building teams if you're on a tight budget. What matters is that you aspire to find people for all these roles and, at the beginning of your career, are prepared to accept compromises in terms of availability in order to get someone to do the job well – or to do the job at all.

Make sure you establish a common language with the people in your creative team before you start work on a specific play. This means spending time together, sharing images, sounds or music. Confusion often arises between directors and set designers because of misunderstandings about the simplest of words (like 'red') or complex words describing atmosphere (like 'sombre' or 'bright'). By going to exhibitions or films together or sharing images from your favourite painter or photographer, you will build a clear language with which to talk about visual information. Spend some time with your lighting designer looking at films that capture lighting ideas that appeal to you both or go through reproductions of photographers that feature a strong use of light and shade. With your sound designer (or composer) listen to music or sounds that interest you both, and analyse why certain pieces have more impact and meaning for you than others. These meetings and discussions will generate a shorthand that will make your working relationships smoother and more efficient. Of course, when you are at an early point in your career, you may find yourself working with more senior designers or composers, who will not have the time for conversations like this with you. In this case, try to snatch a chat over a cup of coffee, and remember to use images or music and not words to communicate what you like or want.

Whenever possible, share the outcomes of your preparatory work with your creative team. If you are pushed for time, the most important ingredient to communicate to everyone is the events around which the action will be structured. In an ideal world, the lights, sound, music, movement, set and costume design will all work to sharpen or underscore these turning points. Work with your set designer to ensure the maximum change to the stage picture after an event and discuss whether the characters landing the main events in each act should be dressed in a particular way or colour so that the eye is subtly drawn to them. The designer Vicki Mortimer and I decided to relocate the action of Act Two of *The Seagull* from a garden to a dining room where lunch was being served. We wanted to maximise the change in stage picture at the main event of the act: The Refusal of the Horses. Before the event everyone was seated, the first course of soup had just hit the table and people were starting to eat. Shamrayev suddenly announced the news about the horses. Immediately people stopped eating, spoons were put down in mid-flow, full soup plates were returned to the kitchen by servants, and the guests gradually all stood up. Arkadina left the room and soon servants were seen passing through with suitcases ready for her to pack to go back to Moscow. As a result, the visual picture changed at the same time as the event: the change was strong and ensured that the stage picture was full of life. The decision also gave the actors many physical activities by which to respond to the event, like folding napkins, carrying cases, leaving rooms and so on. At the same time as the event occurred, the lighting designer Paule Constable subtly altered the lighting state, and the room darkened ever so slightly as if a cloud was just passing across the sun. The sound designer, Gareth Fry, added a barely perceptible low bass rumble to underscore the actions in the aftermath of the event.

Do not start to work on design, costumes, lighting, music or sound until you have studied the play carefully. That way you will avoid making critical errors – such as ending up with a design that works in the model box but will not function for the performers as they work on the detail of each scene, or deciding on a bold anachronism like relocating the action of a nineteenth-century play to the twentieth century without thinking it through carefully.

Design

Design has three main functions:

> to communicate time and place
> to help focus the eye of the audience on the key action or narrative
> to support the actors in transmitting the ideas and genre of the play.

The director's work with the designer could be divided into three stages: before rehearsals up until the model is made; during rehearsals; and in the theatre. This section will cover the first step. The second and third steps are described in Chapters 9, 11 and 12.

The process by which a design evolves does not follow a linear narrative. Instead there are several tasks which are undertaken simultaneously and which finally coalesce into a coherent shape. Remember also that the process I describe is an ideal one that would take place over a couple of months. If you have less time than this to work with your designer, be reassured that you can still cover many of the tasks outlined in the following text.

First, spend time with the designer exploring the play in detail without working on solutions to specific scenes. For example, you might go through the back history list of facts and questions. This will concentrate you both on the tiny details of the material and give you clear separate research tasks. You might research the things that relate to character biographies while the designer is researching the questions about architecture or furniture. It is particularly important to share information about place, time, immediate circumstances, the titles of the acts and events (including the 'main' events of each scene), as the design will need to serve these decisions very precisely. Sharing information like this will throw up many tiny details that will need to be incorporated into the completed design or concept. For example, the room in Act Four of *The Seagull* is cold, so there needs to be a decision about where the heating is and why it is not functioning, or research into walking sticks in the nineteenth century will reveal that they were widely adopted as fashion accessories; this might determine the choice of stick for Sorin. If your time is limited, it is still important to communicate the essential information from your preparation (you should be able to do this in an intense three-hour session).

In rehearsals you will have to answer questions from the actors such as: 'Where does this door lead to?', 'Where have I just come from?' and 'What can I see out of this window?' It is much easier to address or even answer these questions while working on the design process. If you leave them until the rehearsals you may find that the design decisions do not fit the detail of what the actors have to do and say in the action – if you have a short rehearsal period, you could easily waste valuable time sorting these details out. Even if you are working on a genre like surrealism, or an eighteenth-century opera, the performers will have questions about the logic of why they use one entrance as opposed to another (or where they have come from, or are going to), so you need to have thought this through in detail. It is also important that the audience understand the logic of where the play is set or they may spend time during the performance asking questions about where people have come from – or worrying about bigger questions like: 'Where are we supposed to be?'

In Chapter 1, I described how you could draw plans of the circles of place described in the text. Show the rough sketches of the places where the action of the play occurs to the designer. At this point, remember that you are not deciding on the actual set design the audience will see; rather, you are starting to think about each scene as if it were a real place. In *The Seagull*, two of the acts (Acts Three and Four) happen in different rooms of the same house: one in a study overlooking the lake and the other in a dining room. The designer and I went through all the entrances and exits to each room in detail, as well as everything that was said about where people were coming from or going to. For example, in Act Four of *The Seagull*, Masha, Polina and Medvedenko are looking for Konstantin at Sorin's request. Actors and audience alike need a credible picture of where Sorin is and where they think Konstantin may be; the arrangement of the rooms needs to fulfil the logic of everyone's search for Konstantin. We tried to make sense of where the rooms for both acts were located both in relationship to the other rooms (that the audience would not see) and in relation to the grounds surrounding the house.

At the end of this process you will have several detailed maps of the place where the action of the play occurs, although the designer will probably not have translated them into any decisions about the set design.

Next, consider the angle at which the audience might look at the place or places where the action occurs. When the designer Vicki Mortimer and I worked on the design for *The Seagull* we drew a detailed plan of the relationship between the lake, the house, the improvised stage and the rest of the estate. We decided that the audience watching Konstantin's play were sitting with their backs to the house looking towards the improvised stage and the lake behind the stage. We then drew a line on the plan between the stage and the house, and this line marked the position of the proscenium arch. This meant that the actual audience at the National Theatre watched the action as if they were sitting in the lake: they could see Nina's back and, behind her, the faces of the characters watching the play with the house in the background.

However, it will not always be possible to draw a neat line through a realistic plan and place the audience on one side and the action on the other. Theatres can be many different shapes and you will often have to modify your realistic plans to fit the actual footprint of the stage area. Similarly, it will not always be possible to solve the design of a scene by working from a real plan of the geography surrounding that place. In some cases, you will need to work the other way round: it might be necessary to design a scenic solution to fit the footprint of the stage you are working on before deciding on a logic for the realistic environment. Nonetheless, thinking about the design as if it were a section of a real place (or places) provides a useful starting point. However you arrive at the final design, you should emerge from the process with a clear idea of what surrounds the place or places where the action is set, so that the actors can inhabit the rooms or environments the audience see as if they were real.

At this point in the process, think forward to how the characters will use the place or places event by event, and how everything in that place (including the furniture) will be arranged. It is particularly important to think about where key or main events occur. Remember that decisions about the set and furniture are also the first steps that the director makes towards arranging the actors so that the audience can see what is going on – indirectly, you are already starting to direct the play. Check that you have positioned entrances or furniture in such a way that the key bits of action will be well focused and visible if used logically by the characters in the situation. In my experience, it is best to keep instructions to actors in rehearsals about where to stand to a minimum and the way to do this is to plan ahead during the design process. That way, the actors can simply use the space as their characters logically would without worrying about whether their actions are visible or not. Of course, there will always be exceptions to this ideal – moments when you will have to cheat a position or an entrance. I write more about this in the section on blocking in Chapter 11.

The designer will probably start showing you ideas for scenes at about this point – either in the form of drawings or a white card model. There are two basic types of model: the white card model (which is a three-dimensional sketch of the broad architectural decisions under consideration); and the final model (a precise replica of the design the audience will see, with all the walls or surfaces finished perfectly). Often, a designer will present a model of the set within a black box that normally includes both the stage area and the auditorium itself. In large theatres the finished model is the one that goes to the workshop and is used as a point of reference by the people building and painting the set. A white card model is cheap to make so you can easily make changes to it, whereas finished models are enormously labour intensive and expensive to construct. It is not always possible to make a finished model if you are working on a tight budget for a small company. Do not worry if this is the case because a white card model can communicate the essential information required to the builder or painter, as long as it is accompanied by very specific visual reference. When you look at the white card model, be brave about asking to see different possibilities. It is relatively easy for a designer to take large sections of the model apart and cut another bit of white card to make another door or a new wall for you to look at. I also find it very useful to move tiny model figures and pieces of key furniture around the model box, so that I can look at different ways of arranging things or people for each scene.

Make sure that you have a firm grasp of the sightlines in the theatre and, if it is possible, ask your designer to mark them up on the model or ground plan you are looking at. A 'ground plan' is a plan of how the set design fits into the footprint of the theatre space. The word 'sightlines' describes the invisible lines on the stage that mark the boundaries of the area that every member of the audience can see. I was recently working on a new opera and had a real problem with the sightlines. Rehearsals had begun and the set was designed – indeed, sections of it were up in the rehearsal room (as is normal practice for many opera companies). I worked my way through the piece, scene by scene, and finished staging everything in the penultimate week of rehearsals. Then the stage manager sidled up to me and asked, very politely: 'Do you think it is wise to put the action so far stage left?' 'Why?' I asked, thinking that I was completely safe in making that staging decision. 'Because it won't be seen by half the house,' he replied. (The word 'house' describes the audience.) I immediately rang the designer and we discovered, to our horror, that some of the sightlines had not been drawn up on the ground plans. We had to make several rather crude alterations to the physical shape of the scenes at an awkwardly late stage in the process. This is a situation you want to avoid.

A firm understanding of certain visual rules that determine how we look at what happens on stage will help you in your work. If you are working in a proscenium configuration, there is a difference between entering from stage left and entering from stage right. Crudely speaking, if a character enters from stage right they will appear stronger and larger than if they enter from stage left, and if someone moves between the two entrances, their scale will appear to alter. As the actor walks from stage right to stage left, they will appear to the audience to be getting a tiny bit smaller, and as the actor walks from stage left to stage right they will appear to be growing a tiny bit bigger. This is an optical illusion created because we read from left to right. An awareness of this visual 'rule' will enable you to make decisions about whether you want the entrances at key moments of the action to be strong or weak.

In Act Four of *The Seagull* you could decide whether you want Nina to enter stage left or stage right. This decision is crucial to your interpretation of the scene: you can either make her appear more vulnerable from the top of the scene by having her enter stage left or you can decide to make her appear in control by deciding to have her enter from stage right.

The designer Vicki Mortimer and I decided to have her enter from stage left in our production. Remember, also, that actors will experience a sensation of being slightly smaller (vulnerable) or slightly bigger (powerful) depending on which side of the stage they enter from. They will experience entering from stage left and heading stage right as if they are climbing up a hill and, conversely, they will experience a move from stage right to stage left as if they were going downhill. Again notice how you are already starting to direct actors indirectly by the decisions you make at this point in the design process. Of course, if you are working in traverse or using a thrust stage, remember that the meaning will be different for the audience on either side.

Next, start to discuss the genre of the play and the ideas you have identified as they will determine how you treat the place or places the action occurs in. If, for instance, the genre is surrealism you may decide to position the room where the action occurs at a precarious angle or give it a steep rake or, if it is symbolism (as in *The Seagull*), you might decide to create the strange feeling of foreboding by stripping the environment of all the clutter normally associated with the period and revealing the bare cracked and decayed walls of the house. If one of the ideas of the play is the abuse of power (as in Euripides' *Women of Troy*), you might decide to set the action in an enormous industrial environment which will literally dwarf the characters – making them look like tiny dots in a larger mechanical environment. When you are working on ideas and genre it will help if you both look at other visual references (such as films, art exhibitions, reproductions of paintings or photographs) to pinpoint exactly what you mean when you talk about these more cerebral concerns.

Go and sit in the empty theatre auditorium with the designer. Talk about the pitfalls and benefits of the configuration you are working in. For example, if you are working in the round you will need to keep the action moving. So avoid putting too much furniture around the edges that might encourage actors to sit for long periods of time. Remember that there is not one perfect seat from which to view the action. Go and sit in different seats. Think about how to make your visual ideas reach everyone in the audience. This is not just about sightlines, it is about acknowledging that everyone sits in a slightly different relationship to the performance and looks at the work from a slightly different angle. Of course, it is crucial that everyone sees key bits of the action such as main events. For the rest of the time, it is important that everyone looks at things that take them into the world and ideas of the play. Find a way of creating interesting pictures for everyone, especially the people sitting in the different extremes in the house. In *Iphigenia at Aulis* the designer Hildegard Bechtler and I decided to extend the design off stage left and stage right by a couple of metres. On each side, the world of the building where the action took place continued, but it was only visible to the audience immediately opposite it. We made sure that there was something equally visually interesting for each section of the audience to look at. For example, the audience sitting stage left could see a long antique mirror hanging on the wall and a low threadbare rust-coloured sofa on stage right. This was not visible to the audience on stage right. However, the stage right audience saw equally interesting details on stage left: a doorway and small lobby looking out over a hill. Consider, also, the acoustic of the theatre. If you are in a small fringe theatre then it will be possible for everyone to hear everything said, even if it is whispered. However, if you are in the empty Lyttelton, once you move more than two metres upstage you will literally have to shout to be heard by the full house. Design can help with problems like this. For example, you could decide to use only the first metre and a half of a large proscenium stage for all the key action, then use the rest of the stage to create an impression of a distant landscape or collapsed building. Alternatively, you could put a ceiling on a room to help seal it acoustically.

By now the designer will be working towards the finished model. Normally, you will see this model at different stages in its development, and each time you see it you will be confirming the architectural choices you have already decided on, tweaking tiny details and discussing the treatment of walls or surfaces. It is not usual to change your mind completely at this point, although there are instances when this happens.

This is also the moment to consider how different lighting choices will enrich the set design. Think about where the natural light will come from and whether you need to add windows, doors or other apertures through which light can pour. This light will tell the story of the time of day. Alternatively, consider the angle and height at which you want the light to enter the room and therefore how much backstage space you need to give the lighting designer so that they can place their lights. Think about how to use and where to put practical lights for scenes that take place at night. Practical lights are the lights on the set (such as chandeliers or standard lamps or desk lights). Invite the lighting designer to an early meeting to get their feedback on the direction you and the designer are thinking of heading in. There is no point building a set that cannot be lit effectively. Often the input of the lighting designer occurs too late in the process when changes cannot be made to the design. This creates problems when you get into the theatre. For example, the lighting designer may not be able to get a lantern behind a window because the set flat is too close to the wall of the theatre, or you have built a ceiling which has no apertures through which the light can enter.

When you have finished the set design you can start work on costumes. You will already have touched on costumes when you talked through character biographies in your early conversations. Now you will work in more detail on each character, thinking precisely about what they would wear in each scene, and how things like their class, biography and job may inform how they dress. At the same time you will have to think about the overall relationship of the clothes to the scenery, and how you balance the colour, tone and texture of the costumes with that of the set design. At the end of this process, you might receive individual costume drawings or just references from magazines with swatches of material – depending on how much time your designer has and how they like to work.

I always try to delay decisions about costume until I have spent at least a week in the rehearsal room with the actors. This is because the actors' work on character biographies often throws up tiny details that neither the director nor the designer has previously considered in their preparation; these details could have an impact on what the actors wear. Delaying decisions about costume also allows the designer to watch each actor's body carefully to consider the best way to dress them, in terms of both cut and colour. Understandably, actors may also have anxieties about different parts of their bodies that a designer can only find out about when they take an early measurement or chat in a coffee break. One actor could, for instance, be very self-conscious about their legs, and another might be very conscious of their stomach. The costume design needs to be sensitive to these concerns. If everything is decided before rehearsals begin it is impossible to make some of the necessary changes to costumes in response to these issues.

The next steps of the design process occur during the rehearsal period.

Summary
Spend time with the designer exploring the play in detail rather than working on solutions to specific scenes.
As a starting point, think through each place in which the action of the play occurs as if it were a real place.
Think through how the characters will use the place or places, event by event, and consider how everything in that place – furniture or lampposts – will be arranged.
Check that you have positioned entrances, or furniture, in such a way that the key

bits of action will be well focused and visible if used logically by the characters in the situation.

Work with the designer on the white card model.

Have a firm grasp of the sightlines.

Let basic visual rules guide your choices.

Discuss the genre and ideas of the play in order to decide how you will treat the place or places the action occurs in.

Sit in the empty theatre auditorium with the designer, and talk about the pitfalls and benefits of the configuration in which you are working.

Remember that there is not one perfect seat from which everyone will watch the performance.

Look at, and talk through, the finished model at different points in its construction.

Consider how lighting choices will enhance the set design and involve the lighting designer in the process before the design is signed off.

Discuss what each character will wear in each scene in relationship to the individual biographies and the overall aesthetics of the set design.

Lighting

Lighting has four main functions.

To support the design in communicating time and place. For example, a low golden light flooding through a window will suggest dawn, while a sickly yellow light coming from a high angle through a window will indicate street lighting in a city or town.

To ensure that the action is visible to the audience. There would be no problem with visibility if all plays consisted of scenes set in bright sunshine. However, many plays are set in dark environments or take place on dull rainy afternoons. The action would be invisible if these scenes were lit realistically. So, lighting is used to correct this by cheating in extra light onto the actors' faces or bodies.

To shape subliminally what we look at on stage. If, for example, the key action moves from downstage left to upstage right during a scene, the lights could subtly adjust so that they encourage the eye to follow that action. This adjustment is at its most effective if it happens inside the logic of a precise time of day.

To alter the atmosphere or mood of the action if it is used abstractly. For example, a kitchen can be lit to feel safe and sunny or dangerous and dark.

The first function of theatre lighting – communicating time and place – can be prepared before rehearsals begin. The other three functions can only be fulfilled as the moves and actions that the actors will perform are created in the rehearsal room. It may be useful to talk through these four broad functions with your lighting designer and discuss what role you want the lights to play in your production. Ideally, your lighting design should include all four functions, but if you are pushed for time try to ensure that time and place are clear and that the action is visible to the audience. The third and fourth functions require a lot of careful work and time, and when you are starting out you may not always be in a position to achieve these subtler functions.

Involve the lighting designer in all your decisions about time, place and immediate circumstances, as these will determine the lighting for the scenes. Then take them through the events and discuss how lighting can subtly contribute to changing the stage picture during or after an event. Share decisions about the ideas and genre of the play with your lighting designer. Finally, ensure that the lighting designer is involved early on in discussions with the set designer. In three-way meetings between director, designer and lighting designer talk about the way in which the set will communicate time of day and how the lighting will support this, or the use of the practical lights on the set to focus the action.

Summary
Start to think about how to use the four functions of lighting design.
Share all your decisions about time, place, immediate circumstances, events, genre and the ideas of the play with your lighting designer.
Ensure the lighting designer is involved in discussions with the set designer.

Sound

Sound has four main functions.

To describe time and place – like set and lighting design. For example, you could use the sound of cars passing to indicate a road outside a room or a combination of echoey car alarms and speeding motorcycles to suggest urban night-time.

To set up the atmosphere or mood of each scene when played before a scene or in between scenes.

To underscore change and atmosphere during the action. This means using sound abstractly.

To disguise technical problems. If your scene changes take too long and you find that the audience are sitting in the dark twiddling their thumbs, sound can give the impression that time is passing more quickly than it actually is.

Using sound to communicate time and place is the most essential thing to do. However, if you are able to fulfil the other three functions of sound, it will considerably sharpen your production. The third use – underscoring changes in the atmosphere during the action of the play – is the most complex and, in my experience, dovetails best with the process described in this book.

Using abstract sound is a delicate procedure and requires careful positioning of cues, considered choice of sound effects and subtle setting of levels. The best way to sharpen your use of abstract sound is to watch films and start to notice precisely how sound is used. You will be surprised at how many different components make up the overall aural environment. Film uses abstract sound to conjure up different atmospheres or sharpen changes that happen in the action – particularly psychological changes. For example, the film director David Lynch uses sound to create a wide range of atmospheres, from suspense and fear to irony and nausea. The volume of the sound varies from the subliminal to the very loud and is almost constant throughout his films.

Sound is also used in film to create a subjective impression of what it is like to be inside a character's head. For example, the Russian director Elem Klimov used sound in his film *Come and See* to communicate what it is like to be inside the head of someone who has just had his eardrums blown out. Another Russian film maker, Andrei Tarkovsky, used complex aural patterns to communicate how memories lodge themselves in the brain.

Using sound like this in the theatre can help to support the work the actors are doing and sharpen how you transmit your analysis or interpretation of the material. You can play the sound at a very low level so that it works subliminally on the audience or you could play it more loudly so that they consciously hear it. For example, you can use abstract sound to intensify an event. You can choose to underscore the action before the event or the event itself, or the change in the action after the event. Or you could have different qualities of sound for each of the three steps. Alternatively, you can use sound to sharpen the atmosphere of a place. A place such as a kitchen or an office may look safe, but if you add a low menacing bass note it will transform it into a frightening location. Remember that sound must support what the actors are doing; it should not replace or undermine it. Remember also that sound like this affects both the audience and the actors – and that effect can be physical, making people literally feel unsteady or unwell. Abstract sounds played at a low level can help the actors to envelop themselves in the world of the play. However, remember to be cautious and careful when using sound like this. The audience should not be consciously aware of most of the abstract sound you use. Music or sound added to scenes in a heavy-handed way can completely undermine what the actors are doing, and coarsen the contents of a scene. So approach this tool with care and subtlety. Immediately adjust the sound if it gets in the way of what an actor is doing or if it affects the audience's appreciation of a scene – especially their ability to hear what is being said.

Remember also that you are very unlikely to be in a theatre that is completely silent. Go and sit in the auditorium with the sound designer, close your eyes and listen to the noises that the space makes. Ask yourselves what you want to add to or subtract. Some theatre auditoriums are very noisy because of air conditioning systems, the whirr of lanterns or noises from outside penetrating inside. Consider using low-level abstract sound to erase these interfering noises. There is nothing worse than sitting watching a scene set in a field in the countryside and hearing a tube train rumble under the auditorium. Even if you have to replace these noises with louder 'designed' sounds, at least these will be sounds that you are choosing and one that will suit the world of the play.

Summary
Decide which of the four broad functions you want sound to fulfil in your production.
Study how film uses abstract sound to create atmospheres or underscore events.
Use sound to support what the actor does rather than undermining it.
Listen to the sounds in the empty auditorium and consider using abstract sound to eliminate noises which are not in the world of the play.

Music

Music has six main functions:

> to describe time and place
>
> to establish the atmosphere or mood of a scene
>
> to underscore changes during the action
>
> to support set pieces, like dances or parties
>
> to cover scene changes and
>
> to give a production a sense of coherence, by judicious use of the same or similar musical material. It does this by making very different scenes feel like they belong together, or helping to draw out the ideas or themes underpinning the action. This is the most important function that music can fulfil in a production.

You will either work with music specially composed for your production or use existing recorded material. If you work with a composer, remember that it will take time for them to compose what you want. You may have to go through several drafts of a musical idea before arriving at one you both like. Allow time for this process and be patient. Remember also that composers may think about music as something that has its own structure, like a building or a painting. Different composers will feel differently about having their music 'cut to size' to fit a production, just as a painter might feel uncertain about exhibiting, say, the right-hand corner of their latest picture. It will therefore help if you lay out the rules of engagement in advance so that the composer feels invested in the process of rethinking their own work as the rehearsals progress. The almost inevitable process of radical cuts or sudden edits will then be seen as a creative challenge.

Be aware too that a composer's instinct is most often to aim for music that is rich, surprising and holds your entire attention. Many scenes in theatres do not have the space for this intensity and sometimes the best music for a scene is incredibly simple. Maybe it would be uninteresting or banal out of its context, but it serves a function in the scene. This is not always the case but it is worth talking about this before you start work.

Remember, that it is easy to be intimidated by the specialised skills or language that musicians have. Be reassured, however, that most composers are used to interpreting non-technical descriptions of music, so be bold about how you describe what you are after. That said, it is a good idea to familiarise yourself with some of the basics, such as the ideas of major and minor keys, or the difference between a scale and an arpeggio. This can make discussing music with musicians more efficient.

If you use recorded music, be aware that certain well-known pieces of music such as Samuel Barber's *Adagio*, Pachelbel's *Canon* or J S Bach's *Goldberg Variations* carry with them information about other contexts, such as films or advertising, that can confuse an audience or undermine your production. You can of course consider playing with these imported values for ironical purposes. However, if you are using only 'found' music like this, keep an eye on the overall musical meaning. You might find good music that works well for individual scenes in rehearsal, but when you put the whole piece together something seems to be missing. Perhaps the pieces of music you are using are too eclectic, or perhaps you are overusing a particular favourite. The advantage of having a composer or musical director on board is that they can think about this kind of structural concern.

It is worth being cautious about the use of music to cover scene changes. Scene changes often take longer than anticipated, and the director or composer is sometimes forced at the last minute to add more music or sound to fill the gap. This music can have a negative effect on the scenes that follow – for instance, setting up an atmosphere or tone that you did not intend. Try to anticipate problems like this and plan an aural solution in advance. Finally, make sure you apply for the rights to play music that is in copyright early on in the process, in case you discover that it is not free too late to find a good replacement.

In big subsidised houses or the commercial theatre, composed music is usually played live during the performance. If you are working in this context, decide whether you want the band to be visible to the audience or not. The composer him or herself will cast and rehearse the musicians or a musical director will take charge of this process. If you do want live music on stage, remember that most instruments are quite loud. You may find that quite a small band can easily drown out the spoken text, and that your musicians are having to play extremely quietly nearly all the time. Be warned that a band playing quietly sounds completely different to a recording of a band playing loudly but with the sound turned down. This may not be the sound you want. Remember too that musicians are expensive, so it is unlikely that you will be able to work with them that much before the technical rehearsal – unless you have already budgeted for this. If you need extra time with musicians make sure you flag it up early on with the producer.

Ideally your composer or musical director will work hand in glove with your sound designer. The sound and music generated by both will make a tight aural weave. Ensure this happens by encouraging three-way meetings between the director, the composer or musical director and the sound designer. Together you could go through all the events and work out how sound or music can best support the changes.

Remember, however, that music is an art form in its own right, and does not usually need a play to give it meaning. Of course, design and sound design are also art forms, but unlike most theatre designers, nearly all composers routinely make music which stands up on its own as a performance. Depending on how experienced they are, taking a subservient role to the rules of drama is a paradigm shift. You need to be aware of this if you select a composer who works primarily in the field of music, rather than theatre.

Summary
Decide which of the six broad functions you want music to fulfil in your production.
Decide whether you want new music composed or you want to use pre-existing pre-recorded music.
Allow time for the composer to draft the music you want.

Before starting work with a composer, discuss how you want the music to evolve alongside the rehearsal process and the way in which you want it to complement the action/words of the play.

Be bold about describing what you want to a composer.

Familiarise yourself with some of the basics of musical theory.

Avoid using recorded music that carries other associations not intended by your production.

Be cautious about adding music at the last minute to cover scene changes.

If you are working in a large subsidised or commercial theatre, work out whether you want the musicians in view of the audience or not.

Ensure your composer or musical director work hand in glove with the sound designer to create a complementary aural landscape. Encourage three-way meetings between director, sound designer and composer and/or musical director early on.

Video

The use of video is still in its infancy in mainstream theatre – even though it has been used extensively and exquisitely by avant-garde companies such as The Wooster Group and Hesitate and Demonstrate since the 1980s. The field is therefore wide open and is an exciting one to explore. There are as many ways of integrating video in theatre as there are shows that use it but, crudely speaking, it has two broad functions.

To support the set design in communicating the world and ideas of the play. For example, using recorded footage of clouds in the sky moving across a white cyclorama.

To act as a live participant in the performance, with almost equal status to an actor. For example, video footage of a person – recorded or live – may literally replace one of the actors. Alternatively, an actor might 'perform' the upper body of a character, whilst pre-recorded footage relayed on a screen shows what the lower body is doing, as in The Wooster Group's recent production of *Phèdre*.

I used video properly for the first time in 2007 to direct an adaptation of Virginia Woolf's novel *The Waves*. There was a large screen on which the audience watched sections of a film. The images of this film were created live underneath the screen by actors using lights, props, costumes and sound. It was like looking at the shoot in a film studio and the final edit simultaneously. The process taught me many hard lessons about the use of video.

When I first thought about using video I was rather naïve: I thought I could just plug my little home video into some socket and generate live images on a screen. I had no idea of the technical complexity of the process or of the subtlety that could be achieved with live images by using different camera settings (instead of my friendly 'auto' button) and a media server. If you want to use video to generate live images in a sustained or complex fashion, you might have to buy or hire proper cameras, a media server, a projector and a high quality screen. You will also need to employ someone to operate the editing facility and help the actors with the use of cameras and lighting.

A media server can be used with live or pre-recorded footage: it processes the images, grading them or treating them with special effects (such as sepia or black and white, or a gentle desaturation of all the colours). More importantly, you will have to work in a rehearsal room with a proper blackout facility, some replication of the lighting circumstances in the theatre, and with somewhere to hang the projector and screen.

The use of a media server system also allows the use of multiple projection surfaces without the need for multiple projectors. With a suitably powerful projector and the right lens, it is possible to cover a large area of the stage with projection and to isolate specific areas with pinpoint accuracy. When we created *Waves*, we made over 100 different shots. Each shot, be it a close-up of a face, or blood dripping into a bowl or a billowing sheet on a washing line, had to be lit separately and camera settings had to be adjusted between shots. Moving from shot to shot at speed was very complex and required the actors to learn a great deal of new technical information and practise new skills.

Be prepared for things to move very slowly if you decide to use this sort of process. I was always amazed by how much time it would take to generate one image and sometimes it took a couple of hours to get one shot right. As you work, make sure that someone marks on the floor the relationship between the camera, the object to be filmed and the positions of the lights for each shot. Too often, we set up excellent shots and found that we could not repeat them easily because we had not marked all the positions on the floor.

Be prepared for tension between the use of lights for creating the projected images and the use of lights for lighting theatrical action. In rehearsals we used some small practical desk lights to light the shots. When we got into the theatre it was very hard for the lighting designer to add any other lights to illuminate the theatrical action beneath the screen without them interfering with the lighting for some of the film shots. Make sure you think through exactly how you will use lights in the project and, if possible, ensure that the lighting designer is present for the whole rehearsal period. Whether you are creating live images or not, it is important that the lighting designer and video designer work together; they are both using the same medium – light.

The positioning of the projection screens (or the design of projection surfaces) is also important to get right and make sure the video designer works hand in glove with the set designer on this. Finally, it is worth considering alternatives to projecting onto a large white screen at the back of the stage, the traditional domain of the use of video in theatre. A blank white screen may be distracting for the audience when it is not being used to project images. Although specialist screens will give you a very precise image because they are designed either to transmit or reflect light depending on whether one is back or front projecting, remember that you can achieve dynamic and interesting results by using non-traditional projection surfaces, like walls, or different coloured specialist screens, like the black screen we used for *Waves*.

Summary
Decide whether you want to use video as scenery or as a live participant in the action.
Make sure you hire proper equipment and draw up a realistic budget.
Ensure that you have blackout facility in the rehearsal room, proper lighting equipment and somewhere from which to hang the screen and projectors.
Talk through the difference between the lighting of the shots and the lighting of the theatrical action with your lighting designer and video designer before starting work.
Encourage the video designer and set designer to work alongside each other.
Consider using different projection surfaces rather than the normal white screen.

Voice

Voice work has two main functions.

To ensure everything the actors say is heard clearly by the audience; even if, like me, you are as interested in behaviour as you are in language, audibility is essential.

To remove any evidence of physical strain in the process by which the words are amplified.

There are of course many other subtle uses of voice work, but for me these are the two main functions. However, it is important to add that vocal work is not an area that I am particularly experienced in, and my own work does sometimes suffer as a result – especially in terms of actor audibility. Problems with the audibility of the work I make tend to arise because of the level of immersion in the situation that I ask from the actors. This immersion leads to a reduction of all forms of conventional theatrical expression, both physical and vocal. This is not a problem when a performance is taking place in a small studio venue, but it can be a problem in a theatre of around 500 seats or more. If the voice is lifted to a level at which everyone can hear it, then the sound made by the actors can become rather distorted or shouted, however carefully that voice is prepared. More importantly, this process of amplification can iron out some of the psychological detail and subtlety which can only be expressed in quieter or softer vocal registers. I often struggle with ways of getting the balance between vocal detail and volume right, and I would ask you to bear this in mind when you read what follows.

There are many different approaches to voice work. It is important that you find an approach that is philosophically sympathetic to your process and that you work with people whose methods can dovetail with yours. For example, if you work with intentions, make sure that the voice person uses this terminology when working with the actors. If they are working on a speech with the actor outside the main rehearsal room, give the voice person information about the intentions of the speech as well as the situation in which it is spoken, including time and place. Too often an actor returns from a voice session with increased awareness of their own voice, meaning that when they start working on the scene they jettison everything else they have been asked to think about. They speak the words very clearly and loudly but you cannot believe what they are doing in the situation. Together with the voice person you need to find a balance between situation and audibility, characterisation and vocal clarity. And remember that lack of clarity vocally can be linked to unclear thinking, which is the director's responsibility, and is not always the result of how the actors are using their voices.

Make sure you integrate voice work into your rehearsal process from the beginning, especially if you are working in a large theatre or space. In large subsidised theatres or companies, voice specialists are often brought into the rehearsal process too late to be fully useful. For example, voice specialists are sometimes brought in during previews because there have been complaints about audibility either from the audience or from the management. Alternatively, they join the process because an individual actor is struggling with a speech impediment or accent. The voice person might lead a couple of quick sessions with the group or individual and then departs. This can be counterproductive. Some actors respond easily to this new input and others feel very undermined by it. Avoid this by getting the voice person to do regular vocal sessions to build up the actors' muscles for the size of theatre they will be acting in. If you are working in small or medium-sized spaces where amplification is not a prerequisite, you can be more flexible about whether you do voice work or not. However, the actors will always benefit in terms of clarity and stamina if their vocal muscles are regularly exercised.

That said, be prepared for actors to have strong negative reactions to voice work. This is because of experiences during their training. Sometimes they have had to cope with criticism about their voices and they find any voice work hard to embrace – even though they are no longer in a training context. Other actors have had negative experiences in their professional life and they too might react strongly against voice work. Therefore it helps if you introduce the voice person and their function very carefully and clearly at the outset.

The body and the voice are intimately linked. If there is tension in the body, especially in the neck and shoulders, it will affect the voice. The actor will sound strained and tight, as if the sound were a large object being forced through a small funnel. If this is the case, you will get tense watching the actor, and the character that the actor is playing will not be credible. So wherever possible, work on movement and voice together. Ideally, you will have a voice person and a movement person, and they will work harmoniously with shared goals. The movement person will warm the group up physically and the voice person will take over and exercise them vocally.

If you do not have the funds to employ a voice person, you can give the actors time to work on their own voices daily or at regular intervals in the process – for example, once every two or three days. Most actors will have vocal exercises that help them and, given space, will readily embrace the opportunity to warm up. You do not need to dedicate much time to this – just 15 minutes once a day will be enough if you are pressed for time. Movement can also be integrated into this warm-up, as described below.

Summary
Find a voice person whose working methods can dovetail with your process.
Introduce voice work into the process early on and not at the last minute during your first few performances.
If you cannot afford a voice person, give the actors time to warm up their voices regularly throughout the rehearsal period.
Be prepared for strong negative reactions to voice work and combat this by introducing the voice person and their function carefully and clearly.
Work on voice and movement together with sessions that segue into each other. If you can't afford voice and movement specialists, simply give the actors time to do each step on their own.

Movement

Movement work has three main functions.

> To warm up the actors so that they can prepare physically at the beginning of the rehearsal day or call. This warm-up can last from 15 minutes to one hour – depending on how much rehearsal time you have. Warm-ups are useful at every stage of the rehearsal process.

> To prepare the actors' bodies for the specific demands of the play you are directing. For example, in Euripides' *Iphigenia at Aulis* the chorus stood for two and a half hours. This put pressure on their backs and legs. The movement director, Struan Leslie, put together a series of daily exercises for the rehearsal period that helped them build up their physical stamina for standing. This helped the company to avoid injuries and gave the actors confidence to follow through what was being asked of them in performance.

> To build up the physical or dance skills used directly in the action. In *Dream Play*, the actors trained in ballet and waltz daily with the choreographer Kate Flatt. Both dance forms were used in the performance in choreographed sequences. Any specialised movement or dance skills need to be built up over time and cannot be introduced to the actor at the last minute.

It is important to make a clear distinction between a warm-up that prepares the actor for acting, and game playing. Games include competitive sports (such as football or volleyball) or children's games (such as tag, blind-man's buff or hide-and-seek). Over time, theatre practitioners have modified children's games to fit the needs of particular ensembles working on particular projects and these games have become the staple diet in many rehearsal rooms. There are games designed to help the actors remember each other's names or to build up trust between company members. Games can be useful in breaking the tension early on in rehearsals or getting rid of excess energy in the room. However, do not mistake them for a proper physical warm-up and use them sparingly as their function is limited. Remember that actors can hurt themselves playing games, especially if they have not done a proper warm-up before they begin. Furthermore, games can encourage a competitive environment in the rehearsal room that can be detrimental to a working ethos, encouraging performers to compare themselves negatively to each other. I used a lot of games when I started out but I found that they often left the actors unfocused or overtired in the scene rehearsal that followed. I would also advise against using status games to feed the actors work on the play, as these can encourage a simplification in the actor's thinking about relationships.

When I started out I thought I had to be able to lead the vocal and physical work myself. I read several fantastic books on both subjects by people such as Patsy Rodenburg and Jerzy Grotowski, and I then tried to get the actors to do the exercises described in the books. Over time, however, I realised that it was best to rely on people who were trained in these specialised fields to lead the work directly or to simply let the actors do their own warm-up. Most actors know what they need to do to warm up their bodies properly, but if you force an actor to do a vocal or physical exercise against their wishes, or inaccurately lead an exercise you have read in a book, it can seriously damage an actor's voice or body – or undermine the usefulness of the movement work.

If you want to work with a movement specialist, look for someone whose skills and process can complement your work. Before asking someone to take charge of movement, go and see their work in performance to check you like what they do. Then talk to them very precisely about what you need. Things can often go wrong in rehearsals because the director was not clear at the interview stage about what was actually needed from the movement person. Once engaged, describe the steps of your process in detail and discuss what you want them to do at each step. Remember to share the language of your process; that way you will avoid the actors being pulled in two different directions by the director and the movement person. If they talk about an exercise or technique that you do not understand or cannot visualise, ask them to show you practically what they mean. Most importantly, be clear about whether you want them to contribute to the production beyond a warm-up or any specific choreographic requirements. If the boundaries are not clear, the movement person may start to input inappropriately into all areas of the physical life of the production.

If you cannot afford a movement person, get the actors to do warm-ups individually at the beginning of each day or call. If you also do not have a voice person on board, combine this movement warm-up with vocal work. I suggest that you do not do this as a group activity. Rather, give the actors the space to work individually. Let them each find a place in the rehearsal room to do their own physical and vocal warm-ups simultaneously. This means you will be relying on the training the actors have received at their various drama schools. You can give them between 15 and 30 minutes to do this, depending on the length of your rehearsal process.

I would advise against taking part in the warm-up. Instead, use the time that the actors are warming up to prepare the work you will do with them after the warm-up is finished. Remember that you can also learn a lot about your actors by sitting and discreetly observing how they use their bodies or voices in a warm-up.

Always remember to let the actors know that you are going to do movement work the day before you plan to do it, so that they can turn up wearing appropriate clothing. And if the work is particularly demanding physically, consider doing a 'warm-down' at the end of the day, where you give the actors 15 minutes to stretch and shake the tension out of their bodies. This is particularly important if they are doing a play that is physically demanding or involves imagining a psychologically distressing situation (such as *Women of Troy* or *Iphigenia at Aulis*, where many of the scenes concern the death of children). This can leave a lot of physical tension in the actors' bodies after a rehearsal or performance.

Summary

Decide which of the four main functions you want movement to fulfil in your production.

Be clear about the difference between movement work and game playing.

Do not lead movement or vocal work yourself, unless you have been trained in either field.

Find a movement person whose skills and process can complement yours.

Let them know precisely what you want them to do before they accept the job.

Once engaged, let them know exactly what you want them to do at each step of the rehearsal process.

If you do not want, or cannot afford, a movement or voice person, set aside time in rehearsals for the actors to do their own combined movement and vocal warm-up.

Use the warm-up time to prepare the work you will do with the actors afterwards.

Always warn the actors that you are doing movement work the night before so that they can wear appropriate clothing.

Consider doing a 'warm-down' if the work has been physically demanding or involves them imagining a situation that is psychologically distressing.

Katya Kabanova by Leoš Janáček

CHAPTER 7

Selecting actors and testing starting points for rehearsals

This chapter has two steps:

Casting
Workshops

Casting

Casting is about choosing the right actors for the play and the right actors for your rehearsal process. If you cast an actor who is right for the part but who will not undertake your process, you may waste valuable time in repeated conflicts about working methodology, meaning that the actors who want to work in your process will be caught in the crossfire. The result will be a production where the actors do not inhabit the same world. On the other hand, if you work with an actor who is absolutely willing to work alongside you but cannot possibly deliver the character, everyone will be in the same world but one person will not be believable. Try to get a balance.

When you do auditions, spend at least 30 minutes with each person. Many actors find auditioning frightening and, as a result, they cannot easily do themselves justice. Giving them a little more time to relax can lessen the hold the fear has on them. They will then do better work and you will be able to measure their appropriateness for the role more accurately. Also have cups and water to hand for each person – fear can cause dehydration and interfere with an actor's ability to speak.

Divide the auditions into four loose sections:

Talking with the actor about jobs on their CV
Asking them what they think about the play and the character they are
auditioning for
Explaining the job as you understand it – the role and the process
Giving them different tasks to play on a short scene from the play.

Take the time to read each CV before the actor enters the room and select one or two jobs from their CV to ask them about. Ideally, that job should be one that you know something about (for example, you might know the director or the text or seen the production). If, for instance, you know the text, then ask them how they dealt with a specific moment. Talking about work they have already done will also relax the actor. Next, ask them what they think about the play you are auditioning them for. The answer to this question will measure the degree to which the actor is interested in the overall play as compared to the character they are being seen for. A complete absence of any thoughts about the overall play should ring a tiny alarm bell in your head. Then ask them what they think about the character you are seeing them for. Here, look out for actor's affinities with the character that could get in the way of them playing the role. An actor might want to use character to exercise or exorcise a private problem that would be better dealt with in therapy. For example, the actor who starts to cry as they talk about the role or who offers an inappropriate and lengthy parallel between their own life and the character's life is a cause for concern. Ask the questions about the play and the character before you give them an idea of how you are approaching either. That will stop the actors from trying to please you by matching their answers to your reading of the material.

Next, give a brief description of your working process and ask whether they would be comfortable working in that way. Most actors will say that they would love to work in the way you describe because they want the job – so scrutinise them carefully as they answer this question, and look for any information that may belie what they are saying. For instance, you may see a sudden eye flicking, or an involuntary movement of the hand to the mouth or a twitch of the foot. Describing how you work will also provide you with an insurance policy for the future. You can remind them of what you said in the audition if they complain about the working process during rehearsals.

Then describe the job you are seeing them for. Be clear and straightforward about what the job is and, in a desire to secure them, do not mislead them into thinking that it is something that it is not. For example, when you are auditioning actors for small roles, do not pretend that the role is bigger than it is – or that you will add things to it when you have no intention of doing so. Similarly, do not adjust your description of the process in order to secure an actor. Do not pretend that movement sessions, which are central to how you work, are optional because a famous actor clearly doesn't like the sound of them. Lies like this will catch up with you in the rehearsal process when the actor will see things for what they are.

Finally, move on to reading the text. It will help enormously to have another person to read with the actor so that you can objectively watch the work done by the actor you are auditioning. This is not possible if you are involved in the reading itself. If you have a casting director, they will normally read with the actors. If you do not have one, get someone else in to read – perhaps a friend or an actor already in the cast. The scene you select for this should be simple and easy to grasp after a first reading. Ideally, the scene should be between two characters and the tasks you suggest to the actor should be straightforward and clear. The feedback you give should be direct and reassuring – whether their work is good or bad. Each actor auditioning for a part should read the same scene and do the same tasks. This will help you to assess them fairly and accurately, especially at the end of a long day of casting. Remember that if you read several different scenes when casting one character, you can sometimes mistake the fact that someone is reading a different scene for a better audition.

First, ask the actor to read the scene through for sense only, as this gives them a chance to say the text out loud without the pressure of having to deliver a performance. Next, set some simple tasks. The tasks should include instructions about time, place and intentions. Here is an example of the tasks you could set the actors auditioning for Konstantin in *The Seagull*. Ask each actor to read the scene in Act Two when the seagull is laid at Nina's feet; ask them to play that it is a very hot day and that lunch is due in five minutes. They will read the scene three times and each time ask them to play a different intention:

> to make Nina feel guilty
> to wake Nina up to the reality of what she has done
> to entertain Nina.

Ideally, the third intention should be a curve ball designed to see how imaginative and flexible each actor can be.

After they have read the scene, thank them for their work and ask if they have any questions they would like to ask you about the production or process. A word of caution here: be prepared to field some challenging questions at this point. I am often asked questions such as: 'Why do you want to direct this play?', or 'What drew you to the play?' or 'How are you going to stage the play?' So prepare for this beforehand. Being able to answer questions like this simply and with confidence can help the actor to feel secure about you as a director. After all, the audition process is a two-way street – you are also being assessed by the actor.

After seeing each actor, take a couple of minutes to jot down your thoughts about their work. At the end of a long auditioning day you can easily forget your precise thoughts about the first actors you saw. Write the notes clearly so that you can read them back easily at the end of the day. Do this before asking for feedback from the person with you in the audition. You will then catch your precise responses unalloyed by anyone else's opinion.

A surprising number of actors have dyslexia, so let everyone auditioning know which scene you will be working on beforehand. That way they can all have a fair chance to do their best.

When you are making decisions after auditions, try and keep the following in mind:

> the actor's appropriateness for the role
> how casting the actor might work in relationship to other casting decisions
> > you are making
> their interest in how you work and
> how they will fit into a group of people who need to work together.

Listen very sensitively to your hunches or instincts about the actors you meet. If you sense an actor is difficult or aggressive or hung up in some way, you are more than likely to be right. Hunches are hard to explain or defend to casting directors or producers. However, if they are not followed up, they can lead to casting errors that damage productions. If you cast someone who proves difficult or destructive you will often look back and remember how a negative thought about them flitted through your head during the audition.

If you have any doubts about an actor, ring other directors who have worked with them. Most directors are more than happy to talk about people they have worked with – even very famous directors. Phone calls can reassure you about a choice or confirm your doubts.

If you are casting actors who are older or more experienced than you are, try not to be overawed by their knowledge or status. Remember, it is possible to be respectful and yet retain your distance. Similarly, try not to let your own insecurities about your right to direct determine your behaviour. Early on in my career when I auditioned older actors, I remember putting so much energy into persuading the actor I could direct, that I gave myself no time to judge their ability to play the part. It took me several years to be confident enough to put my energy when auditioning into selecting the best actor for the role.

Summary
Spend at least 30 minutes with each actor.
Ask them about they work.
Ask them what they think about the play and the character.
Be clear about what the job entails.
Describe your working process and check they are comfortable with it.

Ask them to read a scene from the play and set them simple tasks to do.
Have a third person in the audition to read with the actor.
Let the actors know which scene you will be working on before the audition.
Ask them if they have any questions for you and be prepared to be challenged.
Ensure that every actor is auditioned in the same way.
Jot down a record of your thoughts after each audition.
Listen to your hunches.
If you have doubts, ring directors the actor has worked with previously.

Workshops

While rehearsals are about delivering a production for an audience, workshops are about exploring ideas. Use workshops to investigate grey areas in your interpretation of the text, or to test-run new steps and tools in your process. The discoveries made in the workshop will provide you with clear starting points for rehearsals. In a rehearsal process you cannot change your mind all the time about your working method or the interpretation of the text. This will make the actors unstable and stop them building a performance strong enough to go in front of an audience. In a workshop you can chop and change as much as you like because you do not have to build anything durable.

Get into the habit of doing a workshop before every rehearsal period. There will always be some corner of the work that will benefit from investigation or a step in your process that needs re-evaluation. For example with *The Seagull*, we explored different solutions to the production style of Konstantin's play using movement and music. With *Dream Play*, we studied the composition of dreams and searched for a language with which to communicate them on-stage. Workshops also allow you to kick the material around in a more adventurous way than you could in a rehearsal period. For example, with Chekhov's *Three Sisters*, we investigated ways in which slow motion and waltzing could work alongside psychological realism.

Workshops are best done with between four and six actors. It can help to have an even number so that you can set them tasks in pairs. If you have already cast your production, use all or part of your cast – depending on the size of the company. If you are not cast, work with actors you are considering casting – but do not use the workshop as an audition. Alternatively, you could use actors you have worked with before, as you will get more done working with actors you already have a relationship with.

Enter the workshop with a series of simple questions and guide the actors towards answering those questions by giving them concrete things to do. If there are conflicts or abstract debates, encourage the actors to translate them into a practical exercise. For example, I started a workshop on Strindberg's *Dream Play* by telling the actors that I wanted (a) to explore what dreams were composed of, and (b) to find a language with which to communicate them on-stage. I had six actors in the group. First, I asked them all to recall a dream they had had recently. Next I asked them to attempt to stage the dreams. They could use the rest of the group or work singly. The rehearsal room was pretty bare so they had to use chairs, tables or any other objects they could find in the room.

One by one I watched the 'staged' dreams. Other members of the group watched with me – if they were not in the exercise in hand. After each attempted staging I asked the actors watching to tell me what they noticed about the composition of dreams and the staging solutions. We compiled a list of the ingredients of dreams. We noticed, for example, that there was always one dreamer, that people from the dreamer's waking world often appeared in different roles and that there were jump-cuts from place to place. Then we noticed which aspects of dreams were possible to stage and which were not. For example, it was easier to stage a dream in a domestic setting (like a kitchen) than in an exterior location (like the sea). Next, we took the aspects of dreams we had listed and worked on them one by one. For example, we spent an afternoon looking at different practical ways of doing jump-cuts between locations. Next, I asked them to concentrate on working on dreams in domestic settings. Then I gave them some of the dreams described by Carl Jung and Sigmund Freud to work on.

Subsequently we started to apply what we had learnt to the play. For example, we selected the candidates for the role of the dreamer from the dramatis personae (the banker, the writer and Agnes). Then we tried staging some of the shorter scenes as if they were being dreamt by each of the three different people. Earlier in the workshop we had noticed that most people who appear in dreams come from somewhere in our waking lives. We soon realised that we needed to build a strong back history for each of our dreamers so that we could people the dreams accurately.

By the end of the workshop I had a clear idea of how to use work on dreams to direct the play. I knew that we had to avoid ambitious settings, like water or sky. The exercises on jump-cuts made us realise that the set had to be able to move from location to location in a split second. I knew I had to select one character to be the dreamer and that the banker was the best candidate. In turn I understood that this dreamer's actual biography had to be constructed before we could build his dream world. You can see that the workshop followed a simple logic that emerged from the two initial questions.

A workshop for testing out new directing tools can follow a similar format. For example, you could take ideas or exercises you have read about or been taught but are not yet confident enough to use in a rehearsal situation. Boil down the things you want to investigate into three or four simple questions. A workshop on intentions might include the following questions.

> In life how do we get what we want from other people?
> How do you find what a character's intention is from a play script?
> How do we notate the intention?
> Does every word or action in the play need to be harnessed to an intention?

The questions will focus your work with the actors and provide you with simple points of reference to return to if the exploration loses focus.

Summary
Be clear about the difference between a workshop and a rehearsal.
Isolate any aspects of the text or staging which you are unclear about.
Enter the workshop with a series of simple questions and make sure that the work you do attempts to answer the questions.
Draw up a list of things to take on into the rehearsal room.
Use workshops to test-run new directing tools or exercises.

Katya Kabanova by Leoš Janáček

CHAPTER 8

Preparing the rehearsal environment

This chapter has four steps:

Working with stage management
Selection of rehearsal rooms
Establishing communication structures
Getting the rehearsal room ready

Working with stage management

Building a good stage management team is crucial to a healthy atmosphere in the rehearsal room and a smooth transition into the theatre. Different cultures have different ways of arranging their stage management. In larger UK theatres such as the National Theatre, there is a team of three or four stage management – a stage manager, a deputy stage manager and one or two assistant stage managers. By comparison, a production on the fringe in the same country will probably involve one or two people covering all the stage management functions.

Whether you have a team of four or two, someone will be cueing the show, and it is this relationship that you need to get right. This person is technically called the deputy stage manager and they sit with you during all your rehearsals. They have a copy of the script and in it they write down all the moves that the actors make. When you get into the theatre they write down where all the lighting and sound cues occur. This copy of the script is called 'the book', and will be used by the deputy stage manager to cue the lighting and sound operators. The way in which they cue will affect the rhythm of the entire performance. Therefore, this person must have a clear sense of what you want artistically, in terms of both the overall pacing of the evening and the tiny details of the timing of different entrances or sound cues. Do you, for example, want the entrances to be anticipated and sharp, or slow and delayed? Or do you want the sound to come in a split second earlier, or later, on a certain line?

I have found the difference in the work of various deputy stage managers astonishing. I can feel their energy and personality in the rhythm of the shows they operate. Since 2003, I have worked almost exclusively with one deputy stage manager, Pippa Meyer. This is because she has nerves of steel, completely understands what I need rhythmically and works very closely with the actors. If they make the slightest change in what they are doing she follows them with her cueing. It is a fine art.

If you have a choice over who does this job for you, interview different people for the role. If you do not have a choice, take the time to talk to your deputy stage manager before rehearsals start and explain precisely how you want them to be in the room with you and how you work. Then, as you get closer to the technical rehearsals, sit down and talk through precisely what you want in terms of the timing and rhythm of all the cueing. Never assume that a deputy stage manager will tune into your way of working or your timings. If you encounter a deputy stage manager who you work well with, try to employ them again.

If you are working in a large-scale theatre in the UK, the other stage management roles might be structured as follows.

The **stage manager** is responsible for the overall running of the show. They will often not be in rehearsals with you, as they are coordinating with everyone outside the rehearsal room such as production management, props buyers, designers and so on. They organise any meetings needed and communicate any problems thrown up by the rehearsal process to the rest of the creative team. When you get into the theatre, they run the technical rehearsal and they remain backstage for every performance, ensuring that everything runs smoothly.

The **assistant stage manager** is mainly responsible for recording and organising the settings of props, furniture and so on.

Before rehearsals begin it is useful to have a meeting with some or all of your stage management team to discuss how you like to work. There are many different ways of organising the culture of the rehearsal room and it will help enormously if your team can prepare the room and tailor how they execute their roles so that it suits your specific needs. Talk through the steps of your rehearsal process and how you would like the room set up for each step. It will help, for example, to go through the props list with your stage management team and discuss which props you need in rehearsals, and when. If you are working in a small theatre, they can then find those props themselves; in a large organisation they can ask the relevant department to source them. Remember to pass on any requirements from the movement director (for instance, gym mats for exercises) to your stage management. You should also discuss the point at which you would like the stage management team to do the mark-up.

The mark-up is a way of notating the set design: it is a series of lines marked on the floor with plastic tape that indicate the boundaries of the landscape or architecture that the set describes. The stage management will usually stick it to the floor of the rehearsal room on the first or second day of rehearsals unless you tell them not to.

Sadly, when you are starting out, not all stage management teams, or individual members of teams, may be prepared to listen to, or follow, a different way of working – particularly if you are a younger and less-experienced director. Do not always expect the relationship to be an easy one to negotiate. However, the good experiences will far outweigh the bad and, of course, a good stage management team is a completely invaluable asset to any director.

Summary
Get the relationship with the person cueing the show right.

If possible, interview different candidates for the role of deputy stage manager.

If you do not have a choice, ask to meet the deputy stage manager, and talk them through your working process and what you need from them.

Before rehearsals begin, arrange a meeting with your stage management team to talk through how you like to work.

Ensure that the stage management prepare the rehearsal room to suit your specific needs.

Do not be overwhelmed if the stage management team do not always immediately support your way of working.

Selection of rehearsal rooms

In many theatres you will not have a choice over your rehearsal room. If you are working on the fringe, your budget might mean that you have to hire the draftiest church hall known to mankind. However, if you do have any room for manoeuvre, consider the following things when making the choice of rehearsal room.

Make sure that the room is large enough to mark up the ground plan of the set plus an additional one or two metres all round. This allows the actors to start the action a few steps back from the beginning of the scenery or the point at which the audience will see them. This physical runway ensures that they are already inside the character and situation before they begin the action of the scene and therefore stops them using the first few feet of their entrance onto the set to enter the world of the play. Remember, also, that it is difficult to practise entering a room or a building convincingly when you cannot get behind the door because it is flat against the rehearsal room wall. Read the section on mark-ups in Chapter 11 if you need further clarification.

Ensure that there is somewhere for making hot drinks, storing milk and that there is a secure place for the actors to leave their belongings outside the rehearsal room. If this is not possible, divide the rehearsal room into different sections that fulfil these functions. For example, you could put some flats up in the corner of the room and store your kettle, fridge and so on behind them. You could position a curtain elsewhere to create a place where the actors can leave their things during rehearsals and drink or chat during tea breaks. A rehearsal room should not be a place that blurs the boundaries between free time and work time. Nor should it be cluttered with everyone's belongings. This will clutter the actors' heads and make it difficult for them to imagine the world of the play.

Next, check that the acoustic of the room is not booming or echoing. Then, find out about the temperature. If it is winter, enquire about heating, and if it is summer, ask about any cooling or fan systems. Make sure you turn on all the lights in the room you are considering using as a space. Some rooms are lit mainly by glaring strip lights. This makes it difficult for actors to concentrate during long rehearsal days. If the lights are not good, ask if you can rig some simple theatre lights and use them instead. If you are planning to use sound during the rehearsals, check that a sound system can be installed and that there is a safe place to store the equipment overnight. Check, too, that you can put things up on the walls.

At the beginning of your career you will find yourself in many rehearsal rooms that are far from ideal and do not have any of the facilities – or possibilities – that I am suggesting you look for. When I started out on the fringe in London, I worked in freezing cold rooms where I had to wear hat, coat and scarf, and keep moving all the time. I also worked in boiling hot cupboards, where I sat with barely nothing on, fanning myself with the script. In most cases, I just had to put up with it, but whenever I could I would try to raise a little extra money towards a better room. I learnt very quickly that a pleasant, comfortable and clean room really enhances the actors' work – and makes them feel as if the situation is professional, especially if you are not able to pay them. When money is tight, rehearsal room hire is very low on people's agendas. If possible, place it a little higher up – if, for example, you have a choice between an expensive costume and a rehearsal room, put the money on the rehearsal room.

Summary

Ensure that the rehearsal room is large enough to mark up the ground plan of more than the room or rooms, place or places in which the action occurs. Allow for at least one or two metres between the wall of the rehearsal room and the threshold of where the set starts.

Make sure that there is somewhere for making hot drinks, etc. and a secure place for actors to leave their belongings.

Check that the acoustic of the room is good for the spoken word.

Check the heating, if you are rehearsing in winter, and the cooling systems, if you are working in summer. See what lighting is available in the room and, if it is not good, ask if you can install any other lights.

If you plan to use sound, check that you can install it and that there is a safe place to store the equipment overnight.

Remember that a warm and welcoming rehearsal room is a real asset if you are asking actors to work for little or no money. Put it a little higher up on your list of priorities.

Establishing communication structures

It is essential that everything that happens in the rehearsal room is communicated clearly to all the relevant people – be they designers, prop makers or set builders. Whether you are working for a theatre with a large infrastructure or for a small profit-share company on the fringe, establish robust and efficient systems of communication with clear priorities.

The first means of communication is rehearsal notes. These are the notes that the stage management sends out on a daily basis to everyone involved in making things for the production. They contain all the new things that crop up in rehearsals, and include costume ideas, set design modifications and new props. Make sure that you are sent rehearsal notes and that you read them. Communication problems can often occur because of an inaccurate rehearsal note. If you are devising work from scratch or making substantial changes to the text in rehearsals, ensure that the stage management contextualise new ingredients. For example, instead of just saying a prop is required, ask them also to explain how it is used and why it has been added. This creates a little extra work for the stage management but ensures that all the relevant people digest the new information clearly and efficiently. Even if you are working on the fringe with a small budget, use rehearsal notes to establish a culture of communication between the rehearsal room and anyone working for you outside that room. It will help you run a tight ship, especially if funds are low. It also establishes an atmosphere of professionalism even if you are unable to match that by proper wages for everyone.

The second means of communication is a regular production meeting, chaired by the production manager. These meetings should happen once a week in a lunch break or at the end of the rehearsal day. They are attended by everyone involved in making the production: prop makers, production managers, technical directors, lighting staff, sound department, wardrobe people, dressers, make-up and so on. At these meetings unclear rehearsal notes are clarified and all technical demands discussed. It's important to be clear and simple about why you need any new ingredients such as a prop or a piece of furniture. If any financial concerns arise at the production meeting, first try to find out exactly what is causing them. Then ask whether there is anything that can be done to solve them. Whatever the outcome of your enquiries, do not give an immediate decision. Rather, go away to think about whether there is a creative solution to the problem. If necessary, arrange smaller meetings with specific individuals to thrash out problems. Even if you are working with a small group of people on the fringe and have limited funds, try to meet regularly with everyone helping you to make the production. This will ensure good communication and planning.

It can also help to have smaller meetings regularly with the core creative team – set designer, lighting designer, sound designer and composer and/or musical director. This will allow you time to brainstorm creative problems that do not need an immediate technical solution. With devised work it can also help to send out artistic notes. These are notes that describe in detail how the work is being developed in the rehearsal room: they are particularly important if there is no script before rehearsals begin.

Summary
Establish robust and efficient systems of communication with clear priorities, whether you are working for a theatre with a large infrastructure or for a small profit-share company on the fringe.
Set up a system of rehearsal notes and ensure that all new ingredients are clearly contextualised.
Establish a system of production meetings with a clear chair person and clear agenda which prioritises things efficiently.
Establish a system of regular creative team meetings to brainstorm creative problems that do not have immediate technical solutions.
If you are devising work, establish a series of artistic notes to complement your rehearsal notes.

Getting the rehearsal room ready

In an ideal world you will have now found a comfortable, well-heated rehearsal room with a good acoustic larger than the footprint of your set design. You will also have an area inside the room, or adjoining it, in which to make tea and coffee and another area where the actors can put their belongings. Ask your stage management team to buy tea, coffee and biscuits for the first day of rehearsals (provide these free on the first day, then encourage the stage manager to organise a kitty to which everyone in the room should contribute). The stage management will also have organised the furniture and props you asked for at the meeting you had with them before rehearsals. Hopefully, these will include a lot of things that you will use in the performance itself. The room should be tidy with all these objects stacked neatly in the corner or along the walls.

Now set aside a table for your research material. Here you can share the research you came across whilst you were doing your initial research or the books and photographs you came across in the design process. It can be tempting to put some of the research or design material up on the wall before the actors arrive. Instead, have the walls bare for the first day, then start to stick things up as they emerge or are discussed in the rehearsal process. That way the actors will understand the function of each reference. Next, ensure you have a table that is large enough to seat the full ensemble around. Try to ensure that the room is neat, clean and ready for work.

In my experience it is best not to have the mark-up on the floor at the beginning of rehearsals. This is because you will not be doing any practical work in the locations where the play is set for the first 40% of rehearsals. I write about when – and how – to put down the mark-up in Chapter 11.

Summary
Make sure that the stage management buy tea, coffee and biscuits for the first day.
Ensure that all props or rehearsal furniture are stacked neatly in the corner of the room.
Put all your research material discretely on a table at the side of the room.
Make sure you have a table large enough to seat the full ensemble – and chairs.
Ask the stage management to defer putting the mark-up on the floor until later on in the process when you start doing improvisations or scene rehearsals in the place where the action of the play is set.

PART TWO

REHEARSALS

Jephtha by George Frideric Handel

Rehearsals

This section of the book describes how to use all the preparatory work you have done with the actors. Rehearsals should allow the actors to build things step by step over time, gradually and slowly. The main skills required from the director are patience and long-term thinking. Even if you are rehearsing for only two weeks, the process should be one that evolves carefully and gently. It is like building a house in which different materials are laid down layer by layer from the foundations to the roof. The materials must be put in place carefully and in a logical order, or the building will not stand up properly. So, try to take small steps rather than big leaps. Do not expect an immediate outcome from the actor and do not respond to their work in an early rehearsal as if it were the final result that the audience will see. Instead, watch it as a step towards that result. And be patient with any early errors or stumbles. Actors need time to build their characters and to practise what they have to do in the scenes. They cannot always respond to an instruction with an immediate solution or result. If you wait a couple of days you may well see the outcome unfold. If not, simply keep giving the instruction until it does. Similarly, if there is a big problem in the scene, do not think you have to solve it in one go. Instead, chip away at it over time.

Remember too that rehearsals are about making work that lasts well into the run of the performance of the play – not creating one-off exciting moments that cannot be repeated. So make sure that the process is not about the search for a sudden revelatory discovery or epiphany that will unlock everything. Actors often talk about 'finding the character', as if the character were a suit of clothes sitting in a room somewhere just waiting for the actor to open the right door and put it on. I once worked with an actor who would turn up to rehearsals every day with an entirely new proposal for his character. One day he would play his own age and tempo; the next day he would be older and do everything at a faster tempo. Or he would turn up having diagnosed his character with a new psychological problem, like depression or separation anxiety. Finally, at the penultimate rehearsal, he said,

'I think I have got it' and did a fantastic run-through. This actor was so brilliant that he was able to draw up a biography behind this successful, last-minute, choice, and the character was entirely grounded and real. His ability to do this was an exception. Most actors who 'find' their characters late on in rehearsals, present work to the audience that is thin – and remains thin from the first performance to the last. This is because it takes time for any actor to construct a credible character. Epiphanies are often built on a fleeting emotion and are rarely possible to recreate nightly. Create a rehearsal room culture that encourages the gradual construction of strong and durable characters and situations.

The next three chapters assume an ideal rehearsal time of six to eight weeks. This is, I know, very different from many situations that directors will encounter early on in their careers, where rehearsal periods can be as short as two or three weeks. Therefore, at the ends of Chapters 10 and 11, I have included a description of how to use the steps described if you have a shorter rehearsal period. Make sure you read the full chapter first before looking at the essential ingredients for a short rehearsal period. Be reassured, however, that it is perfectly possible to use the techniques in these chapters to great and precise effect in a less-than-ideal time span – and, even if you only have time to use one or two of the exercises described, remember that your directing will already be considerably enhanced by the preparation you have done on your own before rehearsals begin.

The Oresteia by Aeschylus

CHAPTER 9

The initial few days of rehearsal

This chapter looks at the initial few days of rehearsals with the actors and describes how to establish the way you want to work. Start in the right way and it will set you up for the whole process. Make an error in the first few days and it can cause lasting damage. This chapter covers nine separate areas:

> Organising your thoughts about actors
> Twelve golden rules for working with actors
> Establishing the language of your process
> How to give feedback to actors about their work
> How to sit in the rehearsal room
> Introducing the text to the actors
> The first day of rehearsals
> The model showing
> Introducing sound, costumes, props, furniture, lights and scenic elements
>   to the rehearsal process

Organising your thoughts about actors

The thoughts you have in your head about actors when you enter the rehearsal room will dictate how you work with them. If, for example, you have the thought 'Actors are difficult' you will enter the room in a defensive manner, anticipating problems even where there are none. If you have the thought 'Actors are special' you will enter the room worried that you are at a disadvantage – not special enough yourself – and may well start to treat them with kid gloves.

Sort out your private thoughts about actors before you start rehearsals. Take a few minutes now to fill in the sentence 'Actors are ...' with some simple adjectives. Put down all your thoughts, however relevant or not you think they are. You will find that your adjectives include positive words like 'imaginative' and 'brave' and negative words like 'demanding' and 'difficult'. In some cases you will use words like 'special', 'artists' or 'instinctive' which classify actors as a unique and special breed. In other cases you will find that you use words like 'frightening' that reveal your own anxieties about how to work with them. Look at all the words you have used to describe actors. Weed out the words like 'frightening', 'difficult' or 'special' which will make you feel inadequate or put you at a disadvantage. In their place add new words to help you work more easily with actors. Use simple and clear words, like 'adults' or 'skilled craftspeople' or 'responsible'. Always try to be objective: it is a professional situation.

The acting profession, like any profession, contains some people who are difficult to work with. This leads to problems in the rehearsal room. For example, one actor may use the character inappropriately to demonstrate their own pain while another will be driven too strongly by career thinking and take short cuts in their work. The more you direct, the more familiar you will become with different types of problems – and the more skilled you will be at avoiding casting certain types of actors or learning to cope with the challenges they pose on the rehearsal room floor.

Sorting out your own thoughts about actors will go a long way towards helping you cope with difficult actors early on. It will put you in a healthier mental place from which to respond to them. Console yourself with the fact that even the most skilled and experienced directors cannot avoid casting difficult or trouble-some actors – either because of necessity, or because of an error of judgement. Remember that difficult actors are often shaped by experiences with bad directors. Provide a considerate, consistent and respectful atmosphere in your rehearsal room and it will go a long way towards softening the impact of their behaviour.

However, there will always be some people who are impossible to work with. All your attempts to direct them will fail. You did not cast the right person. In these cases, it is important to remember two things. First, do not bend your working process: do not adopt one way of directing for the difficult actor and one way for the rest of the ensemble. That way you can end up losing the trust of the whole group as well as the difficult actor. A change in the working process will not remove the difficulty. So stick to your guns and be respectful but consistent. Second, make sure that the difficult actor does not take up all your mental space. Reduce the space they take up in your head and adjust your expectations to what is realistically possible in the circumstances. Then concentrate on the other actors – and on the things that you can change and develop. Some battles cannot be won.

Do not let this advice about difficult or negative actors give you a picture of the profession that is full of troubled and troubling individuals. Most actors are responsible adults. They will work hard to build the world of the play and the character inside that world.

Summary
Remember that the thoughts you have in your head about actors will dictate how
  you work with them.
Sort out your private thoughts about actors before you enter the rehearsal room.
Prepare yourself mentally for working with difficult actors.

Twelve golden rules for working with actors

1 Cultivate patience and long-term thinking

Work slowly and take small steps rather than big leaps. Do not respond to the
actors' work in an early rehearsal as if it were the final result that the audience
will see. Instead, watch it as a step towards that result. Be patient with any early
errors or stumbles. Actors need time to build their characters and to practise
what they have to do in the scenes. Imagine, instead, that you are building work
that will be clear for audiences throughout the entire run of performances.

2 Be consistent

Be consistent in your use of language, your goals, your behaviour and how you
conduct your relationships. Hold a steady and straightforward relationship to
each actor with clear boundaries. Do not prioritise one relationship over
another and thereby create competitiveness in the room. Give clear and encouraging feedback to each member of the ensemble, irrespective of a status that
could be measured by counting the number of lines a character has or referring
to an actor's television or film credits. This rule will be expanded on in two later
sections: 'Establishing the language of your process'; and 'How to give feedback
to actors about their work'.

3 Do not worry about being liked

You will not make clear work if you are too concerned about being liked by
actors. If this is your goal, you will avoid saying anything difficult, or challenging, for fear of being disliked. Or you will waste time ensuring that everyone has
a good time instead of focusing on sharpening the work the actors are doing.
Even if being liked is the goal, it is unlikely that you will achieve it. The pressures
on the actor building a character in a play are such that they are bound, at some
point in the process, to enter a more conflicted or tense relationship with the
director. Replace the need to be liked with the aim of being respected – and head,
instead, for the goal of making clear work.

4 **Make the text the mediator of any conflict**

Position the text as the arbiter between yourself and the actor if there is any disagreement in the rehearsal room. Read the words together and ask what it is that the writer intends. Look for the simplest impression that the text gives. This will help the actor to see the difference between what they want, what the director wants and what is actually written on the page. You could use phrases like, 'That is a useful observation, but what do we think Chekhov is actually saying here?' to help guide the actor. If you are devising work rather than working with a text, then use the storyboard or the ideas you are aiming for as your mediators.

5 **Do not automatically blame the actor if something goes wrong**

If there is a problem in an exercise, an improvisation or a scene rehearsal, do not immediately blame the actor – either in your head or out loud. Instead, assume it is your fault. Stop and think about what happened. Ask yourself whether anything you said was unclear. For example, you might have given your instruction too quickly so that the actor did not grasp what you wanted. Perhaps you spoke too abstractly so that the actor did not know how to translate your ideas into something concrete. Reflect on whether the timing of your instruction made it difficult for the actor to execute it. Maybe you gave your instruction at the last minute and the actor did not have time to absorb it. Ask whether your mood or preoccupation with other things interfered with how you gave the notes to the actor. Perhaps you were worrying about a budgetary problem when you told them what you wanted them to do so that the actor responded to your worried look instead of listening to what you said. When you have diagnosed the possible cause of the problem, give new instructions and try the scene or improvisation again. In most cases the new instruction will remove the problem or begin to remove it.

6 **Always apologise if you make an error**

Directing errors come in all shapes and sizes. For example, you might give an unclear note which confuses what the actor does, or might have called an actor to rehearse a scene but fallen behind your original schedule, leaving the actor sitting in the room twiddling their thumbs for the whole rehearsal. If you make an error, apologise immediately and keep the apology simple and brief – then move on. Do not be tempted to hide an error because of embarrassment or pride. If you do this, then the actors will follow suit creating an unhealthy working environment in which everyone wastes energy pretending that they are right. On the other hand, do not apologise every other minute for minuscule errors that only you notice. The actors will think you are insecure.

7 **Do not use anyone as a kicking stool**

Do not use someone as a kicking stool. Using someone like this can start on the first day of rehearsals or it can happen subtly over time. You might be aware you are doing it or you could be doing it unconsciously until someone points it out to you. Kicking stools are often assistant directors or stage management or actors playing small roles. Treat someone badly and everyone's respect for you in the rehearsal room will be undermined. You will also create a climate of fear. The actors will be frightened that you will suddenly turn on them in the same way. As a result, they will stop offering you the best of their creativity.

You will unsettle the actors if you let any negative emotion get a strong hold on you – even if it is justified. Negative emotions include anger, frustration and despair. These emotions will affect your judgement – you will not see things or talk clearly about them. Call a coffee break if you feel an emotion getting a hold on you like this. Tame the emotion, then start work again. If you regularly experience the same negative emotion, work on yourself outside the rehearsal room. Find out what is causing this repeated emotion and then, when you experience the first signs of its appearance at work, learn to inhibit it.

8 **Do not put time pressure on actors and do not waste time yourself**

Never give the actor the impression that there is no time or very little time – even if that is the case. Short rehearsal periods in particular create anxiety about time and this leads the director to say things like: 'We only have four weeks, so we have to work really fast.' This makes the actor feel that there is no time to build anything properly or explore. It puts them under pressure and makes them product-driven. They take short cuts and lose faith in the steps of the process. Keep your anxiety about time to yourself. Tackle an actor who wastes time head on and have a quiet word with them in a tea break or at the end of a rehearsal day. Point out what they are doing – for example, constantly arriving back late after tea breaks – and the effect it has on the group. Ask them politely to stop. Do not indulge an actor who wastes time. Similarly, do not constantly look at your watch in the rehearsal room. Instead, ask the stage management to put a clock on the wall in a position that you can easily look at it without anyone noticing. You can keep a strict eye on time without affecting anyone with time anxiety.

Do not waste time yourself. When you are starting off as a director, it is easy to waste valuable time explaining your ideas or justifying your process. You might ask the actors to do an exercise, then spend ten minutes explaining the thinking behind that exercise. The ten minutes of explanation is a sign of anxiety about your inexperience. Instead, just ask the actors to do the exercise. If someone questions the idea behind the exercise or the process, suggest firmly that they do the task first and then see if the act of doing it answers their concerns. Nine times out of ten doing the exercise will sort things out. If not, explain things as simply and briefly as possible after the exercise is finished.

If you have a brief rehearsal period, study all the aspects of your directing style and process from a time point of view. See if there are any steps that you can trim or compress – or any weak areas you can brush up on so that you are more efficient and flexible with your use of time. This will save you time without the actors ever needing to know you are concerned about it. Again, do not constantly look at your watch in the rehearsal room. Instead, place a clock on the wall as described earlier.

9 **Keep an eye on the actors' 'audience thinking'**
Of course, directors and actors must have thoughts in their heads about the audience – the work is being made entirely for them. However, there are useful thoughts for the actors to have about the audience and thoughts that are not useful. Useful thoughts are: 'I want the character in the situation to be clear for the audience', or 'The audience are flies on the wall'. Thoughts that are less useful are those that get in the way of them playing the characters in the situation and may distort and disturb what the actor is doing. For example an actor might think 'I want to impress the audience', resulting in them unnaturally slowing down what they do and adding some vocal flourishes. Or they might adjust where they are standing in order to be seen by the audience or raise their voices unrealistically. Alternatively, an actor who thinks 'I am boring the audience' will artificially speed up what they do. It is possible that the presence of the audience will make these actors frightened or self-conscious. They will not be able to control what they do and their hands will shake. All these responses create physical and vocal material that is not present in the situation in which their characters find themselves. This additional material confuses audiences.

Learn to differentiate between actions or gestures that reflect an actor playing a character in a situation, and those that reflect a self-conscious actor on a stage. For instance, a self-conscious actor may repeatedly rub one finger under their nose, put their hand over their mouth when they are talking or brush their hand through their hair all the time. These tiny physical tics are not an expression of the character they are playing. Initially, do not point out self-conscious actions or gestures directly to the actor. Instead, continue to give instructions about things like time or place or relationships. These instructions should begin to immerse the actor in the action and the self-conscious gestures should slowly subside. If you are unable to dislodge the self-consciousness over time, draw the actor's attention to moments of unhelpful audience thinking, and ask them to turn the volume down on their thoughts about the audience.

10 **Keep clear the boundaries between actors' private lives and the work**
Encourage actors to draw clear boundaries between their private lives and their work. Actors will often draw on personal events in their lives to build aspects of their characters – whether you ask them to or not. If you notice them doing this and it is useful for the play, do not pry into the personal events underpinning their choices. If an actor starts to use the rehearsal room as a therapeutic environment, find a way of stopping them immediately you see it happening. You could talk to them directly about the problem, or use the idea of affinities or impressions to stop them from imposing inappropriate emotions from their private life on the character. If the actor starts to talk to you about their personal life, curtail this conversation as soon as possible – unless, of course, it is a serious concern that will affect their ability to do the job, like the mortal illness of a loved one. Remember, you do not have qualifications as a therapist and you may find yourself out of your depth very quickly. Remember also that directing is about making plays clear rather than addressing actors' personal problems. If you mix with actors socially, keep the boundaries clear. Do not drink too much or let your guard drop and disclose personal information that might confuse their relationship with you.

11 **Avoid last-minute instructions**
You have given the actors five things you want them to play and you have suggested that they take a few minutes to digest your instructions. They are now ready to practise the scene. They are standing in the room about to start and you have sat down with your notebook ready to watch their work. Then, you suddenly jump up and say: 'Oh yes, and another thing, can you remember to focus on the time of day.' The actors then do the scene. This last-minute instruction will undo all the five other instructions you gave, as it will be what is played the most because it is uppermost in the actors' minds. It will also be played thinly because you have not given the actors any time to digest the instruction properly. So, if you have a last-minute thought, do not give it to the actors just before they rehearse a scene. Instead, jot it down in your notebook and give it to them the next time you practise the scene.

12 **Hold your nerve**
There are moments in every rehearsal process where the director privately – or

publicly – loses their nerve. For example, you might not be able to immerse an actor in the character accurately and you might begin to feel defeated by the struggle to do so. If an actor is unable to learn their lines and it might suddenly feel impossible that they will ever manage to perform the role, it's possible that the first run-through will be a complete disaster with no structure or clarity. How you manage these vulnerable moments will determine the success of the production the audience see. Either you will buckle or you will hold your nerve with renewed determination. Try to hold your nerve; it will be better for everyone involved in the production if you do. They will see there is a problem and that you are working on it. Remember, the more you practise your craft, the more attuned you will be to those moments where you are vulnerable to loss of nerve. This knowledge will enable you to cope better.

There will also be moments in the process when the rehearsal room suddenly and unexpectedly turns into a frightening place. This may occur because a private relationship between two actors (that you know nothing about) explodes in front of you, or perhaps one actor has been consistently undermining another. These events are characterised by sudden bursts of emotion, usually aggression or tears. Another actor is often the target but the director can also be at risk. When this happens, remember that you are in charge and, if things get out of control, it can often be wise to call a break. Make sure you leave the rehearsal room, walk round the block a couple of times, either alone or with someone you can trust (like a stage manager or an actor not directly involved in the event). Analyse what happened and think of the best steps you can take to remind everyone involved that this is a professional environment.

Summary
1 Cultivate patience and long-term thinking.
2 Be consistent.
3 Do not worry about being liked.
4 Make the text the mediator of any conflict.
5 Do not automatically blame the actor if something goes wrong.
6 Always apologise if you make an error.
7 Do not use anyone as a kicking stool.
8 Do not put time pressure on actors or waste time yourself.
9 Keep an eye on the actors' audience thinking.
10 Keep the boundaries between the actors' private lives and the work clear.
11 Avoid last-minute instructions.
12 Hold your nerve.

Establishing the language of your process

This way of working utilises a language that is very particular; it is therefore useful to find a way of introducing it to the actors with clarity and precision. However, even if you are not using the language of this process it is useful to consider how you will introduce your way of working to the actors. You may not even be conscious that you use a particular vocabulary to talk about acting, so before rehearsals begin spend a little time thinking about the words you do use and considering how best to introduce them into the rehearsal room.

It is best to introduce the actors to your language from the first day of rehearsals and stick to that language until the last night. It will be a stable reference point for the actors and supply them with steady goals to aim for. You can introduce them to it either by using key words repeatedly in your sentences or in relationship to a particular step in the process. Alternatively, you could simply inform everyone early on that these are the words you use to talk about the work. Make sure you always give concrete examples of what you mean by any of the words you introduce. Pick an example from the play you are working on or from life to make your point clear. For example, when you introduce the word 'affinity', select one character to describe. For instance, point out that Arkadina has four key aspects to her character: she is an actress, a mother, a lover and a sister. Playing an affinity would mean feeding one or two aspects of the character and not all four. All four have to be in place for the character to function fully in the play.

Actors will walk into your rehearsal room speaking many different languages about their craft. These languages will reflect their training and working experience. When you introduce them to your language (and the process it describes), do not do so in a way that suggests it is the only way of talking about acting because it is not. Rather, assure them it is one of many languages but that these words will help everyone work together if they all agree to use it for the duration of this job.

Here are examples of the key words from this process that you should introduce into your sentences early on. Use the word 'affinities' to guide the actor to look at the character objectively. Encourage them to read the text carefully to listen out for the 'impression' the writer is giving you whenever there is disagreement or confusion. Warn them against being too 'interpretative' about their characters or other characters in the play. ('Interpretative' means making superficial and easy value judgements about the character based on a simplistic reading of a scene.) For example, in *The Seagull* an interpretative statement would be 'Arkadina is mean' or 'Nina is naïve'. Value judgements like this can make the actors play their characters two-dimensionally. Introduce the word 'practise' to describe any work on the scenes. You may use this word instead of the words 'perform' or 'rehearse' as the word 'practise' takes the pressure off the actor to deliver a scene perfectly the first time they rehearse it and encourages long-term thinking. Talk about past pictures and future pictures to help the actors to concretise their characters' past and their desires for the future. Other words such as 'intention' and 'event' or 'time' and 'place' are best introduced when you are giving feedback on early acting exercises, and I write about how to do this in Chapter 10.

Remember too that you do not have to use the terms given in this book in order to use the tools described. Some actors find words like 'intention' or 'event' off-putting. It makes them feel as if they are scientific specimens in a laboratory; perhaps these words do not chime with the way that they experience human behaviour. If an actor reacts strongly against a term, stop using it. Find a simpler way of describing what you want to investigate. Instead of 'intention' ask them 'What does your character want?' Instead of 'event' ask them: 'Where do things change for all the characters?'

Next, establish the words with which the work will be graded and measured. For example, remove the words 'good', 'bad', 'right' and 'wrong' from the rehearsal room vocabulary. These are value judgements that may position you inappropriately in relationship to the actor – as parent or moral arbiter. Replace them with words like 'clear' and 'unclear', 'specific' and 'unspecific', 'focused' or 'blurred'. Establish a culture in which the highest praise an actor can receive is: 'That was very clear.' These words, in turn, position the director in a role closer to that of a member of the audience watching the performance for the first time.

Remember to keep your language in proportion to the circumstances. The use of hyperbolic words of praise like 'excellent' or 'brilliant' can be counterproductive. They lose value with repetition. Similarly, a more sensationalist vocabulary featuring words like 'completely awful' or 'a disaster' will not help the actors build anything. Sometimes directors use this sort of language in response to tiny flaws in a scene. Using such enormous words about minuscule problems does not help anyone take a proper measurement of what they are doing or need to do.

Keep an eye on how actors describe their own work. Some actors can use language that is self-flagellatory or self-deprecating. They can say things such as 'That was completely crap', or 'I failed horribly with that task' or 'I found that note impossible to play'. There are odd moments when these descriptions will be accurate. Mostly, they will not be apt or useful. So gently inform the actors that the words they used did not accurately describe what they did as you saw it. Say things like: 'It was interesting that you used the word "crap" there. I thought that time and place were actually played very accurately. But perhaps you needed to sharpen how you played your intention a little.'

Find accurate words that describe the strengths and weaknesses of the work the actors do and you will encourage a calmer and more measured rehearsal environment. And if you need to adjust your language in any way, then always try to reduce the scale of any problem by adding 'tiny', or 'little' or 'slightly' to your notes.

Finally, be careful to avoid stock phrases that carry negative meanings. For example, the phrase 'text bashing' is often used to mean practising lines during the rehearsal period. It gives the impression of either the text or the actor being beaten up in some way. It certainly does not make the actor feel that this is another step in a process by which they will become immersed in a situation or character. Rather than using this phrase, describe the actual task using simple language. Let the actors know that they will be running or practising their lines.

Summary
Introduce the language of your process on the first day of rehearsals and stick to that language until the last night.
Use key words consistently in your sentences, or introduce them in relationship to a particular step in your process or simply inform everyone that these are the words you use.
Stress that your language – and the system it describes – is not the only way of talking about making theatre. It is just something that this ensemble will adhere to for this one job.
Let the actors know the key words you will use to give them feedback about their work.
Keep your language in proportion to the circumstances.
Avoid stock phrases that carry negative meanings.

How to give feedback to actors about their work

Learning to talk precisely to actors about their acting is critical to good directing. The first step towards achieving this is to be uniform in how you give feedback after all acting exercises, scene rehearsals, run-throughs and performances. Problems occur when there is one way of giving notes to the actor in rehearsals, another in a technical rehearsal and another in performance. The relationship between the actor and the director breaks down at the points at which the language changes, because the actor feels a sudden shift in how they are talked to and what the director expects. Remember, too, that uniform targets and language will increase the actor's ability to be self-criticising – and, longer term, self-directing. This means that they can note themselves more precisely, either individually or as a group, during the run of performances when you are not there.

Here is a checklist of the areas of the actors' work you should be giving notes on. Keep an eye on all these ingredients at every step in your process from the first day to the last night, and the work will be built properly and fully.

> Time
> Place
> Immediate circumstances
> Events
> Intentions
> Character (including pictures of past events, tempo, thoughts
>   about themselves and future pictures)
> Relationships

Chapters 10 and 11 will show you how to set up every task on this list practically with the actors.

When you are watching the actors' work look very precisely at what they are doing. This means you have to look at their whole body and not just their face. Pay attention to every tiny physical detail such as a flick of an eye, a twitch of a foot or the way they sit down heavily on a chair. Observing physical details precisely is a skill that you can train yourself in. Much of the information about things such as time, place or events will be contained in detailed physical information. If, for example, someone is hot they might make tiny adjustments to their clothing or how they are sitting throughout the scene. If someone has just heard some bad news, they might sit stock still for a moment and then hold onto the table with their hands in order to steady themselves. You should also pay attention to what the actors are saying and how they say it – but remember that the information about what is going on inside someone comes from a combination of their physicality and their words. It can be all too easy to fixate on listening to words and forget to look at bodies.

Always give feedback to actors after they have done any practical acting work for you, at any stage in the process, even if you just give a brief note about time or place. Give notes in simple, short sentences. For example, say: 'Your intention was not clear when you entered the dining room up until the moment when you sat down' or 'You did not give me the impression that it was 12 noon and hot through-out the scene.' Be specific and concrete. Mix criticism with praise, and vice versa – for instance: 'You played the immediate circumstances very precisely when you were carrying the suitcases but less precisely when you wrote the luggage labels.'

Do not give a note if you cannot think of an economic and concrete way of saying it. This is a sign that you are not entirely certain of the problem the actor is having or the direction you want them to head in, or what you want them to focus on. In these cases, watch the scene again and see if you can isolate what they need to do to improve the work.

Be even-handed and make sure you note all the actors involved in the scene or called to the note session – even if you just give a single note. That way everyone feels that their work and contribution is valued. Notice if one or two actors are constantly getting more feedback than the rest of the group. These actors may feel inadequate or put on the spot and this feeling may disable them from improving what they are doing. Address the balance by giving them fewer notes for a while. This might take the pressure off the actor and can lead to clearer results. Alternatively, you could store up notes from one session and slowly drip-feed them to the actor over a longer period of time.

Give feedback on the work both when it is clear and when it is unclear. Directors can often focus on the things that are not clear and forget to give feedback on the things that are going well. This can breed insecurity in actors who might read an absence of positive feedback as a sign of disapproval or bad work. When you give feedback about work that is going well, remind the actors of what caused the clear work. For example, inform them that it was the new intention which clarified what they were doing or that it was a sharpening of the picture of an event in their back history that led to a clear piece of work. Actors need to be able to repeat clear work. They will do that more efficiently if you remind them of what caused the clarity, instead of describing what the outcome looked like. But do not give false reassurance by giving positive feedback about work that is not going in the right direction.

Always give feedback openly in a group, rather than giving it privately to individuals in the corner of the room. That way everyone hears all the notes and no one can be unsettled by a new choice played by a colleague. This openness also removes favouritism and hierarchy, as you are seen to treat everyone equally. It is worth bearing in mind that if you give notes individually, an actor may duck your note and point the finger of blame at another performer. They may say: 'I can't do what you are asking me because actor X isn't playing their intention.' Alternatively, the actor may use the one-to-one situation to talk at length about personal problems in their lives – thereby positioning you in an inappropriately therapeutic relationship. There are some very rare moments when you need to break this rule and deal with an actor outside the group – for example, if an actor is really struggling to understand an instruction or taking you to task at length about a note they are resisting. If this is the case, arrange a time to talk to them privately and make sure you keep the conversation efficient and brief – and inside rehearsal room hours.

Actors take notes or instructions in many different ways. Some take them quickly, without saying anything. Others need to talk with you at length to grasp exactly what it is you are saying. Be patient. A note is pointless unless the actor has grasped and absorbed it. Sometimes talking about the note is simply a way of the actor digesting it properly – so do not mistake the conversation for disagreement.

If an actor strongly disagrees with your feedback, retract it. Look at the scene or exercise again and see if you have made an error of diagnosis. If you have made an error, simply acknowledge the mistake. If not, study the problem again. If you realise that the resistance on the part of the actor to your note is due to a desire to play something other than the text, give the note again – explaining that you have looked at the scene more carefully and feel that the note will help. Alternatively, look for a different way of giving the same note. If you give a note and the actor says that they were playing it, ask them to play it again but more sharply. Or tell them that you will watch this 'corner' carefully to check that you did not make an error.

The time it takes to give feedback varies at different stages of the process. For example, after an early rehearsal of a scene you should spend no more than ten minutes giving notes. But after a run-through you might spend between one and two and a half hours on a notes session. In Chapters 11 and 13, I write specifically about how to handle note sessions after you run the play in the rehearsal room or after public performances in the theatre. I also write about the effect of the impending performance on the actors' ability to take notes.

Find an efficient way of writing down notes and make sure that every note you write down is legible. Accept that you might miss some things in the action because you are writing notes. Accept too that your note-taking will hit the actors' radar and that some actors will be affected by the movement of your pen as it writes, however immersed they are in the situation. If you are anxious not to disrupt their work by writing a note at the point at which it strikes you, practise holding notes in your head until there is a better moment to write them down. Develop a shorthand so that you don't have to write down so many words for each note. I use the letter d with a circle round it Ⓓ to denote a design issue, the letter t with a circle round it Ⓣ to denote the word 'thought', the letter i with a circle round it Ⓘ to denote 'intention', Ⓑ to denote 'biography' and so on. Don't describe the problem you are noting in detail. The note is a brief *aide-mémoire* to remind you of the problem when you read the notes back. Remember: never give a note if you cannot decipher your handwriting; instead, put a question mark next to it and move on. Look back over your hand-writing at the end of the day to see if you can decipher it.

It takes time to learn to note actors well and give feedback efficiently. Practise this skill by noting the work of actors in other productions you see. Take one or two items from the note checklist at the beginning of this section and watch productions with them in mind. Take mental or literal notes as a way of strengthening your directing muscles. It will also stop you falling into easy value judgements about the work of other directors. Instead, you will be able to pinpoint accurately where the strengths and weaknesses lie in the directing or acting – thereby improving your own skills.

Summary
Be uniform in how you give your notes throughout the rehearsal process and public performances of the play.
Have a fixed checklist of targets to note, which remains the same throughout the process.
Give feedback to actors for any practical acting work they do for you.
Give notes in a simple and concrete language.
Mix criticism with praise.
Do not give a note if you cannot think of a clear and concrete way of giving it.
Be even-handed with your feedback.
Give notes to the actors when the work they do is clear.
Give all notes openly in the group and ensure you give feedback to everyone involved.
Allow for the fact that actors need to digest notes in a wide variety of ways.
If an actor disagrees with a note, retract it and study the scene to see if you have made an error.
Be prepared for the fact that giving feedback will take different amounts of time at different stages in the process.
Find an efficient way of taking down notes in your notebook.
Practise note-taking by taking notes at productions by other directors.

How to sit in the rehearsal room

Many directors are not aware of the impact of the way they sit or what they do in the rehearsal room on the actors. For example, some directors sit slouched back in a chair with their arms crossed. This gives the actors the impression that they are judging the work or that they are bored. Others lean forward with legs crossed and one leg jigging up and down. This gives the actors the impression that they are tense and nervous. Others look repeatedly at their watches, which gives the actors the impression that there is very little time to rehearse or that the director is bored. None of these directors intends to give the impression described and they would be embarrassed if it were to be pointed out to them. However, all these sitting positions and physical activities affect how the actors work.

Notice how you sit as you watch the actors act and ask yourself whether you are sitting in a way that is conducive to their working well. If you are uncertain, adjust your position and see if it makes any difference to the actors' concentration or application.

Summary
Sit in the rehearsal room in a way that makes the actors feel you are interested in their work.
Notice how you sit and ask yourself whether it is conducive to the actors working well.

Introducing the text to the actors

Ideally, the actors will have the text you want them to work on before the first day of rehearsals. If you have prepared the text for the actors (as described in Chapter 4), make sure this is circulated prior to rehearsals so that everyone is working from the same document.

When you first sit down to read the play, explain the reasons behind any cuts you have made to the stage directions and suggest firmly that the actors accept them rather than wasting time comparing different versions of the published text or other translations. In my experience it is better if the text is a fixed and stable ingredient in the rehearsal room. Valuable time can sometimes be wasted comparing versions or translations – with very little useful outcome. This is particularly important if you do not have a long rehearsal period.

Only make changes or cuts to the text during the rehearsal period when it is absolutely crucial – for example, if the story is unclear or if the overall structure does not function. Keep cuts to a minimum and time the moment you give them carefully. Badly timed cuts can destabilise the actors and make their work thinner. Try to wait until the work is secure under the actors' feet before you make cuts, and try to deliver all the cuts in one clean go. Then stick to them and move forwards. Avoid a situation in which you make cuts every day in rehearsals: it will stop the actors from being able to build work that is solid or lasting. Remember that I am writing here about ways of approaching the text of dead writers; the presentation of the script of a living writer requires very different handling.

Summary
Explain the reason behind changes to the text on the first day of rehearsals, but make it clear that the script in hand is now a non-negotiable element of the process.
Only make changes or cuts to the script if it is absolutely necessary.
Make cuts in one clean sweep late on in the process when the work is secure under the actors' feet.

The first day of rehearsals

First days are about managing everyone's fear efficiently so that they can do a proper and useful day's work. If someone is frightened, they do not take in information well or respond precisely to tasks, so consider the things you can do to reduce the fear. The formal read-through in front of an invited audience is the staple diet of many first days and can be completely terrifying for actors – they either mumble, paralysed, into their polystyrene cups of coffee, or construct elaborate clichéd performances that are difficult for them to leave behind.

In my experience, the read-through is not a useful thing to do and I would suggest, instead, that you construct a day with a series of simple and relaxing steps in which no one is put on the spot. Do not mistake this for a licence to waste a day of rehearsal. It is perfectly possible to treat the first day as a proper working day and do creative work at the same time as tackling fear. Here are some suggestions about what you might usefully do on the first day of rehearsals.

Begin by telling the actors what you are going to do during the day so that they have a plan in their heads. In particular, let them know you will not do a read-through. Then do a gentle movement session, as physical exercises can soften the hold that fear has on the body. If you have a movement director, they will be able to lead this work or you could allow the actors 20 minutes or so to warm up on their own. Follow this warm-up with something physical that relates to the production and brings the actors together in pairs or as a whole group.

Whilst working on *The Seagull* and *Three Sisters*, the actors learnt social dancing – waltzing and tango. This broke the ice between people and also meant that they started to work on something for the show. Remember, however, to let the actors know that they will be doing movement work before they turn up, so that they bring the right clothes. Because some actors like to change in and out of clothes for physical work, make sure you have organised somewhere for them to do this. Do not assume that men and women will be happy to do this in the same area.

Read the play together but without actors reading their own parts. Go round in a circle with each person saying a line at a time. Make sure that the stage directions and all the adjectives in brackets are read. Encourage the actors to read the text for the sense alone and reassure them that no performance is required. You, the stage management and other members of the creative team can also take part in this reading, and this will bind everyone working on the project together. This is how the read-through would go if ten people were reading the first scene of *The Seagull*.

Person 1: Reads dramatis personae.
Person 2: *A section of the park on Sorin's estate. A broad avenue leads away from the audi-*

ence into the depths of the park towards the lake. The avenue is closed off by a stage which has been hurriedly run up for some home entertainment, so that the lake is completely invisible. Right and left of the stage is a shrubbery, a few chairs and a garden table.

Person 3: *The sun has just set. On the improvised stage, behind the lowered curtain, are YAKOV and the other WORKMEN; coughing and banging can be heard. MASHA and MEDVEDENKO enter left, on their way back from a walk.*

Person 4: *Why do you always wear black?*

Person 5: *I'm in mourning for my life. I'm unhappy.*

Person 6: *Why?* [reflectively] *I don't understand. You've got your health. Your father may not be rich, but he's not badly off. I have a much harder time than you. I get 23 roubles a month all told – less deductions for the pension – and I don't go round in mourning.*

Person 7: [They sit]

Person 8: *It's not a question of money. Even a beggar can be happy.*

Person 9: *Theoretically. In practice it comes down to this: my mother and I, plus my two sisters and my little brother – and only 23 roubles a month coming in. You mean we don't have to eat and drink? There's no need for tea and sugar? No need for tobacco? I don't know how to manage.*

Person 10: [Looking round at the improvised stage] *The show will be starting soon.*

After you have read the whole play, divide the ensemble into smaller groups and give them each a specific task. Working in small teams helps people get to know each other and begin to learn how to work together. For instance, you could ask a group to collect information about a particular circle of place (as described in Chapter 10). Finally, lead a brief session about the writer. Talk through the three or four essential facts about their life that you prepared (see Chapter 3) and discuss how they shed light on the play. Remember that this exercise needs to be handled in a different way if you are working with a living writer.

At the end of the day, set the actors a simple research task to do overnight. For example, ask them to find three facts about the time that the play is set in. With *The Seagull* I asked the actors to find three facts about Russia in the late 1890s. With Martin Crimp's play *The Country* I asked the actors to locate three facts about the British medical profession in 2000. When setting this task, give an example of the desired outcome. Homework like this is a useful way of helping the actors to think in the right direction for their work outside the rehearsal room. You can use this tool throughout the rehearsal period. Actors will always be thinking about their work outside rehearsal hours – sometimes they will do this in a way that is not useful. They may, for example, worry away at one tiny moment in the action or about their ability to do the whole thing at all. Clear homework tasks are a way of filling their heads with thoughts that are useful for what they have to do. However, approach the use of the word 'homework' with caution. Some actors have negative associations with this word because of unhappy experiences during school years. Use the word lightly, or, if people react strongly against it, find another way of putting it.

Directors themselves also have to cope with the effects of fear on the first day. Fear may make you talk faster than normal; this acceleration in thoughts and words will mean that you are not 100% clear in what you are saying. This can confuse the actors. Fear might make your thoughts jump around, or you might find yourself talking too much. Your attempts to hide your fear may create further problems – for instance, you might stop noticing the reaction that others have to what you are saying.

During a workshop, a young director once described how she coped with her fear on the first day of rehearsals. She said that she tried to give the impression of being more organised and efficient. I asked her to re-enact this, with the rest of the group playing the actors. The impression she gave was of being abrasive and rude. She was not conscious of this and was mortified to realise it. Fear can also stop you from being able to remember really important and simple things, like people's names. So make sure you plan the day so that you can manage your own fear.

First, only use work or exercises that you have prepared carefully so that you know the outcomes of any tasks set. Second, create a balance between tasks where you lead the group and tasks where the actors work on their own. This will give you breathers during the day when you can steady yourself. Finally, there are some tasks like introducing people to each other that you cannot avoid, so make sure you think about them the night before.

Most theatres will want to schedule time for the actors, stage management and the creative team to meet up with the artistic and administrative staff of the building. This event is really important, as it allows the other people in the building to welcome the actors and means that the actors get to know the faces and jobs of people they will meet in the various corridors of the theatre. If you can, try to avoid doing it on the first day (and avoid in particular starting the day with this event). Fear can be multiplied tenfold by an awkward social situation like this. Instead, schedule it at the end of the day or, ideally, a couple of days later. Then everyone directly involved in the rehearsal process will have got to know each other a little before they have to meet everyone in the building or organisation or production team.

All these ideas for arranging the first day can be put in place in most working environments, but there will be instances where you have to do things such as a read-through, a meet-and-greet or a model showing on the first day. This might be because you are working for a commercial management or because the artistic director is going away on holiday and can only do a meet-and-greet on the first day. Remember to set these events up sensitively and with an understanding of the fear everyone experiences on the first day. Organise the read-through so that the actors and the people listening are all sitting around a table, instead of a more pressurised layout with the actors on one side of a room and the 'audience' on the other. Then ask the actors to read the play mainly for sense and remind them that they are not under any obligation to perform. This will reduce fear and temper any tendencies to shape a final performance.

Summary

Realise that fear is the main obstacle to work on on the first day.

Do not do a formal read-through.

Only use exercises that you have prepared beforehand.

Start the day with movement work.

Follow this up with something physical that relates to the production and brings them together in pairs, or as a whole group.

Read the play together with no one reading their own parts.

Divide the ensemble into smaller groups with specific tasks, as working in small teams helps people get to know each other.

Lead a brief session about the writer.

Set them a simple research task to do overnight as homework.

Plan the day so that you, the director, can manage your own fear well.

Do meet-and-greets at the end of the first day or later in that week.

Do not worry if you have to fulfil things like read-throughs on the first day; just be sensitive in how you set them up to the fear everyone experiences on the first day.

The model showing

The main aim of showing the model to the actors is to imprint on their imagination a clear picture of the places where the action of the play will occur. Give the actors time to absorb what they are looking at and to ask all the questions they have. Remember: the next time they see the set will probably be in the theatre, so if you rush the model showing it may not allow them to form a picture of the environment to feed their work in rehearsals. This may create problems when you enter the theatre, as there will be a gap between what they have been imagining in the rehearsal room and what they find themselves standing on. This gap will make it hard for the actors to believe in their actions at this critical stage in the process. Similarly, do not show the model on the first day as the actors' ability to absorb it usefully will also be hampered by the fear that tends to accompany the beginning of the rehearsal period.

Once, in the last week of rehearsals, I had a very confusing conversation with an actor who had no idea what the set design of the room in the final scene looked like. I was perplexed because he had seen the model on the first day of rehearsals five weeks previously. I said to him: 'But surely you saw that it was like this in the model?' He replied: 'It might as well have been a bright pink rake with purple sliders for all I cared. I was much too frightened to notice a thing. The whole day was a blur.' I realised then that model showings were best left until the second or third day of rehearsals.

Make sure you discuss how you are going to show the model with the designer as it can be a nerve-racking experience for some designers. The best way of alleviating that pressure can be a shared presentation with the director and designer explaining it together.

The model showing can also be used to give a picture of what the show will look like to those people involved in producing the show. If you can, do this model showing separately to the showing you do for the actors, as these two showings have very different aims.

In some cases, you will not have a model to show – either because you are devising the performance or because there was no money to make it. Instead, find a way of articulating the picture you have in your head of the look of the places where the action occurs, by using either photographs or reproductions of paintings – even if the images you show are only hunches about the final outcome.

Summary
Give the actors time to absorb the model and ask questions.

Do not show the model on the first day of rehearsals, as the fear will mean some actors may not absorb it at all.

Discuss the best way of presenting it with the designer.

Do not combine a model showing for the actors with a model showing for all the people in the theatre working on the show but not in rehearsals.

If you do not have a model, try to show some visual information that indicates the direction you are heading in.

Introducing sound, costumes, props, furniture, lights and scenic elements to the rehearsal process

Whether you are working for a large subsidised organisation or a tiny fringe theatre, you will have less time to rehearse technically in the theatre than you have to work in the rehearsal room. Of course, this is not the case in some European countries such as Sweden and Germany, but in the UK and USA this is the norm. This puts a lot of pressure on everyone to do the technical rehearsals incredibly quickly and efficiently. The actors, in particular, have to absorb several new ingredients – lights, sounds, scenery, costumes and so on – in a very short period of time. All this new information can overwhelm actors and dilute the work they have carefully built up over the rehearsal period. Introduce as many of these ingredients as possible into the rehearsal room as early as you can, as it will ease the transition into the theatre. It will also save you time in the technical rehearsals so that you can focus on those elements that are simply impossible to put into the rehearsal room (such as a lighting rig or large set) or even something simple (such as a wind machine or flame effect).

Sound effects, especially abstract effects, can ambush actors if you have not integrated them into rehearsals, so it helps to introduce them at some point in the process. Consider, for example, having a sound desk and sound operator in the rehearsals for the last week or so, and play all the sound cues as the actors rehearse. That way sound will be integrated with the actors' work in a relaxed environment.

Consider gradually introducing costumes and footwear throughout the rehearsal period so that the actors can practise walking and moving in what they will wear in the theatre. Rehearse with actual props and furniture whenever you can. 'Actuals' is the word used to describe a prop or item of furniture that will be used on stage in the production. Many rehearsal props are stand-ins rather than the real thing. It is ideal for the actor to practise as much as possible, and for as long as possible, with the 'actuals' – the props or furniture they will eventually use. The more they have done this in the calm environment of the rehearsal room, the more precise and fluent they will be with them in the pressurised environment of the theatre. Be assured, however, that a stand-in prop or costume is better than nothing.

Do not attempt to rig lights in the rehearsal room. Most rehearsals do not take place in the theatres in which they will be performed, and they do not have complex lighting rigs or lighting operators. They will not be able to deliver anything that resembles the final lighting states and attempts to approximate theatrical lighting in a rehearsal room can confuse the actors.

Keep in mind the fact that few rehearsal rooms have good blackout facilities.

There are exceptions to this rule, when, for example, you are working on complicated multi-media performances using video. In these cases you will need the rehearsal room to function closer to show conditions with full blackout and many of the actual lights. This way of working needs careful planning and costs a lot of extra money. Make sure that you have prepared your producers for this additional cost. It is useful, however, to have practical lights that work in the rehearsal room such as bedside lamps, candles, lanterns or desk lamps. You can use them during the day (if you have a blackout facility) or at night. Either way, looking at the action with only the practical lights on will help you work out how to focus that action and what extra lights the designer needs to cheat in from the rig when you get into the theatre.

Of course, the degree to which you can achieve any of this depends on budgets. Some of my earlier suggestions might be impossible in a fringe theatre or small touring company. However, there will always be things that you can integrate and, even if all you do is to get one or two costumes into the rehearsal room for the last few days, it will alleviate some of the pressure of the technical rehearsal.

Remember to prepare the actors for everything new that you are planning to do in the theatre. Avoid surprising them with entirely new ideas. If, for instance, you have made changes to the set or costumes after the model showing, share this with the actors in the rehearsal room. Try not to let gaps develop between what the actors imagine a costume or room looks like and its actual appearance, and avoid introducing them to a large new scenic element in a technical rehearsal. At that point in the process, you want your actors to be steady and calm, not thrown off balance by an unexpected change.

Summary

Introduce as many of these key ingredients into the rehearsal room as you can, because it will ease the transition into the theatre for the actors.

Consider, for instance, installing in the rehearsal room a sound desk and operator, and introducing elements of costumes, footwear, actual props, furniture and some scenic elements.

Do not install any element of a lighting rig in the rehearsal room; instead, use practical lights that will be there in the performance.

Prepare the actors for anything new you are planning to do in any of these areas before you enter the theatre.

The Maids by Jean Genet

CHAPTER 10

Building the world of the play

The rehearsal process divides into two periods. In the first period work with the full acting company to build the world of the play. This takes up about 40% of your rehearsal time. In the second period break the play into small sections and only call those actors who are in each section. This takes up the remaining 60% of your time in the rehearsal room. This chapter deals with how you build the world of the play and includes advice on the following areas:

> How to divide up the rehearsal day
> Introducing facts and questions
> Research
> Place
> The writer and the genre
> Practical work on ideas
> Practical work on emotions
> Character biographies
> First practical work on character and character tempo
> Relationships
> How to set up improvisations with the actors
> How to use visualisation exercises
> How to do all this with a short rehearsal period

This list gives the impression that every step in the process needs to be completed before you move onto the next. It also gives the impression that you have to work in a precise order. Neither of these things is entirely true. For example, you might choose to begin practical work on ideas whilst you are still working on facts and questions. The completion of your research could overlap with the beginning of your work on character biographies. Play these things by ear. The ingredients that have to go in linear order are:

> back history facts/questions
> character biographies

first practical work on character
relationships
improvisations (events in the past, trigger event, then immediate
circumstances).

This chapter will show you how to use material you have prepared with the actors. Be careful about how you refer to this prepared work. Use it to guide and focus the actors – not to make them feel that they have nothing to contribute. Make them feel, instead, as if they are building the world with you and, wherever possible, encourage them to work things out for themselves. Do this by asking questions instead of making statements. This is particularly important when it comes to work on characters.

How to divide up the rehearsal day

I structure my rehearsal day to include three main ingredients: work on the play around a table, movement work and acting exercises. Avoid spending too much time on a single activity, particularly table work. Remember that actors will enjoy transforming ideas discussed around a table into practical work on the floor. Indeed, practical work is central to building a character or exploring the type of acting you are asking the actors to do.

Here is an example of how to divide up the day. This is a template to guide you rather than a structure that needs to be adhered to rigorously. The exercises described will be explained later in the chapter.

10am	Movement work: warm-up
11am	Work around the table: read Act One and start to list all the facts and questions
1pm	Break
2pm	Acting exercises: practical work on ideas
3.30pm	Movement work: social dance
4.15pm	Work around the table: actors share the results of the research tasks set the night before
5pm	End

At the end of each day, you might set the actors some simple tasks to do overnight, in the same way that you did on the first day (see Chapter 9). This task could emerge from your work on facts and questions, and ideally it should connect with the character the actor is playing. For example, in *The Seagull*, the actor playing Sorin would research the use of walking sticks or the actor playing Masha could investigate the price and use of snuff.

I have already suggested that you delay marking up the ground plan of the set on the floor whilst you are building the world of the play. The rehearsal room will be used to enact exercises or improvisations that occur in several different places other than the location or locations where the action of the play is set. For example, improvisations of past events will take you to other family homes in different countries or cities and so will exercises on the ideas of the play. The presence of brightly coloured tapes used to do mark-ups on the rehearsal room floor will constantly distract the eye and the imagination of the actor, as they enact events in entirely different places.

Summary
Structure your rehearsal day to include three main ingredients: work on the play around a table, movement work and acting exercises.
Avoid spending too much time on a single activity, particularly table work.
At the end of each day, you might set the actors some simple tasks to do overnight.
Do not put a mark-up down.

Introducing facts and questions

Getting the actors to read the play for back history facts and questions (concerning everything that exists and happens before the play begins) is the most efficient way of establishing a rehearsal room culture in which everyone thinks about the play precisely and objectively.

Ask the actors to read the play in the same way that they read it on the first day – with everyone in the circle reading a line at a time. Before you start reading, tell them that they will be making four lists:

facts about everything that exists and happens before the action of the play
    begins
questions about everything that exists and happens before the action of the
    play begins
facts about the immediate circumstances of the first scene
questions about the immediate circumstances of the first scene.

Ask four people to keep a list each. Do not try to finish this task in one session and try not to rush it. Perhaps the tasks might be divided up over three or four days – or even longer if you have more time.

It is worth keeping in mind the fact that the lists you wrote as you did your preparation will not be exactly like the lists that you draw up with the actors. Their perceptions will add new facts and new questions to your pre-prepared list.

However, your knowledge of the outcome of the exercise will mean you can draw the actors' attention to facts they are neglecting or questions they are not asking.

If there is any dispute about whether a piece of information is a fact or not, immediately notate it as a question. If you are unable to 'land' the information as a fact, there is clearly some ambiguity or doubt about the information. Include it on the list of questions and return to it later when you are able to tackle it with more precision. Try to make sure that the actors do not attempt to answer any questions as you do the task. Let them know that these questions will be answered at a later point in the process. Actors may ask questions that do not relate to the four lists you are working on. They may, for example, have a query about the action of the play or the sense of a particular line. Take a note of their queries and reassure them that these things will be addressed at a later point in the process – either when you analyse the action of the play or when you come to do the first rehearsal of the scene.

During this exercise, some actors may start to talk at length about their character or other aspects of the play. This is because it is the first forum for discussion that the process has allowed them. Curtail these conversations by asking them to boil down their thoughts into one simple question. Add this question to the list and move on. At the end of this process give the actors a photocopy of the four lists. These master lists will prove extremely useful when the actors come to construct their character biographies.

Summary
Read the play together and draw up four lists:
- facts about what exists and has happened before the action of the play begins
- questions about what exists and has happened before the action of the play begins
- facts about the immediate circumstances of the first scene
- questions about the immediate circumstances of the first scene.

Use your knowledge of the outcome of the exercise to guide the actors through it.

If there are disputes about whether information is a fact or a question, add that information to your 'questions' list.

Discourage actors from answering questions at this stage and reassure them that they will be answered later on in the process.

Take a note of any questions relating to other steps of the process, for discussion later on in rehearsals.

Stop actors from using this exercise to talk at length about other concerns.

Research

Research ensures that the actors build a shared, concrete and detailed picture of time and place. It is integral to the rehearsal process, even when a play is brand new. The research you did when you prepared the text means that you can allocate essential tasks to specific actors and guide them towards books or articles that will help them to answer their research questions economically. You will also be able to correct them if the information they return with is not quite accurate.

On the first day of rehearsals you might have asked the actors to undertake their first simple research task overnight – to find out three facts about the year (or years) in which the action of the play occurs. These facts might reference political, social or artistic events. On the second day gather the group around the table and ask each actor in turn to share their facts. Do this for a maximum of an hour. For example, here are some of the facts that actors working on *The Seagull* brought back into the rehearsal room.

> In 1891 there was a famine which affected 14 to 20 million people.
> Tchaikovsky died in November 1893.
> Between 1850 and 1900 the population of Russia doubled.
> In 1890 Russia experienced its first mass strikes.
> In the 1890s the Russian literary symbolist movement began.
> At the time Alexander III was tsar. He was a reactionary autocrat who presided over a repressive regime. In 1894 Nicholas II inherited the throne.

As the actors go through their facts, encourage them to relate them to the play. In *The Seagull*, a useful fact is the famine of 1891 (two years before the action of the play begins). When someone reports this fact make sure that all the actors directly affected by this event jot down the date for use in their character biographies. Encourage each of them to think about what their characters might have been doing during the famine, and to translate their answers into concrete events in their character's past. Then point out a moment in the action which is 'explained' by the famine: the dog in Act One is probably tied up all night to protect the precious grain from thieves made desperate by bad harvests.

These facts will begin to create a shared picture of the world in which the action of the play takes place. In *The Seagull*, it was important for the actors to realise that the action takes place in a repressive time in Russia, following the assassination of Alexander II in 1881; that travel was difficult because there were only 25,000 miles of railway; and that the country was just recovering from a disastrous famine. Even if this is the only research that you have time to do, it will really help to launch the actors into the same world.

This task will also reveal which actors are confident with research and which are not. If, for example, you notice that one actor is very vague and generalised with their information, you will know that you have to guide them very carefully when you set the next bit of research. On a more practical level, you might discover that an actor does not have access to the Internet or a library. You may have to provide this person or people with Internet access or set them tasks which they can do with books that you lend them.

Next, go through the two lists of questions on your back history lists and earmark all the questions that need to be answered by careful research. Then allocate the research tasks to the actors regularly as homework over this part of the rehearsal period. Wherever possible, give them tasks that relate directly to their characters. Only give the actors one research task at a time, then schedule regular one-hour sessions where they feed back their research to the group. Continue to relate the research facts collected by the actors to the action of the play.

You might ask: 'But why do I have to get the actors to do any research at all? Why not just photocopy all the research I have done and hand it to them to read?' This is because research is best digested when the actors find out the information for themselves; it helps them to go on a journey to find the information, and the discovery can be satisfying. This feeling of personal satisfaction means that the information lodges in their thoughts more strongly. If the information lodges, then it will put clearer pictures in their heads and influence how they do things in the scenes for the better. Remember too that research is more effectively absorbed if a series of different people deliver it. If the director or a specialist presents all the research to the ensemble in a monologue, the rehearsal room can start to feel like school and the research can end up going in one ear and out the other.

Actors can sometimes get lost in research. If this happens, guide them to extract what is useful from what they have investigated and to disregard the rest. Remember that research must deepen the actors' understanding of the world or their character or what their character has to do in the play.

Now put a large piece of paper on the wall and write up a list of dates and events that result from the research. You can add to it every time a new discovery is made or an important date is found. Later on in the process you can add the important dates from the characters' biographies. This is a good job to give your stage management, or an actor playing a small part or an assistant director. Put up any visual information that emerges from the actors' research on the wall of the rehearsal room.

Show any videos or DVDs you have collected as part of your pre-rehearsal research. Give time for a discussion afterwards and do not assume that the actors will perceive things as you do; people will not always see the point or usefulness of material you show them. A discussion beforehand will let them know what you want them to take away from the viewing for their work on character or place.

Arrange any field trips in the first week of rehearsals so that they can feed the actors' imagination at the point at which they are starting to build the world and the character. If you leave it too late, then they will have a strong imaginary picture that can be in conflict with the reality of a place. Ensure that the whole group makes the trip and try to encourage the rest of the creative team to come along – the designer, lighting designer, movement director, sound designer and composer. After the trip make sure that you give time for the group to discuss their impressions and discoveries.

Summary
Set an initial research task early on in which you ask the actors to find out three simple facts about the year in which the play is set.
Get the actors to share these facts in the group, relate the facts to the action of the play and assess the actors' research skills.
Mark all the research questions as they emerge from your back history lists of facts and questions.
Regularly allocate research tasks from the back history list of facts and questions.
Use your own research to guide the actors in the right direction for the information.
Give each actor research tasks that are specific to the characters they are playing.
Remember that research is best absorbed by actors if they do it for themselves.
Run regular group sessions where individual actors report back their findings to the group.
Collect key dates from the research on a large piece of paper and mount this on the wall.
Show relevant DVDs or videos and allow proper time for a discussion afterwards.
Do field trips.

Place

Building a complete picture of the place or places in which the action of the play occurs helps the actor to enter and believe in the world in which their character exists. However, remember that in the actor's head, the place might be less interesting to play than emotions or character biographies, so you may have to work a little harder to encourage them to pay attention to this aspect of the play.

Introduce the actors to place by setting up a simple exercise. When you prepared place you worked on differentiating between different circles of place. Use this information to set up the following exercise.

Divide the ensemble into smaller groups and ask each group to make a list of facts and questions from the text about one circle of place. If you are rehearsing *The*

Seagull, one group might work on the interior of the house, another on the estate, a third on Russia and a fourth on references to locations outside Russia. When they have completed their lists, ask them to draw up a rough map or plan of each circle of place – or find a map of an actual place (such as Russia or Europe) and mark all the places mentioned. Each group then shares what they have done with the full ensemble.

There will be gaps in their work and, in some cases, the actors will need to do additional research before they can complete the task. Put the maps on the wall and, as the group's knowledge of the text deepens or research questions are answered, redraw or sharpen these maps. Then use them as points of reference for improvisations about past events that occur in the place or places where the action of the play is set or, later still, for scene rehearsals.

From this point onwards, ensure that the actors have a strong sense of place whenever they do any practical acting work. Before each exercise ask them to make sure that they know exactly what surrounds them and encourage them to use chairs or other objects to mark the edges of different places. For example, two chairs can mark a doorway while four chairs could mark the corners of a large bedroom.

Similarly, put place high on your checklist whenever you give feedback on any acting work and be precise about when the actors play place accurately and when they do not. When they start doing scene rehearsals, always make sure that the place where the action occurs is marked out clearly and that the actors have spent a couple of minutes reminding themselves of what they can see around them.

Do not always sit in the same place in the room to watch the work the actors do. This will encourage them to present everything in that one direction, meaning that they might adjust or distort what they are doing so that you can see it. Instead, watch the scenes or acting exercises from different angles as if you were directing theatre-in-the-round. Encourage everyone else watching to do the same. But be careful not to encroach on the place where the action begins. Make sure you are not sitting in a doorway that will be used or squatting in the corner of a room where the cooker is supposed to be. You can always move if there is something you cannot see. Moving around like this will encourage the actors to inhabit a fully imagined world rather than worrying about where the audience will be.

Summary
Introduce the actors to place with a simple exercise on the circles of place.
Put the maps of each circle of place drawn up by the actors on the walls and hone them through rehearsals as you discover more about each place.

> Ensure the actors have a strong sense of place when they do any acting exercise and put place high on your list of things to note when you give feedback on that work.
>
> Do not sit and watch all the work the actors do from one fixed place in the room.

The writer and the genre

Deepening the actors' understanding of the writer helps them to understand specific details about the text and locate the ingredients from the writer's life that may be useful in constructing their characters.

The writer will have been introduced on the first day of rehearsals when you shared the essential facts about their life and suggested how they might shed light on the play. Now you can share more detailed information gathered when you researched the writer during your preparation – for instance, any biographical facts that relate to a specific moment in the play or useful things that the writer said about the play during their lifetime. Point out any connections that help certain actors get under the skin of their characters. With *The Seagull*, the actor playing Nina could usefully read up on Lika, one of Chekhov's girlfriends at the time. It is possible that the characteristics of this woman are built into the character in the play. Sometimes the relationship between events in the writer's life and events or characters in the play they have written will not help the actors play the play. If the writer has taken a few tiny incidents from life and sewn them together in a different order to how they occurred, this will have created an entirely new reality. If this is the case, then discourage the actor from researching the connections. Again, your preparation means that you save the actors from wasting time in fruitless research.

Suggest that specific actors undertake more detailed research into aspects of the writer's life that may be useful for their own character biographies. For example, the actor playing Dorn may want to do research into Chekhov's medical training or the actors playing Sorin, Polina and Shamrayev may want to research how Chekhov managed his own country estate. These research tasks enable the actors to fill in the gaps in their knowledge of their character's training and work experience with material drawn from Chekhov's own life. If the writer is alive, follow their lead when it comes to sharing information. Any discoveries you have made about the connection between the writer's life and the play must not be used in the rehearsal room without the writer's approval.

Next, let the actors know about the genre of the play but try to avoid long intellectual debates about '-isms'. Simply introduce the genre, then give a couple of examples of how it manifests itself in the action of the play, and reassure them that you will work on how to embody the genre when you rehearse the scenes. In the section on genre in Chapter 3, I wrote about directing *The Seagull* as symbolism and how I increased the force of a gust of wind in two of the acts in order to realise the genre. You can explain this to the actors in real terms, by talking about the sudden gusts of wind that can occur before a thunderstorm or you can talk to them directly about the goals of the genre.

If you are working on a particularly demanding genre like surrealism, it may help to do some practical exercises at this point to help the actors get to grips with the genre. For example, you can ask the actors to re-enact some of their dreams, and after you have watched these re-enactments you can discuss the concrete components of those dreams and the elements that you can take forward to your work on the scenes.

Summary

Look at the simple facts about the dead writer's life and discuss how they can shed light on the play.

Share more detailed information about the writer – for instance, any biographical facts that relate to a specific moment in the play or useful things that the writer said about the play during their lifetime.

Suggest that specific actors undertake more detailed research into aspects of the writer's life that may be useful for their own character biographies.

With a living writer, only go through a similar 'research' process if the writer agrees to it.

Introduce the genre simply.

Lead some simple, practical exercises to help the actors get to grips with a difficult genre.

Practical work on ideas

Working practically on the ideas that underpin the play will bring those ideas to life for the actors in a vivid and tangible fashion – and will show them how to translate the ideas into concrete actions they can do in the play. It will also remind them about the relationship between real-life situations and what happens in plays, and will encourage them to use observations drawn from real life to build their work on scenes or characters. All good actors draw directly from life to make their work, but sometimes it can help to remind them of the level of precision required to replicate that behaviour well. The exercises will therefore allow you to introduce your interest in, and expectation of, detailed and accurate physical information. This will be the first acting work you watch and give feedback on, so it also allows you to introduce gently ingredients that you will use later on in the process, such as intentions, events, time or place.

First gather the actors around a table and ask them to suggest the key ideas of the play. Tell them that you are looking for simple words or phrases, or a 'primary school' description of an idea rather than anything sophisticated or intellectual. Jot down all their thoughts; you will find that some suggestions are spot on, others are close and a few are not right at all. When the list is completed, gently guide the group towards the three or four ideas you isolated when you prepared the play. Perhaps the name that you have given to an idea might not chime with the group, in which case you should change the name. For instance, the group might not respond to the words 'destroyed dreams', preferring 'broken hopes' instead. What matters is that the idea is located.

As a rough guide, I try to make sure that an idea relates to more than half the characters and is visible in the action of the play. If the actors propose an idea that is clearly not in the play, encourage them to test that idea against all the characters and the action – just like you did when you were working on the ideas in your preparation period. Very quickly it will become clear that an inaccurate suggestion does not affect the characters or the action significantly enough to qualify as an idea.

When you have drawn up a final list, ask the actors for the 'main idea' of the play. That is what the play is about. This entire process should not take long; try to guide the actors towards the answers efficiently and quickly. Do not let the group get stuck in a long digression or get into arguments. If this happens, suggest that everyone accepts an initial list as a starting point from which to work.

Next, work practically on the ideas. Select an idea and ask the actors to think of a moment in their lives that relates to or embodies that idea. Ask them to imagine that their life is like a very long film and encourage them to present a few minutes of that film exactly as it happened, without edits or corrections. Ask the actors to recall what happened, how it happened, when it happened and where. This extract could last between two and ten minutes. Give them an example of what you mean from your own life in order to make the exercise clear. In *The Seagull* the theme of destroyed dreams may make the actors think of a moment in their lives when they found out that they hadn't got into a drama school, or a moment when they discovered that a desired job had gone to another actor. It might be a phone call with an agent or a conversation with a teacher. The theme of unhappy love might be represented by a moment when an actor was rejected by someone they loved or a particular event in a relationship that was making them unhappy.

Reassure them that the moment they choose can be banal and domestic (a couple arguing about who puts the rubbish out or a moment when they sat on the sofa alone and switched on the television). Remind them, too, not to adjust what happened to make it resemble a scene from a play. Most importantly, warn the actors not to use any events that are recent, very painful or not properly digested. Remind them that the rehearsal room is not a therapeutic environment. If any of the ideas are particularly bleak (such as death or illness), make the exercise optional. Give the actors an evening to think about the task; tell them that they will be re-enacting what happened with other members of the ensemble the next day.

The following day go round the group and find out how many people feature in each actor's slice of life. Then set up the exercises so that everyone in the ensemble is occupied either being themselves in a slice of their life or being other people in someone else's slice. Give each actor time to share the information about the event with the people who will enact it with them. Do not be surprised if this process takes 20 minutes or so. Stress that it is not necessary to change anything about the situation in order to 'share' it with an audience. The aim is to reconstruct an event that happened in their lives as precisely as possible and not, as I wrote earlier, to do a 'scene from a play'. When they are ready, ask them to show each slice of life in turn. You will either watch these exercises on your own (because all the performers will be involved in re-enacting the slice of life) or watch them with the actors who aren't involved in that particular re-enaction.

After the exercise has finished, discuss it for five minutes. First, encourage the actors to make links between what happened in the exercise and moments or characters in the play. The re-enaction might feature a real event that speaks to a particular scene in the play, or it might throw up a physical detail such as the way someone shifts in their seat just before telling another person they are no longer loved. Drawing their attention to links and details like this will help the actors study human behaviour more carefully and think about how to achieve the same level of accuracy in the playing of their characters.

If you are watching the exercises on your own, you will have to point out the parallels between the slice of life and the play. If you are watching them with other actors, you could ask them questions like: 'Was there anything in this slice of life that speaks to a moment in the play?' Make the connection for the group if they cannot see it at first. Actors are not used to talking to each other directly or in a group about their work, so they may be a little coy in volunteering feed-back. If you keep asking the questions, the actors will finally become confident about doing so, particularly when they realise that they are not being asked to criticise other people's acting but to notice small, concrete details about human behaviour.

You can also use these exercises to introduce the key ideas of your process and the words you use to describe them (see Chapter 9). You can ask the actors who watched the exercise with you questions such as 'Where did it take place?' or 'What time of day did you think it was?' and thereby introduce place and time. When you see a moment in an exercise when there is a particularly clear event or intention, point it out. For instance, a slice of life relating to the idea of 'unhappy love' might feature a couple walking hand in hand by a canal in Venice. The woman points to a beautiful hotel and says, jokingly: 'That's a good place for an affair.' The man says: 'Yes, it is.' The woman suddenly stops in her tracks and lets go of the man's hand. She says seriously: 'Did you have an affair there?' The man pauses and then says: 'Yes.' They both turn their heads away from each other.

In this exercise the change or event starts when the man says 'Yes, it is' and ends when he says 'Yes'. Point out what happens physically and textually to mark the bookends of the event – how the woman stopped in her tracks and let go of the man's hand and how they both turned away from each other.

Ask the group who watched the exercise to tell you what they thought the intentions of the man and woman were before and after the event. These responses to exercises give an analytical tool a concrete context in life. Suggest to the actors that this is what you will be looking for later on in the process when you come to analyse the text for events and intentions. This exercise will be an invaluable reference point when you begin that work.

Remember, however, not to let the discussion between the people watching these re-enactions wander into an in-depth analysis of the actor's life (prompted by the exercise), as this can feel invasive and judgemental for the actor concerned.

At the end of the discussion, give the actors time to jot down any of the physical details discussed that may be useful when they come to do the play (such as the way someone moved a foot when they said 'I love you', or the way their whole body shook as they walked away from a dying person). Jot down these observations; you can then refer to them later in the process when you are working on the scenes. For instance, you might say to the actor playing Masha: 'Do you remember when Beth shifted in her seat before someone told her that they did not love her in that exercise on unhappiness in love? Try to add that physical detail just before you say to Medvedenko that you do not love him.'

You can take a different idea a day or do one idea over two days – depending on the amount of rehearsal time you have. Do not work on ideas in one block for longer than two hours. They take a lot of concentration to execute, to watch and to extract information from. You could intersperse ideas exercises with research tasks or reading the play for facts and questions.

Summary
Arrive at a consensus about the ideas of the play with the actors.
Isolate the main idea.
Work through the ideas practically one by one. Ask each actor to re-enact an event
   from their lives that relates to each of the ideas in turn. Do this over a few days.
After watching each exercise, give feedback on the work and encourage the group
   to draw parallels between the exercise and the play.
When you see an example of any of the steps of your process, such as an intention
   or an event, point it out to the actors. Draw their attention to ingredients such
   as time and place.
Allow the actors time at the end of each re-enaction to jot down any useful details.
Work on ideas in two-hour blocks. Do not do more than that in one day.

Practical work on emotions

Studying how emotions affect the body can also be a good way to undertake practical acting work early on in the rehearsal process before the actor is ready to do
work on their feet in character. As with the practical work on ideas, these exercises
make the actor see the need for physical precision in their work and encourage
them to look at what happens in life more precisely as a way of fuelling their work
on stage.

When you are preparing the play you will notice that the characters experience
some emotions more strongly than others. For example, in Euripides' *Iphigenia at
Aulis* one of the dominant emotions is fear: every character experiences fear at a
critical moment in the action, and large chunks of the action occur in a life-threatening context where fear drives behaviour. If you are directing this play, you can study
how this emotion affects the body.

When I started work on *Iphigenia at Aulis*, I asked the actors to think of a situation in their own lives when they were afraid. I reminded them, as with their work
on ideas, to choose a situation that was no longer raw. The next morning I asked
them to re-enact this situation, in the same way that they re-enacted the slices of life
for their work on ideas. They re-enacted the situation either on their own or with
other members of the ensemble. I asked the rest of the group to notice how the
actors bodies behaved as the frightening stimulus hit them. In the discussions that
followed each example, I discouraged any psychological analysis and drew out the
observations made about people's physicality.

One actor re-enacted a moment from his life when he had to film a scene with
a lion. There was a training session in which he had to enter the lion's cage. He
entered, stood stock still for ten seconds, then kept wiping the palms of his hands

on his thighs, taking tiny steps forwards and tiny steps backwards, without moving towards the lion at all. He then turned his head repeatedly back and forth from camera to lion. His body temperature increased and he turned red. We could see his increased heartbeat as a vein on his neck pumped hard. His breathing was very shallow and we could see that his mouth was dry when he talked.

In another exercise, an actor's car was stopped at a checkpoint in Northern Ireland. A gun was pointed into the window. The woman and the man in the car both became completely still for about five seconds. After this their movements were very slow and careful. You could see the actor moving his toes up and down in his trainers. The woman continued to hold the steering wheel very tightly, and the muscles in her fingers, hands, arms and shoulders were all very tense.

When you are discussing these exercises with the actors afterwards, relate them to a moment or event in the play if you can – just like you did when you discussed the exercises on ideas. After the lion re-enactment, I asked the ensemble whether there were any moments in the action of *Iphigenia at Aulis* in which some or all of the same physical 'symptoms' might be seen. One person suggested that we might see Agamemnon's body behave in this way as he approached the altar where he was to cut Iphigenia's throat. Another person suggested that the sudden stillness for ten seconds might usefully be related to what the women in the chorus do when they are told the news that Iphigenia is to be sacrificed. The actor playing Clytemnestra suggested that she might have some of the same physical 'symptoms' as the woman in the car in the exercise set in Northern Ireland as she heard the news about Iphigenia's death. She thought, for example, that she might hold onto Iphigenia in the same way that the woman held the steering wheel. In this way, you encourage the actors to think about using very precise physical information from real-life situations to communicate moments in the action of the play.

Of course, selecting one dominant emotion does not exclude the wide range of other emotions expressed in the play. However, drawing attention to one emotion sets the tone for the precision with which all emotions are to be investigated and re-enacted in the production. It reminds the actors that the body is one of the main means by which the audience 'read' emotions – and understand what is going on inside a person. Like the exercises on ideas described in the previous section, this work on emotions provides you with a set of precise points of reference for later on in the process. If, for instance, when you are rehearsing a scene much later on in the process, you feel that an actor is not playing fear with enough physical accuracy, you can say something like: 'Do you remember when Ben did the exercise about the lion and how he kept wiping the palms of his hands down his trousers and taking tiny steps backwards and forwards? Think about how your character would express fear in his body.' This will remind the actors to add those physical details to what they are doing.

This exercise is not about making actors exaggerate or stylise what they do physically. Rather, use it to get them to enact the precise physical shape of a certain emotion, being true to its scale and tempo from life. You will be surprised by how large these gestures and actions can be. When we were working on fear for *Iphigenia at Aulis*, one actor re-enacted a moment from his life when he opened the door of his flat and saw a rat at the top of the stairs. He jumped back three metres. After doing the exercise, the actor was surprised to discover just how far he had jumped. His impression was that he had just taken a step back. We subsequently integrated this large jump into the production as a reaction to the news that Achilles was to marry Iphigenia.

Summary
Find the emotion that dominates in the action of the play.
Ask the actors to think of a moment from their own lives where they experienced that emotion.
Ask them to re-enact this event for the rest of the group to watch.
Draw everyone's attention away from the psychological information and towards the physical information.
Connect this physical information with moments in the play.
Use the exercises as reference points later on in the rehearsal process when you are working to achieve physical accuracy.

Character biographies

Every director will have to field questions from actors about the lives of the characters they are playing. This is an unavoidable stage of the rehearsal process – you will always have to discuss or answer questions such as: 'When did we meet?', 'How long have we known each other?' and 'When did I last see my uncle?' Working collectively on character biographies early on in the process will mean that these questions will have been addressed by the time you rehearse the scene and that everyone concerned will have a shared picture of the past.

You will already have sketched out each character biography on a separate piece of paper. You will now put the actors through the same initial steps that you took to arrive at these biographies and you will set them the following task overnight. Ask each actor to collect all the facts and questions about their character from the back history lists you made of everything that exists and has happened before the action of the play begins. Then ask them to put the facts in a loose chronological order. Suggest that they go for the simplest and most logical order, just as you did when you prepared the biographies; actors, like directors, have a tendency to over-complicate the character's past. Remember, too, that characters often share a past; therefore, there is no point in the actors working out the fine detail of their biographies in isolation from each other. They might turn up with completely different orders of events which will not fit together and you will have to spend a lot of time unpicking their hard work. For that reason, it is best to get the actor to prepare a simple and brief list of facts for their character's biography. Ask them to put dates by the events in the biography if they can. If they are unsure about where a fact sits in the character's life, they can leave it out. Encourage them to leave their list of questions unanswered. Allocate work on the biographies of indirect characters to actors playing smaller roles or to actors playing characters with a strong relationship to the indirect character – for example, ask Medvedenko to work on the biography of his father and mother. Set all these tasks for completion outside the rehearsal room.

The following day, sit around a table with the whole group. Start at the top of the dramatis personae and work through each character in turn, checking the order of the facts that each actor has prepared about their character and answering some of the simpler questions. Each actor should emerge from the session with a clear chronology of the key events in their character's past.

Use your already-prepared character biography sheets to guide the actors. Ask each of them to talk you through their character's biography and stop them if they have put a date in the wrong position. Rather than telling the actors that their choice of dates is 'wrong', it might be advisable to give a context for your own suggestion. You might, for instance, say: 'I'm not entirely convinced that putting the death of Nina's mother so long ago is useful. It might be better to consider putting it a little closer to the action of the play so that your stepmother is newer.'

Try to cite a moment in the play when this repositioning will help the actors to play a line or intention. In this way, you will always keep them focused on the connection between the events in the past and what the character says or does in the present action of the play. If the actor disagrees with you, read the relevant section in the text together and look for the clearest impression the words give. Then work through the indirect characters in the same way (in the order in which their names crop up in the play).

Keep the whole group involved in the process by encouraging them all to look for links between the character you are working on and their own character's past. Make sure that major events, like a marriage or a death in the family, are written down on all the family biographies – even if only one member of the family talks about the event in the text.

Use your prepared work on relationships to guide the actors to think about the relationships they have in the play as they build their biographies. Even if two characters have very little direct interaction in the play itself, encourage them to recognise that there may be events in the past that connect them – and therefore help them build a relationship. For instance, if you were working on *The Seagull*, when you arrive at Nina's date of birth you could turn to the actor playing Dorn and ask: 'Do you think you delivered Nina?' When Nina talks about her mother's death ask Dorn the question: 'Do you think you nursed Nina's mother?' Remember that Dorn has a line in the text in Act One where he talks about Nina's father in an aggressive way and the actor needs to have something in his biography to support this feeling. The actor playing Dorn will add the date of Nina's birth and her mother's death to his list of facts about the past. Remember too that Dorn is in several scenes with Nina and they need to have a picture of their past relationship to play together accurately.

Also, remember to use the work you did on relationships, described in Chapter 5, to alert the actor to how a particular incident may have formed their character's thinking about either themselves or another character. For instance, point out how Arkadina's thinking about money was shaped by her early experiences of disinheritance and poverty. You only need point out a few key moments like this in a couple of characters' biographies for the rest of the group to get the idea. You can then refer to other connections like this later on, when you are working on a scene where there is a particularly strong connection between present behaviour and a past event.

Ensure you pay each character the proper time and attention – but do not allow any one actor to hijack the group session and use it to talk at length about their character. If this starts to happen ask the actor to put their concerns in the form of a simple question and add it to their list of questions to be addressed at a later point. If there is a major dispute between two actors about when and how a shared event happened in the past, ask them to take the fact out of the equation for the time being. Both of them could turn the fact back into a question to be addressed in the near future. Then move on briskly.

By the end of this process, you do not have to have filled in every detail of every biography or answered every question. There will always be things that need further research, or more careful thought, or a closer reading of the text at a later point. However, do not leave too many loose threads. All the actors must leave this group process feeling that they have a fuller picture of their character's past than their initial sketch of facts gave them and that they have pinned down the key shared events in the past. They should also have started to think about their relationship to all the other characters.

The group session is a laborious and time-consuming activity. Only embark on it if you have completed careful preparation on all the characters (as described in Chapter 1). Stay calm and focused – and always keep the exercise moving without giving the actors the impression that time is limited. It will help if you do not attempt to construct all of these biographies in a single session. You might prefer to work through six characters in one three-hour session and another six in a subsequent session. Remember to invite the designer to these sessions. Watching how the actors deepen the character biographies will help sharpen choices about costumes. Remember, too, that the process is not a one-way street – the actors will often come up with lovely new details that you never thought of, meaning that you might have to adjust the information on your own prepared biographies.

Summary

Ask the actors to collect all the facts and questions about their character from the master list of facts and questions that you have created together. Encourage them to put the facts in a loose chronological order.

Allocate actors to do this work on the indirect characters.

Gather the ensemble together and go through each character in turn. Use your prepared biographies to steer the actors to build a biography that will help them play the play. Help them to arrive at an agreement about shared events in each other's biographies.

Keep the whole group involved in the process by encouraging everyone to look for links between the character being focused on and their own character's past.

Use the work you did on relationships to draw the actors' attention to the relationship between past events and the characters' thinking in the present action of the play.

Pay each character equal attention.

Manage problems in this process by asking the actors to put their concerns in the form of questions to be answered later on in the process.

By the time you reach the end of this work, make sure that you do not leave too many loose ends in the character biographies.

Ensure that your group sessions on character work are underpinned by the research and preparation you completed before rehearsals began.

First practical work on character and character tempo

These exercises allow the actors to dip their toes into their characters in a non-pressurised context, as well as giving you an opportunity to see how they have absorbed the work you did together on their biographies. You can start these exercises once you have completed the group work on character biographies. These exercises also allow the actors to test-run the increased physical precision that the exercises on ideas and emotions have introduced into the rehearsal process.

Ask each of the actors to look at their character biography and to think of a specific time and place where their character was doing a simple activity on their own – such as polishing their shoes, cooking a meal or making a bed. Make sure that they pick a time that predates the trigger event of the play and ask them to avoid major events. Encourage the actors to map out the place where their character is using chairs and to use any props that they find in the room, or to simply imagine the objects they need. The whole group can do their exercises simultaneously in the rehearsal room while you sit and watch.

After they have finished the exercise, ask everyone to say briefly what they learnt about their character. If you have noticed anyone heading in an inaccurate direction, point out any additional ingredients they might need to think about or encourage them to work on an aspect of the character that needs strengthening. In *The Seagull*, the actor playing Shamrayev did several exercises which involved cleaning his army kit and drill practice so that he could strengthen the military side of the character (he had been an officer in the army before he became an estate manager).

Do these exercises regularly for a week or so, depending on how long your rehearsal period is. They should only take about 20 minutes to set up, execute and discuss.

Here are some examples of the sorts of exercises that the actors did on *The Seagull*.

> It was August 1871 and Dorn was alone with baby Masha. He held the child.
> It was May 1888 and Konstantin was trying to write for the first time.
> It was July 1873 and Arkadina was putting on her make-up for her performance at Poltava.
> It was November 1890 and Polina was doing Konstantin's ironing.

Introduce the idea of character tempo during these exercises. This is the speed at which the character thinks and does things physically. Sometimes actors will play their character at their own speed. This might be faster or slower than the tempo of their character. Immediately you see this happening, point it out. Actors can build their characters in the wrong tempo early on: it is a very hard thing to unpick. The problem will emerge later on in the process when the scenes themselves are played at inaccurate speeds because one person is not playing their character's tempo precisely.

You will start to arrive at some conclusions about tempo as you work on character biographies and relationships. You may notice, for example, that Sorin talks about sleeping a lot and moves with a stick. This may start to give you an impression of a slow tempo. Analysing events and intentions will deepen your understanding of tempo. You may notice, for instance, the speed at which Konstantin responds to events in Act One, such as the way in which he attacks his mother when he is talking to Sorin, or the sudden excitement of his response to Nina's footsteps, or the way in which he abruptly stops the performance of his play. Bit by bit the speed of his responses will lead you to the conclusion that he has a fast tempo. The precise speed or tempo of each character will crystallise in this way as you move through your preparation tasks.

Summary
Ask the actor to think of a specific time and place where the character was doing a simple activity on their own.
Get them to mark up with chairs the place where this happened. All the actors will mark up their places simultaneously in the rehearsal room.
At the end of the exercise ask them what they learnt and give any feedback.
Introduce the idea of character tempo.

Relationships

I like to look at what is happening between people on stage and I think of relationships as being like invisible and beautifully patterned spider webs, linking people together – if you were to put your hand gently between any of the characters you would almost be able to feel that web. Sometimes when I watch productions I see actors execute a finely honed sense of a character without having a clear picture of their relationship with the other characters in the scene. When this happens, some part of me always loses interest in what is going on.

Work on relationships encourages the actors to think about the interactions they have with everyone in the play, from the least significant person to the most important. The work you did on each character biography will already have drawn the actors' attention to all the relationships they have in the play. The more you can deepen their thinking about these relationships, the more credible those relationships will be in the performance that the audience finally watch. (If you do not do this work, the actors may be guided by their affinities and at best only play the most important relationships or, at worst, play only one relationship out of ten. For instance, the actor playing Arkadina might only play her relationship with Trigorin and Konstantin, thereby neglecting more than eight other relationships – including her sick brother, Sorin, and her old flame, Dorn.)

Do not set the actors the task of writing down quotes from the play that relate to their thoughts about each character, as you did when you prepared the play. Instead, ask each actor to write down the unfinished sentence 'I am …', just as you did when you were preparing relationships (see Chapter 5), and to fill it in with three or four simple adjectives or nouns that describe how the character thinks about themselves. Encourage the actors to consider these sentences as thoughts that the character would never reveal to anyone. Give them 15 minutes to do this, then gather the group and go through each character in turn. Each actor will read out their sentence and you will respond to what they propose.

You will notice that the actors sometimes write down value judgements on their characters. For example, in *The Seagull* the actor playing Konstantin might put down 'I am a child' or the actor playing Shamrayev might put down 'I am aggressive'. These are things that other people might say about the character but they do not exist as thoughts inside that character's head. Weed out these words or replace them with more accurate adjectives. For instance, Konstantin may think 'I am worthless' which, in turn, makes him behave like a child, or Shamrayev might think 'I am undervalued' which makes him appear aggressive.

If the actors write down several words that all mean the same thing, together select the one word that best encapsulates the thought. For instance, the actor playing Konstantin may write: 'I am *untalented*, a *failure*, *nothing*'; the three italic words can be conflated into the single word 'worthless'. Some actors may also smooth out their character's thinking by removing thoughts that contradict each other. Ensure that they do not do this; if they have omitted contradictory thoughts, then get them to add them back into their sentence. Each actor should emerge from this exercise with a simple, accurate and clear sentence with between three and four adjectives or nouns.

If the group take to this exercise and see the usefulness of it, you can take it to the next level by setting them a similar but longer task overnight. Ask them to fill in a series of sentences in the same way about each of the other characters – again writing down only three or four nouns or adjectives. In *The Seagull*, Arkadina would fill in the following sentences: '*Konstantin is …*', '*Sorin is …*', '*Dorn is …*' and so on. Ask the actors to consider their relationship with every character on the dramatis personae in order that they avoid any of their own affinities. Again, let them know that the adjectives they put down describe a thought that their character would never disclose to anyone.

The next day ask each actor to read their completed sentences back to the group. Use your preparation to help them fill in gaps and remove inaccuracies. Sometimes actors concentrate only on key relationships and neglect others. This is because of affinities, habit or lack of guidance. This exercise ensures they keep all their relationships in the play alive – however big or small they might be. It also ensures that the actors start building their relationships in the right direction for the play. Finally, the exercise reveals any gaps in their thinking about other characters. Actors can get bogged down with finding the right adjective or disputing adjectives you suggest so try to lead this exercise with a light touch and do not dwell too long on it. The main aim at this point is that they start to consider all the relationships they have in play.

Try to be imaginative about smaller characters with little to say. Give them some guidance before they do this task. I asked the actors playing the servants in *The Seagull* to consider the personal hygiene, sexual habits and tidiness of the people they worked for. Servants would always have known intimate details like this about the people employing them and these details would have informed what they thought about their bosses.

Summary
Ask the actors to complete the sentence 'I am ...' with simple adjectives or nouns that describe how their character thinks about themselves.
Ask them to read back their sentences in turn in the group and help them distil an accurate list of nouns or adjectives.
If the group take to the exercise, set them the task of listing the adjectives that describe what their thoughts are about every other character.
Help point the actors playing smaller characters in a useful direction when you set this task.

How to set up improvisations with the actors

Improvisations will build strong pictures of the past in the actors' minds, and these pictures will help them play the present action of the play more accurately. Chapter 5 suggested ways of selecting and planning improvisations. Only begin doing improvisations when you have worked on character biographies and relationships. Remember to work through the improvisations in chronological order whether you plan to do two or twenty.

Start by doing any planned improvisations that precede the trigger event. It is best to do improvisations about the trigger event and improvisations on the immediate circumstances of the first scene later on in the process, as described in Chapter 11. Remember to save the improvisations of what happens in between the scenes for when you are actually rehearsing the scenes of the play. Then you can insert these improvisations in between your rehearsals of the relevant scene. The immediate circumstances to each scene could be improvised just before you work on that scene, so that the memory of what happens prior to the action of the scene is fresh in the actors' minds. The description that follows explains how to set up any improvisation with the actors.

Gather the actors together and give them your prepared instructions for the initial improvisation you want them to do. This will be the first time you give instructions directly to the actors and the first time you bring the key ingredients of this process together in one acting exercise (immediate circumstances, events, intentions, place and time). Try not to rush when you give your instructions and take the time to answer any questions the actors may have.

When they have absorbed what you have said, give them time to build and mark out a clear picture of the place where the action of the improvisation will happen.

You will watch the improvisation either on your own or with other actors (not in the one being enacted). Encourage everyone watching to sit around the boundaries of the place where the improvisation is set as if it were theatre-in-the-round. Encourage the people watching to move if they cannot see something. Ask the actors to keep going with the improvisation until you stop them (although you might allow a maximum of ten minutes). Stop them when they are losing belief in the situation or becoming vague about any of the instructions – for example, if their picture of place has fallen away or if they have stopped playing their intentions. Working out when to stop an improvisation is a fine art. You will make mistakes but those mistakes will help you to improve.

At the end of the improvisation, give feedback that relates directly to the instructions you gave when setting up the improvisation. Point out where an event or intention was not sharply played, where the place was clearly played and where it was not. Highlight the things the actors did that were heading in the right direction for the play and point out the things that were less helpful. For instance, if a character like Sorin did not use his stick in the improvisation, remind him to think about his physical condition a little more; and if the actor playing Masha used her snuff very accurately, let her know that she did.

If you have a large ensemble you can set up several improvisations at once. Give each group your prepared instructions in turn, then allow time for them to set up place. Then do the improvisations in chronological order. You can ask the actors watching the improvisations to give their feedback on simpler aspects of the improvisation such as time and place.

If an actor resists your idea for an improvisation, you can either change your idea or go ahead regardless. If the actor is prepared to try your idea, ask them to do the improvisation but stress that it is only an initial sketch. Let them know that you will try out another version if yours does not work. Nine times out of ten your version will persuade them. If that actor disagrees vociferously then ask them to propose an alternative map of what happens and try it out. You will then have to come up with precise instructions on the hoof.

Summary

Only begin doing improvisations when you have worked on character biographies and relationships.

Work through the improvisations in chronological order.

Give your prepared instructions slowly and give the actors time to absorb what you have said.

Give the actors time to set up the place where the improvisation will happen.

Ask the people watching the improvisation to sit around the boundaries of the place where the action occurs as if it were theatre-in-the-round.

Give feedback at the end of each improvisation that relates to the instructions you gave when you set them up.

If an actor disagrees with your idea for an improvisation, either change your plan or ask them to do it with the assurance that they can try out their idea afterwards.

How to use visualisation exercises

Visualisation exercises are another way of creating pictures of past events to support the action of the play. They can also replace improvisations if you are pressed for time. They can be done in the rehearsal room or as homework overnight.

Ask the actors to sit still with their eyes open, and to imagine that their eyes are like a camera moving through a place, interacting with other people or objects. Give them an event to visualise. In *The Seagull*, Masha might visualise the first time she bought snuff or Konstantin might visualise seeing Arkadina perform in one of Trigorin's plays. Frame by frame the actor will imagine how the event unfolded. If the actor struggles to do the exercise with their eyes open, then suggest they close them.

Visualisation exercises are particularly useful for past events that happen to one character alone, but they are less useful for past events that affect more than one person. In those cases, a shared picture created by an improvisation would be more useful. In *The Seagull*, for instance, it would be good for Konstantin to visualise killing a seagull in between Act One and Act Two because no one else is involved in this event. However, it would not be useful for Nina and Trigorin to visualise the pregnancy, birth and death of their child in between Acts Three and Four because they need shared pictures of what happened.

Summary

Ask the actors to sit with their eyes open (or closed) and visualise an event in their character's biography, as if they were a camera filming an event, frame by frame.

Remember that these exercises are less useful for events that happen to more than one person.

How to do all this with a short rehearsal period

The danger of compressing or cutting the steps of this process to fit a shorter rehearsal period is that you will build characters that do not have clear pictures of the past or the future, or that the characters you construct don't exist in a real time and a real place. Bear this in mind as you select that ingredients you choose to work on.

Introducing facts and questions: If you are pushed for time, do not do immediate circumstances' questions and facts as a rehearsal room task. Prepare the details of the immediate circumstances and give them to the actors before the relevant scene rehearsals. Compress the time you spend on compiling your list of back history facts and questions with the actors into one three-hour session. Then keep the exercise moving along sharply and avoid lengthy discussion. As soon as you see a discussion developing, nip it in the bud by asking the actors concerned to boil down their points into simple questions. If you find yourself running out of time ask the group to focus on facts alone.

Research: Ask the actors to come up with three simple facts about the world of the play. Do this as homework on the first day. Gather as a group and listen to each of the facts together for half an hour; this will help you to build a shared picture of the world. Then throughout the first week set individual actors essential tasks that they can do overnight. For example, it is not possible to play Masha without knowing about snuff. Ideally, any research undertaken should be shared in a feedback session with the whole group, but if you do not have time for that the research will still help individual actors to build their characters. Perhaps find a forum where the key ingredients of the research tasks can be shared. If there is any essential information that everyone needs to know, give it to the actors in an A4 sheet that can be read overnight. In *The Seagull*, every actor is on stage for Act One when Arkadina refers to the derelict estates; they all need to know a little basic information about why those estates have collapsed and the broader economics of estates at the time.

Place: Do the initial exercise on circles of place on the first day. From then onwards, you should still be able to attend to all the work on place without needing to set aside any special time in your process. Do this by always giving clear feedback on place in any of the acting exercises, improvisations or scene rehearsal that you do.

The writer and the genre: You will have introduced the essential facts about the writer on the first day and you do not need to do another group session on the writer. Instead smuggle in bits of relevant information during the work on character biographies. For example, when you reach Dorn's biography ask him to take a look at Chekhov's life to work out how he trained as a doctor. Then you can set the relevant actors research tasks about people in the writer's life that provided the basis for their characters, rather than convening a session to share information about the writer's life with the whole group. Let the actors know what the genre of the play is and work on it as you do your scene rehearsals.

Practical work on ideas: The group session in which you come to an agreement about the ideas of the play should take you a maximum of half an hour. Select the main idea, then ask the actors to think overnight about a slice of their lives that relates to that idea. The following day re-enact the slice of their lives in a single three-hour session. When you give feedback, stress the relationship between life and the action of the play, and draw the actors' attention to any key ingredients in the process (time, place, intention, event and the precise physical actions and gestures people use). Attend to the other ideas when you are rehearsing scenes or building character biographies. You might let the actors know if they are not building their character with all the ideas that underpin the play in mind. The actor playing Arkadina might be playing the idea of unhappiness in love over and above the theme of family; this will manifest itself in her playing only the love affair with Trigorin and not being a credible mother with Konstantin. Suggest that she build her thinking about family a little more.

Practical work on emotions: Cut this step altogether.

Character biographies: It is essential for the actors to undertake the simple character biography exercise as homework and for you to work through those biographies in a group session. You should be able to do this in a single group three-hour session. If you accelerate this exercise, there may be more loose ends than normal so make sure that you sort them out as you work on the scenes. If you are really strapped for time, do the sketch biographies yourself and give them to the actors as a starting point for discussion.

First practical work on character and character tempo: These exercises take only about 15 or 20 minutes, so try to do at least three of them spread over a few early days. If you really cannot afford the time, cut them out.

Relationships: Skip the group exercise on relationships and, instead, use your preparatory work to guide the actors when they are working on scenes together or building their character biographies. For example, you could point out to two of the actors in a large group scene that they do not have a considered relationship with each other. Ask them to clarify their thinking about these characters.

Improvisations: If you have little time, you could consider cutting all improvisations and discussing instead what happened in the past at the relevant point in a scene rehearsal (or asking them to visualise the events). For example, when a character describes an event in the past, stop and talk about it, or give them a few minutes to visualise the events or ask them to think about how the event happened overnight. If the pictures of the past are shared, give the relevant actors time in rehearsals to visualise the event together. Remember, however, that a structured improvisation may take up less rehearsal time than a discussion.

Visualisation exercises: It may help you to set up a few of these exercises, but they are not essential.

The Maids by Jean Genet

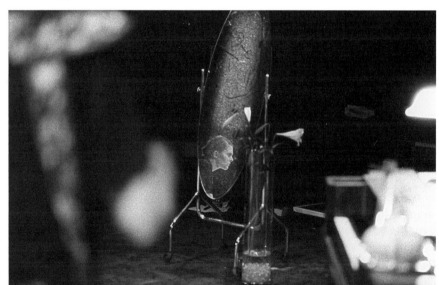

CHAPTER 11

Working on the scenes of the play

This chapter looks at how you put the play on its feet. This work will take around 60% of your rehearsal period. It covers everything from the analysis of the action of the play to the last run-through in the rehearsal room. It includes advice about the following:

Analysing the action of the play with the actors
The mark-up
Improvising the trigger event and immediate circumstances
How to structure the rehearsal day
Rehearsing a scene for the first time
'Blocking', or making the action clear for the audience
The second and third rehearsals of a scene
Run-throughs
How to manage the final days in a rehearsal room
Working on set, costume, sound, lighting design and music during
    rehearsals
How to do all this with a short rehearsal period

Analysing the action of the play with the actors

The group will already have read the play once through for facts and questions about everything that exists and has happened before the action of the play begins. Now, you will read it through together again with four specific tasks in mind:

isolating the events and giving them titles
writing down the facts and questions about what happens between each act or
    scene
writing down the facts and questions about the immediate circumstances of
    each act or scene (i.e. what occurs in the 24 hours preceding the action of
    the scene)
finding a name for each act.

By now the actors should be familiar with the word 'event', as you will have used it when giving feedback on their exercises on ideas and emotions, and when structuring their initial improvisations. However, it will not hurt at this point to remind them of a simple definition of the word: a moment in the action where everyone changes what they are doing or playing. Then, let them know that the name of the act or scene should be the simplest description of what is happening throughout the whole act or scene.

Read the play in the same way that you did initially with no one reading their own parts and each person reading a line at a time. Ask them to stop whenever they spot information that might help with any of the four tasks. If they pass over any information, draw their attention to what they have missed. It is best to ask the actors about the title of each act or scene before you start reading them together. Make sure that everyone in the group writes down the title of each scene and the name of each event. Also, make sure that everyone is clear about when each event begins and ends – and that everyone writes down the same words to describe each event. Use your prepared script to guide them.

I often find that the actors' insights mean that I have to correct the positions of some events, or add a couple of new ones I missed when I did my preparation. I also find it useful to ask them what they think the simplest title for an event is and only offer up the solution I have prepared if they are struggling to find one. If an actor disagrees strongly about an event or its title, suggest that they put a question mark by it and assure them that you will re-examine it later on in the process. Do not waste time in a group session on lengthy debates.

Make sure everyone in the group keeps up with the exercise. Remember that it takes people time to write down titles or draw a line around an event and name it. Do not move forward until everyone has completed each task. Do not attempt this work in one long session; rather do it over a couple of days. Intersperse it with movement, practical work on themes or improvisations. It requires a lot of concentration from everyone. Stay open and responsive to the actors' ideas and perceptions; at the same time use your preparation to keep them on track.

This session is also an opportunity for the actors to bring up the queries they had about the action of the play or the sense of a line. They may have jotted down queries of this nature when you worked on the initial lists of facts and questions and immediate circumstances earlier on in the process. Address any straightforward queries in this session. Defer more complex queries until the scene rehearsals.

At the end of the process, give them a definition of the trigger event and ask them to identify it. Next, ask them to identify the main events of each act and the most significant event in the entire piece. Complete the process by asking the actors to learn where the events come in the text just as they would learn their lines.

Finally, remind the actors about intentions and give them the simplest definition of the word: what one character wants to do to or change in another character (or characters). Give concrete examples of what you mean from exercises they have already done in rehearsals or scenes in the play. Remind the group that intentions only change at events. When they have absorbed all this, ask them to prepare for their scene rehearsals by working out what their character's intentions are between events. This is something they can work on in their spare time outside the rehearsal room. You will sharpen their understanding of this tool when you come to do your first few scene rehearsals. Do not spend too much time unpacking intentions at length at this point.

Summary
Read through the play again with the company and isolate four things: events, titles of acts, what happens between scenes and the immediate circumstances to each scene.

Make sure that everyone writes down all the information and do not rush ahead, leaving people behind.

Adjust your already-prepared answers to accommodate new discoveries or new proposals put forward by the group.

Do not waste time on lengthy disputes over answers to the tasks set.

Intersperse this task with other practical tasks.

Identify the trigger event, the main events in each act and the most important event in the whole play.

Ask the actors to learn where the events occur.

Remind them of the simplest definition of an intention.

Set them the homework of preparing their intentions between events in preparation for the first scene rehearsals.

The mark-up

Ask the stage management to put the mark-up down as soon as you are about to do practical work in the place(s) where the action of the play occurs. This normally happens either when you start to do improvisations on the trigger event or immediate circumstances of the first scene or before the first scene rehearsal. If the action of the play takes place in more than one location, the stage management will lay down a series of plans on top of each other, with different-coloured plastic tape to denote each place.

Ideally, as described in Chapter 8, you should be in a rehearsal room that is large enough for a mark-up of the set plus a minimum of two or three metres around the edge of the room. Ask the stage management to put the mark-up in the middle of the room and, in the three or more metres left free around the edge, get them to add as many other rooms, sections of rooms or exteriors as they can, even though these other rooms will never be seen by the audience. For example, if the action takes place in a dining room, add a mark-up of the kitchen or hallway and front door leading off from the dining room.

When we rehearsed *The Seagull* at the National Theatre (London), we had the luxury of a very large rehearsal room. We were able to mark up several rooms on the ground floor of the house, including the two rooms where the action of Acts Three and Four was located: the dining room and Konstantin's study. The other rooms marked up (the bootroom, kitchen, hallway) were not seen by the audience in the final design but they were used by the actors in rehearsals to help them build a picture of where they had come from and where they were heading to during the action.

Of course, this was an unusual size for a rehearsal room and not at all what one might expect early on in a career. If you are only able to mark up the precise foot-print of the set design (or even less than that) do not worry – just bear in mind that you will need to find another way of helping the actors prepare to enter the places where the action of the play occurs. You can, for instance, use visualisation exercises or simply allow the actors a few seconds before starting the scene to remind themselves of exactly where they have just come from and what they were doing in that place.

If you are working on a play in which the action occurs in several different locations and you do not want to confuse the actors by layering several mark-ups on top of one another, use bamboo sticks to delineate the boundaries of each room or place. The sticks can be easily laid down and taken up as you move from place to place.

Ask the stage management to do the mark-up either at the end of the rehearsal day or just before the beginning of the rehearsal day. Then, as soon as the actors arrive, ask them to familiarise themselves with the environment that the mark-up indicates: you could walk round the mark-up with the whole ensemble, reminding yourselves what the lines on the floor represent in terms of architecture or land-scape. Discuss what can be seen or heard outside the place (or places) marked up, or where different exits or entrances lead to and, as always, make sure the actors all know what they can see in each place if they turn 360 degrees.

At this point it is also useful to discuss with your designer any key scenic elements that you may want mock-ups of. Consider, for instance, constructing mock-ups of a scenic element such as a door frame with a door in it, a window frame or some flats representing walls. I have always found mock-ups of doors a really important thing to have in rehearsals, although be warned that the construction of a free-standing door is a fine art: many have a tendency to fall over as soon as they are used.

Summary

Get the stage management to do a mark-up of the set on the floor in the centre of the room and, if possible, to allow between two and three metres between the edge of the mark-up and the walls of the rehearsal room.

Add as many other adjoining rooms or places as possible around the main set mark-up, even though the audience will not see them.

If you only have space for a mark-up, find other ways of helping the actors picture where they have come from and what they were doing in that place.

If you are working on a play set in many different locations, consider whether to use bamboo poles to delineate different places so that the actors do not get confused by several layers of different-coloured plastic tape.

Get the stage management to do the mark-up at the end of a rehearsal day.

Walk round the mark-up with the ensemble the next day and remind yourselves of what the lines on the floor represent in terms of landscape or architecture.

Consider adding some mock-ups of key scenic elements such as doors, window frames or walls.

Improvising the trigger event and immediate circumstances

Now do the improvisations you have planned around the trigger event followed by the improvisations on the immediate circumstances of the first scene. Set them up in exactly the same way that you did the other improvisations (see Chapter 10) and continue to give precise feedback. Do not do any of the improvisations around the events that happen in between acts or scenes, or any immediate circumstances to any other scenes or acts. You will do these improvisations later on in the process when you are working your way through the action of the play.

Summary

Set up improvisations around the trigger event and immediate circumstances to the first scene or act.

Give thorough feedback.

How to structure the rehearsal day

At this point your rehearsal day will change its structure – you will start to rehearse the play itself and only call the actors who are in the sections you are working on. Try to work your way through the play in chronological order and to use the events as a guideline for breaking the play into smaller sections to rehearse. If someone has an entrance during the course of the action, you need to make sure you ask them to join the previous rehearsal so that everyone can practise the event of their entrance. In this way the sections you rehearse will often overlap: this will make the moment when you first thread the sections together in a run much smoother.

Here is the structure of the first scene rehearsal day of *The Seagull*.

10.30am	Masha, Medvedenko, Yakov and workmen
11.30am	Konstantin and Sorin to join
1.30pm	Lunch
2.30pm	Konstantin, Sorin, Yakov and workmen
4pm	Nina to join
5.30pm	End

Give the actors a few minutes to warm up before each call or, if you are pressed for time, before calls with larger groups of actors. During this period of rehearsals, you could also consider calling the full ensemble occasionally for movement or voice work, or to relay any new research material. It's important not to lose the sense of a shared group activity and purpose. Do this once a week for an hour or so. This is, of course, an ideal structure for a long rehearsal period. Do not worry if you have a short rehearsal period and do not have time to schedule these ensemble calls.

Summary

Work your way through the play in chronological order.

Use events as a guideline for breaking the play down into smaller sections to rehearse.

Overlap your rehearsal calls so that the actors can practise the events of entrances and exits.

Schedule warm-ups where you can.

Schedule occasional ensemble sessions for movement work or feedback on research.

Rehearsing a scene for the first time

The aim of the first rehearsal of a scene is to establish all the targets that the actors need to work towards long term and to allow them to enter the material gently. Before investigating the section you will work on, check that there are no outstanding questions about the meaning of what is said in the text. If there are, discuss them and if possible iron them out.

Then let the actors know that this first rehearsal is not about practising the words in the section; instead, it is about practising everything that underpins and generates the words. These 'underpinnings' include intentions, immediate circumstances, time, past pictures, relationships and place.

First, look at events and intentions together. Normally, you will rehearse the play 'event by event', so remind the actors of where the event occurs, where it starts and where it ends. Then ask each of them, in turn, what their intention is before and after the event (and remind them that intentions only change at events). You will have already written these in your script, so you can use this preparation to guide the actors in the right direction. The actors' insights may mean you have to alter the sentence that you originally wrote down.

When you have arrived at an agreement about an intention, make sure you and the actor write down the agreed sentence precisely. It does not matter if the final sentence is different to the one you conceived during your preparation as long as it captures the essence of what you want the actor to play. Some actors will prefer cool and cerebral language such as 'to make Medvedenko feel uncomfortable'. Others will respond best to stronger words such as 'you make Medvedenko feel like a piece of shit'. During rehearsals you will learn how to translate the intention you want played into the vocabulary or syntax that suits each individual actor, and that gets the result you want. The process of deciding on the intentions will take up 50% of this first rehearsal. At the end of it, ask the actors to read the scene through together with the intentions in mind.

Next, remind them of the immediate circumstances, time of day and name of the scene or act that you are working on. Finally, ask them to renew their picture of the place in which the scene occurs. It is best to encourage them to do this on their feet. I usually give the actors five or ten minutes to talk through place together – they normally stand in the mark-up and describe to each other what they can see all around them. (The first time you rehearse a scene like this, it may help if you go through 'place' with the actors by asking simple questions such as 'What can you see through the window?' if the scene takes place inside or 'What can you see in the far distance over there?' if the scene takes place outside. They can also refer to the maps of place that they made earlier on in the rehearsal process (see Chapter 10) and that will now be up on the wall of the rehearsal room.)

Ask the actors to use a mixture of the words they remember from the script and their own invented dialogue when they come to rehearse the section. This brings the first rehearsal closer to an improvisation and means, more importantly, that the actors will never have to hold onto their scripts when they rehearse the play. Their scripts will sit outside the place where the action of the play occurs on a table or chair or on the floor.

The first time the actors practise the scene they will be a little awkward: they will remember some things and forget others. They may even feel a little frustrated or embarrassed afterwards, particularly if this is the first time they have rehearsed a play in this way. Do not be worried if this happens – instead, give them feedback on the tasks you set them (including events, intentions, immediate circumstances, time and place) just as you did when you set up the early improvisations. You may, for example, ask them to sharpen the playing of place and time, but reassure them that their intentions were clear.

Then ask them to 'practise' the scene again and watch how they execute the notes you gave them. If you have time to run it a third time, you can start to add other things to your checklist of things to give feedback on – relationships and character (past pictures, tempo and thoughts about themselves). You could, for example, suggest that the picture of a past event was not quite accurately imagined or guide them towards playing the relationship between the characters with more precision. In most cases, these notes will be about reminding them of things that you have already worked on with them in the rehearsal process. In these early rehearsals, the scene will not be played as accurately as it will be when the audience sees it – there will be gaps and inaccuracies but the actors will have a clear sense of all the ingredients that need to be in place at that future point. Some actors will be able to absorb all the notes you give them at this first rehearsal and others will take time to digest them after the rehearsal. At this point, do not worry if their rate of absorption is slow.

At the end of the rehearsal, ask the actors to undertake any research tasks that have emerged or give them things to think about for the next rehearsal such as sharpening their pictures of certain events in their character's past or filling in any gaps in their picture of place. Then ask them to learn the intentions. Learning intentions is as important as learning words. In life, when you look back on significant events it is often what you wanted to achieve or desired that lodges in the memory more strongly than anything you said.

You will repeat this process for every section of the play, moving from event to event. Normally the majority of the words spoken in the first scene rehearsal will be improvised. Ideally, the lines will be learnt over the second and third rehearsals, so by the time you do a run-through, the only words used will be from the script.

This way of working on early scene rehearsals was a revelation to me when I first came across it. For years I had struggled with the transition from early improvisations to work on the scenes of the play. I loved the fluidity and ease of an improvisation and hated the constipation and tension of the early scene rehearsals. The idea of mixing words from the play with words from the actors' imaginations was a perfect way of building a bridge between these two stages of rehearsals. However, be warned that it does take some actors a bit of time to adjust to this way of working. Some will worry about getting the lines of the play right and you will have to ask them to lower the volume on this concern. If an actor has already learnt their lines, then they should use them – but ask them to bear in mind the fact that they may not get the proper cues from their fellow actors who have not learnt the lines. You may also have to allow older actors to use more of the words from the play than everyone else, because of their genuine concerns about their ability to memorise the text. Actors can also find it hard to juggle everything you are asking them to play at this first rehearsal. They might not always be accustomed to playing notes about time and place as well as intentions and past pictures. Reassure them that this will take time to achieve but that they will arrive at it in the long term.

When you are working on intentions, you may encounter resistance from some actors, who think that pinning down intentions for every step of the action makes their character appear manipulative. If this happens, remind them that in life we are often unconscious of the desires or intentions that drive us, whereas a psychologist, watching from the outside, would be able to tell us exactly what we want at any given moment. The process of diagnosing and naming intentions is therefore often about making unconscious desires conscious for a while so that the forces driving the character are properly understood. They do not then have to be played self-consciously as if every character were like Iago in *Othello*, clearly manipulating all the characters for his own end.

Some actors will also want to change their intentions after their first attempt at practising the scene. Try to resist this request unless they have real cause. Instead, ask the actor to explore different ways of playing the agreed intention. If, by the end of the rehearsal, the actor is still convinced that the intention is not correct, suggest that you both take time before the next rehearsal to think about an alternative. Ideally, the decisions about intentions will change very little from this first rehearsal up until the last night of the performances, so in this early rehearsal, make sure the actors realise that you are laying down a long-term map.

As you work on intentions you will notice that there can be obstacles that modify the playing of the intention. These obstacles can be 'outside' a character such as the heat of the midday sun or they can be 'inside' a character such as heartburn, a heavy cold or the effect of the guilt the character feels about what they have done to the person they are talking to. Obstacles like this will affect how the intention is played but will never dislodge the intention altogether.

Keep an eye on whether the characters need intentions inside the events or not, and add them if you feel it will help to clarify what they are doing. You may, for instance, find that certain events (such as an entrance or exit) take more time than the text intended (this may be because of the way the actors are playing them, or because of an unexpected complication in the set design). In these cases, give the actors an intention during the exit or entrance. Alternatively, some events occur over a longer period of time than others: the actors will need intentions during these events. 'Slow burn' events that take place over several lines may also require the characters to have intentions.

When you get to the end of the scene or act, improvise the off-stage events before the next scene begins. If you do not have time to do an improvisation you can ask the actors to visualise what happened or simply ask them to talk about it briefly to you. Next, improvise any immediate circumstances preceding the next scene you will work on, then rehearse the next scene or act. If you do not have time to improvise the immediate circumstances, you can give the actors your prepared information about these circumstances as part of your instructions for the next scene rehearsal.

Summary
Iron out any outstanding queries about the meaning of the text.
Remind the actors where each event ends and begins.
Discuss the intentions between each event and write the agreed description down precisely.
Remind the actors of the immediate circumstances, time of day and name of the scene.
Give them time to set up place and build a clear picture of it.
Let them know that they will be using a mixture of the words they remember from the text and improvised dialogue.
Do not worry if the first attempt is awkward. Ask them to try it again with the same instructions.
At the end of the rehearsals, ask them to learn their intentions.
Be aware that it can take the actors time to learn this new way of rehearsing scenes.
Discourage them from changing the intentions, unless they have cause.
Consider what the obstacles are that may modify the characters' intentions.
Consider adding intentions inside events.
At the end of each act or scene, improvise what happens in between the scenes and the immediate circumstances prior to the next scripted scene.

'Blocking', or making the action clear for the audience

It is essential that actors are arranged on the stage so that the action, events and key story points are visible and well focused for the audience. This is a major part of your work as a director. 'Blocking' is a word used to describe one way of arranging these 'stage pictures'. Many rehearsal processes begin with blocking: typically, the director and actor discuss where the character should enter and where they should sit, stand, jump and so on. Alternatively, the director might simply tell the actor where to stand and what to do. These decisions are refocused during the rehearsals and the moves are then repeated identically in every performance.

For me, however, blocking is about balancing well-focused action for the audience with fluid and unselfconscious movement by the characters in the situation. If you bluntly tell an actor where to stand so that the audience will see them, it can increase their thinking about that audience and therefore reduce their thinking about the character in the situation. This can lead to self-conscious gestures and actions or awkward movements. And this, in turn, can lead to an uneven experience for the audience: sometimes they will be watching moves that resemble life while at other times they will be watching self-conscious or incongruous moves that are unlifelike. By self-conscious moves I mean, crudely, a moment when a character takes three large steps diagonally down stage and looks out at the audience whilst telling someone he is in love with them. This is not a convincing movement drawn from a real-life situation. Of course, the audience are not always consciously aware of the difference but they do absorb it at some level and it interferes with the belief and interest in what is going on.

I once took a friend of mine who was a neuroscientist to see a production I had directed and, unprompted, he highlighted a central problem about the acting. He said that there were two different types of acting going on: one was lifelike and the other was 'more heightened, self-conscious and theatrical'. He could cope with either, he said, but the moment that the brain struggled most was when the actors lurched between one style and another: in these moments, he lost all engagement with what was going on in the action of the play.

In Chapter 6, I suggested that during the design process you should think ahead to the way in which the characters might use the space, and position scenery, entrances, exits and furniture in such a way that it would lead to well-focused 'blocking' if the characters used the environment logically. This is the first step to getting a balance between unselfconscious, fluid movement from the actors and well-focused action for the audience. When you are first working on the scenes, let the moves evolve naturally out of the logic of the situation. That way much of the action will 'block' itself without the actors needing to worry about it or even know that the process is happening.

It will also help if you try to avoid thinking that on-stage action is only 'focused' when the audience is looking at faces or the front of people's bodies. The worst type of 'blocking' occurs when actors are positioned in a nice semi-circle facing downstage, walking sideways like crabs. Remember that profiles and backs can also be used to focus the action or direct the gaze of the audience to a particular character or object. Crudely put, if you position the person talking facing downstage and you position the person listening facing upstage, then the person talking will be well focused.

Of course, letting the blocking evolve like this will not solve all your focusing issues. You will always need to tweak the physical shape of the action – that is, you will have to ask the actors to make adjustments to what they are doing, where they are standing and so on. However, avoid doing this until the actors are well immersed in the character and the situation. It is easier for the actor to change what they do or where they stand if they are clear about what they are playing. That way, they can absorb the change without it leading to self-consciousness. Wherever possible, see if you can subtly alter the position of furniture or the placement of props to solve the problem without worrying the actors about it. Of course, any intelligent actor will know exactly why the chair or the prop is being moved, but they will appreciate the fact that you have approached the problem through altering the situation rather than by calling a blocking rehearsal. If you cannot make a useful tweak, then talk directly and clearly to the actor about the problem, whether it is a problem with a sightline or an attempt to focus a particular moment.

Remember that organising the actors spatially is only one of the tools at your disposal for making the action clear. This work will be supplemented by the lighting, costumes and set design. These additional ingredients will be added when you start technical rehearsals. But try to keep these ingredients in mind in the rehearsal room: sometimes you can worry away at the physical focus of a scene and forget that it is night and that the practical lights on the set will keep the eye looking at the key action. If you have a problem you cannot solve, think about how a lighting or sound or costume decision might help you find a solution.

If you struggle with making stage pictures that work, spend some time studying painters and paintings. This will train your eye in composition. Study the work of painters who use the human figure either in books or, better still, in art galleries. Artists like Caravaggio, Rembrandt, Vermeer, Manet, Gwen John, Hammershoi, Edward Hopper, Lucian Freud or Paula Rego are masters of composition. Look at the relationship between the figure, the furniture and the environment. Study how natural or man-made light falls across figures. Notice how colour is used to draw the eye to one figure or object more than another. There is no need to make the stage look like a painting, but a working knowledge of composition might help you to focus the action the audience will see.

Summary

It is essential that the actors are arranged on stage so that what they do is visible to the audience.

Let the moves evolve naturally from the logic of the situation.

If you need to make physical tweaks to the action for sightlines, do it late on in the process and try to achieve if first by moving inanimate things such as furniture or props.

Remember that organising the actors in the space is only one tool for creating focus – this work will be supplemented by lighting, sound, costumes and set design.

Learn more about composition by studying figurative paintings.

The second and third rehearsals of a scene

The length of your rehearsal period and the duration of the play will determine how many times you rehearse a scene. Even with a rehearsal period of eight weeks, if you are working on a long nineteenth-century play like *The Seagull* (running at more than three hours) you may find that you only have time for between three and four rehearsals of each section. On average you will probably rehearse a scene three times.

When you rehearse a scene for a second or third time, give exactly the same instructions that you gave at the first rehearsal and continue to give feedback on these instructions. Because you have already discussed, identified and named their intentions, the actors will be able to run the scenes three, four or even five times. Always allow the actors to read or say the lines through once sitting down, before they get up on their feet in the scene.

The actors should continue to mix the words they remember from the text with invented words. Ideally, the words of the play will become more familiar during these rehearsals. Sometimes, however, an actor will suddenly learn their lines before the second rehearsal because they are anxious to have enough time to practise with them. In the rehearsals that follow, undue emphasis may be put on the words said while other aspects of the situation such as intentions and place can wither for a while. Keep giving notes about the areas of their work that are being neglected and, finally, the actors will bring all the elements together.

In your second and third rehearsals, when you get to the end of a scene or act you do not need to re-improvise what happened between the scenes or acts or the immediate circumstances of the scene. Just remind the actors of the improvisation you did when you first went through the action of the play together. Or, if you did not do an improvisation in the first place, remind the actors of what has happened between the scenes and immediately before the next scene you will rehearse.

Begin to watch the scenes from different angles. One day you might watch the action from the perspective of the audience; another day you could watch from stage left, stage right or from upstage. A change of perspective may help you to understand the scene better. It will also encourage the actors to think about the situation in the play rather than the audience: this should lead to more lifelike gestures and actions. At the same time, you must always keep the audience's perspective in mind – there is no point in creating a lifelike gesture if no one can see it. And herein lies the heart of the craft: to immerse the actors in the situation, whilst making sure that what they do is constructed with the audience's perspective in mind. It is this fine balance between creating something lifelike and structuring something artificial that has always fascinated me. Ideally, the director should aim to balance these two tasks very carefully.

The third rehearsal of a scene may well be your final chance to practise a scene before you start running whole acts or the entire play. In most respects, this rehearsal should be identical to its predecessors, but at this point you should consider the relationship of the audience to each scene, meaning that you will have to attend more carefully to visibility, focus and narrative clarity. Do not change the goalposts of the process and start blocking or changing intentions or times of day. Just try to watch the work as if you had never seen it before. Up until now you have been working close to the actors, now move back mentally. When the audience first watch a production directors are often jolted into a more objective or distanced relationship with the work they have helped to make. It can be quite a shock and can happen too late in the process to allow for the necessary changes, so make the adjustment to your perception in the rehearsal room. Then give notes to the actors using exactly the same tools as you have done throughout. Watching and evaluating the work like this will help ensure it is communicated precisely to the audience.

In this final rehearsal give the actors the impression that they still have a lot of time in which to sharpen their work. This is not strictly the case but it helps to keep the actors calm. As they approach the day when they first share their work with an audience, anxiety can affect what they are doing in negative ways. Their unhelpful 'audience thinking' increases and they let go of the layers of precise work they have built up. They might replace this work with shallow choices or they might become less open about trying out new possibilities. They want to consolidate what they are doing – even if it is not finished or clear. Remain consistent. Gently and firmly, encourage them to complete and sharpen the tasks you have been asking them to do throughout the rehearsal period.

Here are some helpful tips for solving problems that may occur in the second and third rehearsal of a scene. In these later rehearsals you may find that some events and intentions no longer seem accurate. Sometimes, an actor will point this out to you before you spot it yourself. You may need to add another event or you might decide that an existing event is in the wrong place. Respond openly to any proposals about changes to events but make sure that the changes are accurate before going ahead with them. Do not create a rehearsal room culture in which events and intentions change every time you practise the scene.

Sometimes you will observe that an actor is trying to cram all the character's past into one scene. This is often noticeable when they are over-emoting. They have correctly observed that the character has a string of painful experiences in the past but they put the pain of all those events into one scene – as if the events had all happened seconds before the action began. If this occurs remind them that memories are stored at different volumes or intensities and that the scene is only a slice in the whole life of a person. The aim of the work is to make that slice as precise as possible and true to the biography that preceded it. Ask them to concentrate on the one past memory that you feel fuels the action most precisely.

Sometimes actors will not know how to use the work you have done on their character's past. As soon as they start work on the play they will jettison this work and concentrate on the scene as if it were a boat floating in a wide and featureless ocean. They might talk about events in the past without having any pictures in their heads. Do not worry about this. Continue to make links between the work they did on the past of the character and the present action. For instance, when their character refers to a particular memory, ask them to recall a clear picture of the improvisation they did which might have created the memory. When they play a new intention, remind them that the fuel for it is a past event between themselves and the other character. Ask them to paint a picture of that event for you or remind them of the improvisation they did around it.

At other times you can watch a rehearsal and feel that the whole scene is unfocused or confused. For example, you might feel that the two actors in a scene are looking rather awkward, or that the tempo of the scene is not quite accurate, or that it all just 'feels like a mess'. Don't panic and don't describe the problem to the actors. Instead, ask them to do the scene again and focus on one or two aspects of the work from your feedback checklist in Chapter 9. For example, ask the actors to 'sharpen their work on events and intentions'. That way they can repeat the scene, practising some of its essential ingredients whilst you watch it again and diagnose where the deeper problems lie. Sometimes the simple act of noting the performers on these essential ingredients will loosen up the scene and remove the block or problem. Reminding them of the title of the scene or act can also help to release a scene that is stuck.

Then there will be times when the actors have the same negative feeling you have about the scene. They will tell you that they are completely confused or that they do not know what they are doing. Do not be alarmed by this response and do not ask them to repeat the scene immediately after they have said this. Instead, sit down and ask them what area of the work is not clear. Again, have the Chapter 9 feedback checklist in your mind. For example, ask them: 'Is the problem about something before the action, like an event in the character's past, or the immediate circumstances? Or is it about the action of the scene itself, like an intention or event? Or is it about some confusion about the place that their characters are in?' These simple questions will help guide you to the area of work that is causing the problem in the scene. Do not let this conversation continue for too long. Once you feel you have isolated the problem, ask them to test the diagnosis by doing the scene again.

Remember to resist the temptation to address everything in one session. Instead, keep some notes back ready for the next time you work on the scene or exercise. Make sure your language reflects your overriding purpose – to make the characters' behaviour clear for the audience.

Throughout these rehearsals keep an eye on what the actors are doing physically. In my experience, the deeper the actors go into the play, the more they forget all those useful observations made early on in rehearsals about how the body responds in real-life situations and the less interested they become in playing things (such as time and place) that have a strong impact on their bodies. They become less precise physically, especially in their lower bodies. They might stand still without moving a muscle from their waist down or their arms and hands might flop in an unnaturally relaxed state at the sides of their bodies. Whenever possible, remind them of anything relevant from the slices of real life they re-enacted when they were working on ideas and emotions.

Remember that as the actors learn their lines you will need to set aside time to practise running them. Do this at the beginning of the rehearsal and get the stage management team to lead this work. This is a technical exercise and it is best done without the director.

At the end of these rehearsals you will be ready to start doing run-throughs.

Summary
In the second rehearsal repeat the same instructions you gave in the first rehearsal and give clear feedback on the same tasks.

Allow for the fact that the actors might still not know every line of the play.

Watch the work from different angles but never lose the audience's point of view in your head.

In the third or final rehearsal start to think as if you were an audience member watching the work for the first time. Give notes in response to the discoveries made by making this adjustment to how you look.

Expect that fear of the imminent performances will affect how actors work. Be patient with them and do not change your way of working.

Alter any intentions or events that are not working.

Help the actors to learn how to use their biographies in the work on the scenes.

If the scene is completely unfocused keep giving instructions from your checklist until you can identify the problem.

If the actors tell you they are completely confused, stop and, together, pinpoint the problem together.

Keep an eye on the physical side of the actors' work.

Set aside time for actors to learn their lines.

Run-throughs

Put smaller sections of the play together before you do a run-through of the entire play. If it is a classical play with a formal structure, like *The Seagull*, run each of the acts individually before you thread them all together in a non-stop run-through. If you are working with a play that lacks a formal structure, pick a logical break point in the play (perhaps the point at which you are planning to put an interval) and run that section first.

Do a run-through at the end of your penultimate week of rehearsals. That will give you at least a week to make any changes in response to discoveries about the overall structure. If you have to do a run-through later on because of a short rehearsal period, make sure you give yourself some time to correct any problems – even if it is just a couple of days.

When you put all the scenes together some of your choices might not work. This is inevitable: do not be overly alarmed if the work is not quite what you want it to be. The first run-through is part of the rehearsal process and it is not about delivering a perfected product. Make the run-through feel like it is another rehearsal (which of course it is). Tell the actors that you are going to practise putting all the tiny scenes together, just as you might thread beads onto a necklace. Let them know that your expectations are low and that the run-through will simply help everyone to learn what they have made so far and to determine what to work on next. If you have a call sheet, describe the run as a 'stumble through' so as to lower the pressure on the actors.

Try to keep people who are only peripherally involved in the process out of your first run. If people like artistic directors or producers come to an early run-through the actors can become unduly anxious. This fear will distort their choices meaning that they will not deliver the choices you have asked them to play well, and that you will not be able to learn as much as you could from the run. Feedback from people outside the process is an essential step in the process, but the timing of that feedback is critical. Ask people to the last run-through, the dress rehearsal or the first or second public performance – the later the better. Sometimes, however, it is impossible to avoid new people coming to watch early runs: the best way to get through these is to remind yourself of the tasks you need to achieve and to stick to them.

After watching the first run-through you yourself might be a little unsteady because of fear, frustration or excitement. Steady yourself before giving notes. Ideally, the run will finish at the end of a day so you can work on your notes overnight. If not, at least take a tea break before doing a note session. Edit your notes carefully, choosing what to say to the actors and what to reflect on. You will often make some big discoveries during the run-through and some of these will first appear to you as broad impressions. Remember that big problems are best resolved by making tiny corrections, so it is best not to share your thoughts about big problems with the actors. Instead, go away and think about how to convert these broad impressions into specific and concrete notes. No matter what your larger concerns are, give the actors the impression that you are happy with the direction that the work is heading in and thank them for their work.

Often note sessions after run-throughs are crammed into the end of the rehearsal day and the director gives notes to the actors very quickly. Try to avoid this; instead, allow time for the actors to discuss any notes that are not clear. This is particularly important if you do not have enough time left to rerehearse everything. I would set aside between an hour and a half and two hours for a note session after a run-through.

Before giving the actors your notes, ask each of them in turn to briefly give their feedback on how the run went and to identify the scenes that they most want to work on. Often an actor will put their finger on a problem they had which will save you from giving them a note. This will also give you a clear idea of where their concerns lie so that you can plan the next week of work accordingly.

Asking actors for their feedback also starts to encourage a self-critical or self-analytical muscle in each actor. Your ideal goal is for them to be self-directing: they should be able to come off stage after a performance and assess what they have done and know how to improve on it or deepen it.

After you have heard their feedback, give your notes. Remember that giving notes after the first run-through is a unique moment in the process. The actors will be more receptive to notes after a run-through than after a normal rehearsal of a scene. It may therefore provide you with the opportunity to solve a long-term problem you have been having with an actor over a choice you want them to make. You may be able to argue that the run-through taught you that the choice they were chasing was not possible. It is also a good moment to make big cuts. Remember, however, that the actors are more vulnerable after a first run-through than they are after a scene rehearsal, so approach changes you want to make carefully. Judge this moment well and you can make several essential changes to the work.

Remember, also, that the closer you come to moving into the theatre, the tenser the actors can be when it comes to taking notes. The note session after the first run-through is the moment when that tension may start to show itself. For example, actors who have taken notes quickly throughout the rehearsals process might suddenly disagree with all your notes or question you at length about one particular banal thing. An actor who is normally verbose in note sessions might suddenly be silent. This is just a sign of growing fear about the opening of the show and each actor will manage their fear in different ways. Be patient and understanding. It will pass.

Summary

Put smaller sections of the play together before you run the whole piece.

Do the first run-through at a point when you have at least two days to make corrections in response to your discoveries.

Do not worry if there are directing errors.

Do not invite people outside the rehearsal process to the first run.

Make the run-through feel like another rehearsal.

Take a break before giving notes to steady yourself and work through your responses – ideally overnight.

Do not give the actors general impressions. Rather, process these impressions and then convert the solutions into small concrete tasks for the actors.

Before giving your notes, ask the actors to give brief feedback on the run, including the scenes they are most keen to work on.

Value the uniqueness of the moment of note-giving after the first run-through.

Remember that actors will be vulnerable after the first run-through, so be careful about how you suggest any changes.

Allow time for the note sessions so that the actors can discuss notes that are not clear.

Anticipate that the actors may respond differently to notes after a run-through.

How to manage the final days in a rehearsal room

This phase of rehearsals should balance the work you need to do with the work the actors are most concerned about. Often these are the same bits, but if they are not, be patient with the actors' concerns. Remove these concerns through rehearsing the scene sensibly and they will enter the technical rehearsals more confidently.

Spend time rehearsing any changes in the intervening hours, days or weeks after the first run-through. Then run the play again, ideally on the penultimate day of rehearsals. This allows you to use the final day in the rehearsal room to work on notes. Again, make sure you allocate enough time to give notes. This will be your last run-through and it is critical that your notes are clear.

As you head towards public performances the actors' fear and unhelpful 'audience thinking' will increase. This will be most visible in the final run-through and it might alter what they are doing. Sometimes the alteration will be subtle and small; sometimes it will be large and glaring. For example, the actors might start to alter where they are standing because they are worried that the audience will not be able to see them or they might start to speak way too loudly because they are anxious about being heard. Previously discreet actions might suddenly become amplified because they are worried that the audience will not be able to understand them if they are life-size. However it manifests itself, you will notice that more mental energy is being spent outside the playing of the character and situation as actors begin to worry about how the audience will receive or understand what they are doing. If this is the case, gently point it out to the actor concerned, ask them to correct the balance and keep giving the feedback on the work from your checklist of notes.

As the director you must also take care of yourself. Do not burn yourself out in last days or week of rehearsal. You will need energy and resources for the next stage – the technical rehearsal. Keep Golden Rules 1 and 12 in mind: take tiny steps, keep long-term goals in view and hold your nerve. These two rules will help you to keep things in perspective.

Summary
After the first run-through, make changes and corrections to the work.
Keep an eye out for changes that are brought about as a result of the actors' fear of the imminent move to the theatre.
Take care of yourself: set long-term goals, take small steps and hold your nerve.

Working on set, costume, sound, lighting design and music during rehearsals

Your relationships with members of your creative team are best serviced if you keep in touch on a regular basis: always share your concerns or ideas as they emerge, however small or apparently irrelevant. Problems occur when the director does not communicate regularly with the creative team, meaning that once you move into the theatre, things might not be as you want them. Perhaps the practical lights that you saw in your imagination are not the ones rigged, or the colour or cut of a costume that you see for the first time on stage is not as you want it. At this point in the process, it is often too late to change things.

There are three ways of communicating with your creative team during rehearsals: first, they can come to rehearsals; second, you can talk at production meetings; and, third, you can ring them.

In an ideal world, all the members of your creative team will witness different stages of the rehearsal process outlined in the previous chapter. In some cases, you may ask them to come to specific rehearsals, for instance the character biography group session. This will give the set or costume designer valuable information about the characters to add to the work on character that you have already done with them. This information can then be translated into the detail of the costume design. If you are worried about a particular scene from a lighting point of view, you might ask the lighting designer to come and watch a scene rehearsal with you. Alternatively, members of your team may attend rehearsals on a more ad hoc basis, working around their commitments to other jobs. Sometimes they will not be able to see any rehearsals and will turn up to the final run-through. This is an essential stage because it offers them a first glance at the overall atmosphere and shape of the performance.

The weekly production meetings will provide you with a forum to discuss the details emerging from rehearsals that affect their particular areas of expertise. Production meetings are a chance to discuss new or unexpected developments. If, for example, you discover that someone needs to jump on a table in one of the scenes, the stage management will already have circulated this piece of information to the creative team as a rehearsal note. At the production meetings you and the designer will discuss how to reinforce the table that has already been designed. You might discover during rehearsals that you need a specific practical light. At the production meeting, you and the lighting designer will then discuss what sort of light is required.

Phone calls to individual members of your creative team about concerns that relate to their different fields will fill in any gaps of communication.

Discussing changes that affect the design is particularly important if the set design is fixed before rehearsals begin. The set will be under construction as you rehearse. As a consequence of the rehearsal process you will inevitably require modifications to the original design: some of these changes will be possible and some won't, depending on how far down the line the set is in terms of the build and paint job. You have to be realistic. However, keeping in touch on a regular basis will give you the maximum possibility for making changes.

Remember that your lighting designer and sound designer will have deadlines by which they have to deliver their lighting and sound plans. These are the plans of where they want all their lights or speakers to be hung from on the rig, or in the set, or on the stage. Be aware when these deadlines are, because they may mark the moment when your respective designers may not be able to adjust so easily to any new suggestions from a rehearsal. That said, be reassured that a good lighting or sound designer will offer you up creative alternatives in this situation.

After the first run-through, schedule time outside rehearsals to meet with different members of your creative team to discuss how their design can develop or enhance what you have made with the actors. Talk to them each individually about their ideas and your needs, scene by scene. Ask your deputy stage manager (or whoever is cueing the show) to come to as many of these meetings as possible. It is important that they start to understand what you want from a sound and lighting point of view; this person will, after all, be responsible for cueing the operation of all these new elements.

Writing down of all the sound, lighting and music cues in the deputy stage manager's book can take up a lot of your technical rehearsal. So get ahead by putting as many cues as you can into the book during the latter stages of the rehearsal period. This is particularly important if you have a very short technical rehearsal period. Either sit with the deputy stage manager and go through the cue points or ask them to meet with the composer, lighting and sound designers separately to put provisional cue points into the book. These provisional cues will provide you with an invaluable starting point, even if the cue points change in the technical rehearsal. If you have a sound operator in the rehearsal room, then cues can go straight into the book as the sound ideas have already been integrated into the action. In this case, your main emphasis before the technical will be on lights and music.

If you do not have time to get any cues into the book, at least talk through the opening sequence – in particular when you want the house lights to go down, when you want the action to be revealed and when you want the sound to start. You will be surprised at how complex this is from a cueing point of view. Planning your opening scene will mean you start your technical in a stronger fashion.

Summary

Communicate regularly with your creative team about the work you are making in rehearsals.

Always update them as new ideas emerge, however small or apparently irrelevant.

Do this by inviting them to as many rehearsals as possible, talking with them at production meetings or phoning them.

Make sure that they see at least one run-through, ideally all of them.

Be aware of their respective deadlines.

Schedule meetings during the last week of rehearsals with all the members of your creative team to discuss your ideas, scene by scene. Make sure the deputy stage manager attends all these meetings.

Ensure that the deputy stage manager notates as many cue points for lighting, sound or music as they can before the technical begins.

How to do all this with a short rehearsal period

A short rehearsal period does not necessarily mean that the process will be compromised. You can still achieve excellence if you are well prepared and use the time you have economically. Here are some suggestions about how to achieve clear work in a limited amount of time.

Analysing the action of the play with the actors: It is essential to go through the text and isolate and name the events. Do this as outlined on pages 169–171 and take the time to clarify all the choices. However, as far as the events that happen between the acts or scenes and the immediate circumstances to each act or scene are concerned, simply give this information to the actors either during the event analysis or just before they work on the scenes. This will provide them with a concrete starting point. They can hone the details of these events during the scene rehearsals.

The mark-up: The stage management can do this without having to use up any of your rehearsal time.

Improvising the trigger event and immediate circumstances: If you only do one or two improvisations in your entire process, build them around the trigger event. Remember that this event generates the action of the play. You do not need to improvise the immediate circumstances if you have no time to do so. Alternatively, remind the actors of the immediate circumstances just before they rehearse the scene to which the circumstances relate.

How to structure the rehearsal day: Adhere to the map of how to structure your days, as suggested in this section. Remember: it is better to rehearse a scene only twice and set up all the targets than it is to rehearse it ten times and short change how you give the instructions.

Rehearsing a scene for the first time: Conduct this rehearsal as described in the section above. To save time, give the actors suggestions for their intentions rather than discussing them together. The actors can test-run them as they do the scene and come up with alternatives if they do not work. Do not do improvisations of the action in between the scenes or acts. Instead, briefly talk through these events. However, be advised that a quick and well-structured improvisation can often be more efficient than discussions.

'Blocking', or making the action clear to the audience: This will be applicable whether you have ten days or eight months to rehearse a play. Try to avoid 'blocking' actors, even if you have very little time: it will not produce lasting work that is interesting to watch. Instead, spend more time during the design process checking through the fine detail of how each character will logically use the space or spaces. Make sure that you and the designer have done all you can to ensure that the design and the placing of things in it will facilitate clearly focused action.

The second and third rehearsals of a scene: Most rehearsal periods allow for three rehearsals of each section before a run-through. If you only have the chance to do two rehearsals, simply ensure that you give very clear instructions and do not waver from them. Be brief in your own feedback so that more time is spent on doing the scenes rather than talking about them.

Run-throughs: Organise a run-through of the work and make sure you have at least one day after the first run-through before you run it again.

Easter by August Strindberg

Ivanov by Anton Chekhov

PART THREE

GETTING INTO THE THEATRE
AND THE PUBLIC PERFORMANCES

Jephtha by George Frideric Handel

Getting into the theatre and the public performances

You will be at your most vulnerable in the period between the technical rehearsal and press night. The approach of the first public performances will affect you in one way or another, however stable or happy you may feel about the work you have made in the rehearsal room. Do not let the anxiety about the imminent performances, or press night, cloud your judgement, or change the way in which you work, or conduct any of your relationships – with either the actors or your creative team. This anxiety can hit you at any point in the process up until press night. Manage this by continuing to stand by the language and goals you set in the rehearsal room. That way you will get the best work from everyone.

At this point in the process, your job is to be at your most consistent and stable. So do not panic and start making drastic last-minute changes. If you do get frightened, take a break for a few minutes, slow down your thinking and ask yourself: 'What are the simple practical steps I need to take to sharpen the work or solve the problem?' Then take those simple steps, one by one.

If the actors start to forget the work they were doing in the rehearsal room, do not get unduly anxious: it will return. Instead, try to remove all the things that are blocking them from believing in the imaginary world. If a member of your creative team becomes unduly anxious and unable to function, stay calm. Focus them on the simple things that need to be done or what is realistically achievable in the time remaining.

Having 'moved in' to the theatre, you will have to keep an eye on many more elements than in the rehearsal room – you will have lights, sound and visual ingredients to focus on as well as the acting. So make sure you organise your note-taking efficiently. To cope with the increase in the number of ingredients you are noting try dividing each page in your note pad into two columns. Put acting notes in one column and technical notes in the other column. That way you can give feedback to different people quickly and efficiently. Keep a clear list of everything you need to work on in each scene. Try nominating a page per scene so that you can jot down random thoughts about work that needs doing on the correct page and refer back to it easily. Carefully plan how and when you are going to address each item on the list.

A production can be like a piece of knitting – if you pull something too hard or suddenly at this stage of the process, the whole thing could start to unravel. Stay clear-headed, prioritise what you need to do and time the moments that you make changes carefully.

Differentiate carefully between the things that can be addressed and the things that cannot. If, for example, you have made an error in casting, acknowledge that you will never be able to transform the actor completely into what you want. You may, however, get them close to your desired outcome. Accept this compromise and put your energy into areas of the work that you can change. My greatest error early on was to worry away at the insoluble problems, often in the area of casting. I spent a great deal of time complaining about things that I couldn't change, or attempting to change them, without affecting the work or solving the problem in any way. After several years of wasting my time in this way, I finally learnt to let these things go and focus on the areas of the work that I *could* affect.

Finally, remember that there are many new concepts and terms that you need to know at this point in the process (see the glossary on pages 233–6, where all the new terms for this stage in the process are in bold type). Take the time to familiarise yourself with these new words or ideas, as there is nothing worse than being tripped up just because you do not understand what someone is talking about or turning up to a session in the technical schedule only to discover that the director is not needed.

Easter by August Strindberg

CHAPTER 12

Technical and dress rehearsals

This chapter deals with the steps by which you will get the play into the theatre and the work you might do on the production up until just before the first public performance. It includes advice on the following:

The schedule for getting into the theatre and technical rehearsals
How to manage the transition from the rehearsal room to the theatre for
  the actors
How to work with your creative team during technical rehearsals
Lighting plotting sessions
Sound and music sessions before the technical rehearsal begins
Technical rehearsals
The dress rehearsal

The schedule for getting into the theatre and technical rehearsals

In most theatres, however small, you will be provided with a technical schedule that describes everything that will be done to get the production into the theatre and ready for the first public performance. This schedule will be discussed about a week before you enter the theatre at a production meeting; go through it with a fine toothcomb to check that the time is being used as you and your creative team would wish. Different projects have different priorities and mistakes can often occur when a generic schedule is imposed on a process that needs a more tailor-made approach.

There are three basic steps to any technical schedule. First, there is the process by which the set, lights and sound elements are installed in the theatre. This starts with getting the set into the theatre, and ends with focusing the lights and checking the sound speakers or band relay. It is not necessary for the director to attend any of these stages of the technical process. Second, there are the plotting sessions when light, music and sound cues are worked on in preparation for the technical rehearsal. It is essential that the director is present for this stage but the actors are not usually called. Finally, there are the technical rehearsals in which the actors join the full technical team to work through the production sequentially sorting out all the technical aspects of the work, from light and sound cues to practising with new door handles on the set to quick changes. Technical rehearsals take place with full lighting, sound, costumes, set, props, make-up, wigs and any special effects such as wind or blood. It is advisable to give the actors scheduled time to get in and out of costumes. Indeed, many unions specify that a statutory 15-minute period is allocated either side of each technical session for this. This can give you an extra half hour or so to do technical work, such as plotting lighting or sound cues, as the technicians and stage management do not need to take these longer breaks.

Different theatres will allocate different amounts of time to each of these three steps, depending on their budgets, union arrangements and repertoire. You may, for example, have a two-day get-in and a three-day technical rehearsal at the National Theatre in London, or only a couple of hours get-in and a three-hour technical at a fringe theatre in the same city. However, in my experience, the length of the first step is always underestimated regardless of the size of the theatre. It is accepted practice that an overrun of this sort should not delay the prearranged start of the technical rehearsal – except under exceptional circumstances. This means that there is nearly always less time to do the plotting sessions than originally scheduled. Bear this in mind when you talk to the sound and lighting designers about how you want to use your time and make sure you have a back-up plan if that time is reduced.

Summary
Familiarise yourself with the three steps of the technical schedule.
Go through the schedule before you enter the theatre to check that everything is scheduled as you and your creative team would wish.
Have a back-up plan for the plotting sessions if the original time allocated on the technical schedule is reduced because of an overrun during the get-in.

How to manage the transition from the rehearsal room to the theatre for the actors

The way in which the director negotiates the transition from the rehearsal room to the theatre needs careful thought. Manage it smoothly and it will strengthen the actors' work and your ability to help them develop that work. Manage it inefficiently and it will weaken what the actors are doing as well as your hold on their work. You will then waste time having to rebuild their confidence and their acting choices.

In Chapter 9 I wrote about reducing the number of new ingredients that the actors have to embrace in a technical rehearsal by adding ingredients like sound, costumes, actual props and shoes into the rehearsal room. If you have managed to achieve this it will help to ease this moment of transition considerably. If, however, you have not been able to integrate any of these ingredients into the rehearsal room, do not worry. Just remember to lead the technical rehearsal with a lot of sensitivity about the fact that the actors have to absorb a huge number of new elements.

On page 188 I wrote about how actors' thoughts about the move into the theatre can increase their thinking about making what they are doing clear to the audience to the detriment of the playing of the character or situation. This problem can intensify as you start work in the theatre. If an actor has not experienced the impact of the imminent public performances in the rehearsal room, then he or she will definitely feel it in a smaller or larger way once they begin technical rehearsals. As I wrote in the section on run-throughs in Chapter 11, the actor might develop a heightened concern about being seen or about being heard even though their positions are well focused and the voice person is happy with their audibility. They might become worried about how the character will be understood, start to doubt their costume or challenge acting choices you thought were solid. These responses are completely understandable and born mainly from fear.

There are four simple ways of helping the actors to reduce this fear.

First, be careful about the language you use in the rehearsal room that relates to the work you are going to do in the theatre. In the final week of rehearsals I refer jokingly to the theatre as 'the other room' and talk about it as a place where we will 'share the work with other people'. This language is my way of helping the actor build a bridge between the two stages of the process. Each director will need to find their own way of doing this.

Second, try not to alter the language you have been using in the rehearsal room in the last few days of rehearsals. During the last few days of rehearsals or once you start working in the theatre words change subtly without you noticing it: 'the play' becomes 'the show', the bird singing becomes 'the first sound cue' and so on. This language propels the actors out of the imaginary world you have been building during the rehearsals and increases their fear.

Third, and most importantly, give the actors the impression that you are calm and in control of the transition, no matter what is happening behind the scenes. There are many technical problems that can occur at this stage in the process (such as a delay in the get-in) and the majority can be easily solved, given time. Only let the actors know about problems that are going to affect their work directly and immediately. Solve any other problems without letting the actors know they exist.

If you cannot solve something, inform them of what the problem is, what is being done about it and when it will be fixed. Stay measured in your descriptions and avoid overdramatising problems.

Finally, look for ways of making the theatre environment feel closer to the rehearsal room. Rehearsal rooms are normally very calm and focused places. No one walks in on a delicate rehearsal and people generally walk in and out of the room quietly. By comparison the backstage area at a theatre can be full of people (crew, stage management, technicians and so on) moving around in a less sensitive fashion during the technical or even the performance itself. Their movement is normally essential but how they move is something that can be delicately policed by your stage manager. There are also ways of cordoning off areas backstage to create tiny islands of calm and concentration where actors can prepare themselves for the scenes either during the technicals or, later, during the performances. See if you can build sealed booths or create fenced-off areas in which individuals can prepare for their scenes, or work in between scenes. Ask the production manager and stage manager to start thinking about ways of achieving this in the backstage area so that everyone can do their work without interrupting what the actors need to do.

When I was directing *Iphigenia in Aulis* at the National Theatre, we set up a series of off-stage booths made out of black screens. We also cordoned off sections of the backstage area for actor preparation. We built a booth stage left containing chairs and suitcases in which Clytemnestra, Iphigenia and their escort sat imagining that this was the carriage that was taking them to Aulis. Stage right there was a room off-stage representing Agamemnon's quarters. Clytemnestra, Iphigenia, Agamemnon and his special advisors all went off into this room at different points in the action and continued to improvise what happened there in between their scenes. At the beginning of the performance, the actors in each of the booths were cued so that everyone started acting at the same time, regardless of when their character entered the on-stage action. The audience saw only one bit of the action: Agamemnon entering a disused hotel.

Working like this is not orthodox practice in many theatres. So if you want to try this method, it is absolutely critical that you explain what you want and why you want it to different departments or individuals. In most cases, you will be surprised by how people working in the theatres respond positively to these sorts of proposals as long as you take the time to explain why you feel they are necessary.

Summary

Reduce the number of new things the actors have to absorb in the theatre by integrating as many of them as possible into the rehearsal room in advance.

Be alert to the changes actors can make to what they do because of their increased fear and audience thinking.

Reduce this tendency by keeping an eye on the language you use about the next stage of the work. Make sure it ties in with the language you have used throughout the rehearsals.

Manage your own fear well and do not worry the actors with technical problems going on behind the scenes.

Investigate ways of making the backstage of the theatre an environment that is closer to a rehearsal room.

How to work with your creative team during technical rehearsals

This will be the first time that the actors work alongside the members of your creative team in the same space. When the creative team visited the rehearsal room they were watching the work, not giving feedback directly about it. Managing the interaction between these two groups in the theatre is a fine art and here are some things you can do to help facilitate it.

By the time the actors arrive for the technical rehearsal ensure that your creative team are working for the same artistic goals as you. Meet beforehand and tell them how you want to run the technical rehearsals and, more importantly, how you want to field their concerns or criticisms. Remember to discuss any areas of the work they are particularly worried about.

During the technical rehearsals, keep the conversations you have with your creative team about problems or concerns out of the actors' earshot. They do not always talk the same language. A remark from a designer such as 'The lighting levels are too bright' will stop the actor from thinking about the hot summer day and make them think instead about being looked at by an audience in a theatre, with a consequent effect on their performance.

Discourage your designer from talking about purely aesthetic concerns or technical problems in front of the actors. If they feel that the lighting levels are too low, or that a prop is not visible to the audience, suggest they let you know outside the actors' earshot.

Finally, set aside time at the end of each day of the technical rehearsals to meet up with your core team and discuss problems or concerns, ideally after the actors have left the theatre.

Remember that a lack of time at this point in the process puts a lot of pressure on all the people in your creative team. Remember, too, that you have had several weeks to do your work with the actors whereas the creative team have to achieve theirs in a few days or even hours. (Your creative teams will often be looking at or listening to their work for the first time at the same moment that you first encounter it.) However hard a lighting designer has worked on a lighting plan, they cannot possibly anticipate exactly what the combination of those lights will look like in the space. However precisely painted the wall flats may look in the paint shop, the designer cannot know for certain whether the construction and paint finish are accurate or not until they are assembled on stage. However appealing the recording of the birds was when listened to in the sound studio, the sound designer cannot be absolutely sure whether it will sound appropriate in the new acoustic of the theatre.

As I said earlier, many technical schedules are over-optimistic and do not allocate enough time to get the set into the theatre. This means that the time given to plot the lights, or do proper sound checks, or paint the set, or do a band call are eaten into and sometimes erased. Be sensitive to the pressure that all these things may put your individual team members under. Ask your set designer what they think needs altering, before wading in with your feedback. Often the things that are worrying you are already down on the designer's list of things to address. If you have worries or if you do not like something that you see or hear in the theatre, explain your concerns simply and clearly. Do not allow your anxiety about the forth-coming opening to raise the temperature of what you say or do. Finally, do not look at the set, or the lights, or listen to the sound or music for the first time with the actors present and do not give your initial feedback about any of these areas in their hearing.

Summary
Meet with all the members of your creative team during the last week of rehearsals to plan how you want to run the technical and how you would like to field their feedback during it.

Keep the conversations about the concerns the creative team have out of the actors' earshot during the technical rehearsals. Set aside time to talk alone with your creative team – ideally after the actors have left the building.

Be sensitive to the pressure that your creative team are under because of the lack of time to prepare or test-run their work.

Do not look at the set, or the lights, or listen to the sound or music for the first time with the actors present. Remember not to give your initial feedback to these first attempts within the actors' earshot.

Lighting plotting sessions

The lighting plotting session is the moment at which you look at the lighting designer's proposals for the lighting states for the first time. The main aim of a plotting session is to get as many of the lighting states into the board as you can before the technical rehearsal starts. (The board is the machine that records the different levels that each light is plotted at.)

You will already have discussed the lighting design in detail with the lighting designer during the last week of rehearsals. The lighting designer will then draw up a lighting plan, which describes where all the lights will be hung on the lighting grid and the direction the lights will be pointing in. After the get-in, the lights will be hung on the grid according to the plan, and then they will be focused and coloured.

A lighting plotting session takes place in the theatre with your lighting designer, lighting operator and stage management. A makeshift table will probably be put up in the auditorium for the lighting designer. Lighting designers will normally work with their lighting plan on the table in front of them. You might see an icon of a lantern on the plan accompanied by a number. You do not need to know how to read a lighting plan or the numbers or functions of any individual light in order to make sure that the work you have made is well lit. However, if you do remember a few of the key lights and their numbers, you might be able to speak about what you want with more precision.

There will also be a computer on the table that connects to the computer system used by the operator in their box. The lighting designer will normally be on headphones so that they can communicate with that operator and with the deputy stage manager (also in their box). You will sit next to the lighting designer. As you confirm each lighting state, it will be given a number, starting with one. These numbers will then be put in the book by the deputy stage manager alongside the line or stage direction that cues the lighting change. Be prepared for this process to take time and try not to be impatient. The deputy stage manager will run the technical rehearsal much more efficiently if each cue is written down carefully and precisely in the book. Some cue positions might be provisional and then altered slightly during the technical rehearsal when it is possible to run cues alongside the action.

There are many ways of using a plotting session, and different lighting designers have different processes. The structure and pace of a plotting session depends on how much time is available. If you have a session lasting three hours, you can approach things at a leisurely pace, but if you have half an hour, you will need to race a little to get the initial states in the lighting board and the book. In my experience it is best to start the plotting session by asking the lighting designer to take you through their main ideas or key lights. You will sit in the dark while the lighting designer flashes up different possibilities. This gives you a sense of the scope of the rigged lights. If you like a particular effect or single light, tell the designer. You can ask the designer to try out that light at a later point if a lighting state is not working for you.

Next, work through each of the states for each of the scenes. Ask your designer to put together their first proposal, then use that as a basis for building the stage you want. Be patient and let the designer work out their ideas for a scene before you give feedback.

Then look at the state together and ask the lighting designer to make any adjustments that you want. Do not spend ages fiddling with the first few lighting states. Put a basic sketch down and move forwards. That way you will have something in the can for your first technical session. Remember that all lighting states look different when you add people.

Taking too much time lighting an empty set is a pointless exercise. Get the broad sketch down and then the lighting designer can adjust it in response to what the actors are actually doing in the scene. Be prepared not to get very far through the show. I don't remember when I last managed to get further than the first couple of scenes in a plotting session. This session initiates the work on lights that will run through until press night. You and the lighting designer will be constantly adjusting the states to make them accurate during this time.

Problems with lighting often occur because of the need to balance realistic lighting of the action and the necessity of lighting faces for the sake of audience visibility. Often the lighting of faces dominates over the lighting of the situation, meaning that too many lights are used at a high intensity. If a scene is over-lit, we forget what is actually lighting the place the characters are in, be it daylight or artificial light. However much light you need to bring up to increase visibility, do not lose the basic structure of the real light source. If you are having problems identifying that structure, squint your eyes to allow a small amount of light in. This removes surface detail and lets you see the basic blocks of dark, light and shadow.

Spend a moment squinting at the lighting state the designer is proposing: if you cannot see any structure under the surface detail, ask the lighting designer to go to blackout and start building the lighting state from scratch. Do not worry about visibility of the actors or the action for a while. Instead ask yourselves: 'What is actually lighting this place? Is it the sun? If so, where is the sun coming from and what angle is it at?' Add the lights that create the sunlight and slowly build the rest of the state around the structure that the sunlight gives you. If a scene is lit by a single practical light, ask the designer to bring that one light up. Identify the shape that the light casts and start to build the lighting state around that shape. Even as you add extra lights you must not lose the impression that the environment is being lit by that practical light.

Summary

Be prepared for the process of writing down lighting cues in the book to take time.

Ensure you emerge from the plotting session with lighting states for the first few cues of the performance.

Do not spend too much time attempting to perfect a lighting state on an empty set; it will look different when people stand in it.

Do not lose sight of the structure of what is lighting the scene, be it the sun or a practical light.

Sound and music sessions before the technical rehearsal begins

The main aim of these sessions is to plot the levels of the sound or music and, if relevant, to confirm the speakers that it is coming out of. The musicians will either be in a band room or they will play in the theatre. (A 'band room' is a sound-sealed room where live music is played and relayed to the speakers in the theatre.) If they are in a band room, you will need to check the level of every cue. If they are playing in the theatre the composer will need to adjust the volume of the playing in response to the acoustic in the theatre.

Technical schedules rarely allocate more than an hour or so to sound or music plotting sessions prior to the technical rehearsal itself. In the majority of cases, you will have time to listen to a few key cues during this session before the sound designer or composer is given a brief chance to set some initial levels for the first ten or so sound cues. Because these sessions are brief you will listen to most of the sound cues and music on the hoof during the technical rehearsal.

Remember that it takes time to programme sound cues or set the levels for the band playing in a band room. This can be a big surprise early on in your career. You imagine that the operator can just press a button, adjust the volume and all will be perfect. This is not the case; it can take several minutes to programme all the settings for one music or sound cue.

As well as a brief plotting session there may also be a lunch break before the technical rehearsal begins which is known as 'quiet time'. This is where the sound designer can plot levels or the composer (or musical director) can listen to the band. You do not need to be at this session – unless you are asked to be. Nor do you need to attend a 'band call', if indeed you are having live musicians playing in the show.

Summary
Be prepared for a brief session to listen to sound cues or music.
Be prepared for the time it takes to programme sound cues.
Be prepared to have to listen to sound effects for the first time during the technical rehearsal.
You don't need to attend 'quiet time' or a 'band call' unless you are asked to by the sound designer or composer or musical director.

Technical rehearsals

Technical rehearsals give everyone involved in the production the chance to work through the play from beginning to end and ensure that all the new technical ingredients are carefully integrated with the work already made in the rehearsal room.

Creating a clear chain of command is crucial for an efficient and functioning technical rehearsal.

First, decide who should run the technical rehearsal: either lead it yourself or ask your stage manager to. In my experience it is better to let the stage manager take charge: it allows you to put your energy into watching all the ingredients come together and discussing things with the sound, set, costume and lighting designers. The stage manager will be on the stage, organising everyone and driving the rehearsal along so it goes according to your pre-planned schedule. This schedule will be drawn up between you and the stage manager and will specify which sections of the show need to be completed in each rehearsal session. Stick to the plan and you will be ready for the dress rehearsal and first performance. You can communicate with the stage manager either by shouting or by using a microphone or headset, depending on the scale of the space you are in or the level of discretion you require. Ensure that the microphone or headset are in good working order before the technical begins. Shouting should be discouraged because it can give the impression that you are being aggressive.

Next, you need to work out how to communicate with your deputy stage manager. They will now be sitting in the place from which the show will be cued. This may put them out of earshot in a sound-sealed booth at the back of the auditorium. In a small auditorium you can probably just talk normally to each other, whereas in a larger space you will have to use a headset or go through your stage manager's headset.

Finally, work out a system of communication with your lighting and sound designers. In an ideal situation, the lighting desk and sound desk will be put up in the auditorium, and the lighting and sound designers will sit at these desks with their equipment and plots. Normally these desks will be set very close to you so that all three of you can communicate easily. The two designers will normally have headsets on so that they can communicate with the operators in their boxes. This might not be the situation in a fringe theatre where the desks may remain in the operating area and the equipment might be rudimentary, or in cases where your designer and operator are the same person. Whatever the circumstances, discuss how you will communicate with the lighting and sound designers before the technical rehearsal begins.

When the actors arrive on the stage to begin the technical rehearsal, go and welcome them immediately. Describe how you will run the tech and ask them to stop as soon as they encounter any technical problems. Next, ask the stage manager to show them around the stage and the backstage areas. This gives them time to get their bearings in the theatre. Then ask them to get into their 'beginners positions'. (This is the place backstage where they stand before they are cued on for their first entrance.)

When they are ready, start working through everything step by step. Let the show run until an ingredient is not as you would want it – for instance, if a lighting cue does not go at the right point, if the lighting state is not what you want or if a sound cue is too loud. Stop, and let the stage manager know why you have stopped. Talk through how to solve the technical problem with the relevant member of your creative team. Ask the stage manager to 'set back' (that is, get everything ready to start again). Then start running the action from the point just before it went wrong.

Do not spend too much time on the first few cues. It is best to motor on – even if there are things that need more work. It helps the morale of the group to feel that things are progressing efficiently and according to schedule. Slow down after the first 15 minutes or so.

Assume that most of your actors are sensible adults and take their concerns seriously. Ensure that you address immediately any concerns the actors bring up. Some of them might seem banal, such as practising a quick change a third time or talking about the logic of a costume, but it is these details that will make their acting clear and the performance run smoothly. It will pay dividends to address these concerns immediately, as they are unlikely to go away.

The average technical rehearsal lasts between one and three days, although sometimes you might only have a few hours. At the end of each session you will have a meeting, as suggested on page 203, with all the members of your creative team to discuss the problems or concerns that have emerged. Remember that most theatres have a show relay system that transmits sound from the stage to the dressing rooms and backstage areas. These relays also send sound from the auditorium backstage. If you meet with your creative team in the auditorium, be cautious about how you talk about any concerns you have; sometimes in the heat of the moment you can speak inappropriately about the actors or reveal fears that would undermine you in their eyes. In some theatres you can turn the relay off.

Summary

Remember that the aim of the technical rehearsals is to integrate the new technical ingredients into the work already made in the rehearsal room.

Create a clear chain of command for the running of the technical rehearsal.

Talk through the best way of communicating with the deputy stage manager.

Decide who should run the technical – you or the stage manager – and establish a means of communicating with each other.

When the actors arrive describe how you will work and show them around backstage so that they can get their bearings.

Stop whenever there is a problem, discuss it and rerun the relevant section. Then move on.

Do not spend too much time on the first few cues; motor on.

Create an atmosphere in the theatre that is close to the calm and focused atmosphere of the rehearsal room.

Immediately address any problems that the actors have.

Hold daily meetings with your creative team at the end of each day of the technical.

Remember that there are show relays in most theatres and be careful what you say in the heat of the moment in the auditorium.

The dress rehearsal

The dress rehearsal is the first opportunity to put all the ingredients you have worked on together at speed. During the technical rehearsals you will stop and start, rarely running large chunks of the action. In the dress rehearsal you will run things at performance speed and this will always throw up new problems: a quick change might not be completed in time, or the speed of a lighting cue may be too slow or too fast.

When you schedule the dress rehearsal allow half an hour at the end of the call so that you can make any corrections before the first public performance. Often, dress rehearsals start late and end just as the call finishes – meaning that there is no chance to correct any problems and that those problems are repeated in the evening performance. Instead, use that half an hour to correct any major technical problems. As you watch the dress rehearsal, prioritise your notes. There might be things you need to change urgently before the evening show. Technical notes can be given to your creative team after the actors are released, in time for that evening's performance. Then there are things which you can work on the following day when there is more time to address them properly.

Finally, there are all your acting notes. In my experience it is unwise to give any acting notes in between a dress rehearsal and the first performance. Instead, save them up for the next day and do not spend the supper break running around dressing rooms or green rooms frantically trying to cram the actors with acting notes. The two hours in between the dress rehearsal and the first performance is the actors' break: they need time to eat, rest and prepare for the performance.

Immediately the dress rehearsal finishes, gather the actors together and reassure them that their work was clear and that you will give notes after this evening's performance. Then ask if any of them have any major technical problems or worries. Address their concerns and your urgent technical notes in the next half hour. At the end of this session suggest that the actors attend a warm-up before the evening performance. This will help them cope with the fear that attends the first public performance. Remind them also to work as a group and avoid 'solo flights'. A solo flight is when an actor departs from what has been rehearsed and starts to impress the audience in another way. After this chat, leave the actors alone.

These steps, of course, describe the perfect way to manage the dress rehearsal and its aftermath. However, there will be instances when you will simply run out of time and are not able to manage things with this degree of measure or care. If this happens, at least gather the actors for five minutes after the dress rehearsal to check that there is nothing potentially dangerous in what they did that needs urgent correction before they perform the show in public.

However, in some cases you may not even get a dress rehearsal or a complete technical rehearsal. When I was working on *Dream Play* at the National Theatre, we ran so far behind schedule that we had to cancel the first performance and do the technical in front of the public (who had turned up for the second performance). This is not a situation I would ever wish to repeat, but it shows how far from the ideal one can sometimes stray as the pressure to deliver a product for a paying audience mounts.

Summary

Be prepared for the fact that the dress rehearsal will throw up problems you have
   not anticipated in the technical rehearsals.

Schedule half an hour at the end of the dress rehearsal to address any major
   problems that emerge.

Prioritise your notes as you watch the dress.

At the end of the dress, ask the actors whether they have any immediate and
   major technical concerns. Address these concerns in the last half an hour
   together with your own urgent technical notes.

Do not disturb the actors in their break time with acting notes.

The Maids by Jean Genet

CHAPTER 13

The public performances

This chapter looks at how to manage the first few public performances, the press night and how to look after the show during the run. It includes advice on the following steps:

>The first few public performances
>Notes after shows
>Rehearsals during your first few public performances
>Press night
>The run of performances from after the press night until the last night
>Analysing your work after the run has ended

The first few public performances

These early performances give you the opportunity to test-run the work in front of an audience and their response allows you to measure the accuracy of your directing choices. Note the audiences' reactions to the performance at the same time as watching the work on stage, paying particular attention to the moments when the audience are concentrated and when they get restless. This will give you a clear idea of the sections that you need to work on most.

Remember to keep your thinking about the audience clear: if they are restless or bored, first ask yourself if your work could be clearer. Do not get caught up in an emotional response to their reaction; do not get upset if they are bored by your favourite moment or get angry if they start eating crisps at an important visual event. If you allow their reactions to affect your concentration, you will get lost in the feeling and not look coolly at the scene to diagnose the problem that is causing the audiences' loss of concentration.

Actors respond to the pressure of the early performances in varied ways. Some will get very frightened, others very excited and others withdrawn. Their responses can alter the relationship you have with them, making it smoother or bumpier. Stay calm: do not adjust your relationship to them or the aims of the working process.

Be warned that the physical impact of the early performances can upset actors' stomachs badly: some actually vomit or have diarrhoea before the performance. They may want to fulfil the goals you have set them but their physical condition makes this impossible.

Equip the actors with skills to negotiate any feedback they receive. The actor is more vulnerable to criticism during these early performances than at any other point in the process. Both positive and negative criticisms impact on them. These criticisms can come from directors, agents, loved ones or in the form of a casual comment by a stranger. They can jump the actors out of the skin of the character and make them doubt everything they are doing or they can make them self-conscious about a particular moment in a scene. A comment made by an audience member could awaken old worries that you have allayed during the rehearsal process or it could create new and unexpected anxieties. Certain actors can even use the feedback given at this stage to support choices that they have wanted to make but which you have discouraged. These criticisms or comments interrupt the process of developing the goals that you have as the director, both for the actor and for the work itself.

Have a brief chat with the actors before the performance, warn them to approach any feedback with caution and remind them that the work is not finished. Ask them to bear this in mind when they listen to any feedback. Warn them that there is a difference between feedback that reflects a difference in taste and feedback that accepts the work on its own terms. They need to discern which type of response they are dealing with. If, for example, a person does not like the way in which a production is designed or paced, this might suggest a difference of taste. Their comments will not always be useful to the development of the work. If, on the other hand, the person clearly understands the direction that the work is heading in but finds a particular moment unclear, then their notes might be useful to the work. Finally, encourage them to talk to you about any feedback that affects their work negatively. A brief discussion can often counter the hold some casual criticism has on an actor and free them to return to working as the play requires.

Make sure you field notes about your own work with care. Learn, like actors, to differentiate between feedback that points to a difference of taste, and feedback that is useful for the work. Similarly, remember that you have not finished making the work. Do not make radical adjustments to something that is half finished; instead, jot down the criticism and finish working on your idea. When you have finished what you planned to achieve, look back at the note to see if it is still on the money. If it is, change what you are doing.

Do not treat all feedback with equal attention; an unsolicited comment in a pub after a show is not the same as one concrete note from a valued colleague.

Choose the people whose feedback you will take seriously and whose notes you will put into practice. Identify these individuals before the run begins and ask them to come on a particular day. You could even give them specific tasks to do whilst they watch your work such as checking that the narrative is clear, or seeing whether a particular moment or actor is working well or not. You will find these people over time and they will make up a small group. Not everyone will talk to you in the language of your process but this does not invalidate their criticism. Translate what they say into your language and sift through it for useful notes.

Never pass feedback you receive verbatim to the actors. Instead, process the notes you value into concrete instructions for individual performers. If an actor asks you about the opinion of anyone significant in the business who came to the production, it is wise to say that they enjoyed the work, whether or not this was the case.

After each early performance gather together with your creative team, stage management, production manager and anyone else involved in making the work (apart from the actors) and go through your technical notes, working out a plan of action for the following day's rehearsal.

Summary

Watch the audiences' reactions to the show at the same time as noting the actors. Notice when the audience are restless.

Do not get caught up in an emotional response to their reactions.

Be prepared for a wide range of different responses from the actors to the first few public performances.

Equip the actor with skills to negotiate feedback about their work from members of the audience.

Ask them to discuss any negative feedback that they cannot shake off.

Field notes about your directing with care.

Never pass on feedback to the actors verbatim.

After each preview do technical notes and work out a plan of action for the following day's rehearsal.

Notes after shows

When actors come off stage they can be very vulnerable and raw. You yourself might not be stable and clearheaded: you might be happy at the things that worked or frustrated by what didn't. You are unlikely to have a balanced view, so do not give notes immediately after a performance. Instead, thank the actors for their hard work and arrange a note session for the following day. Then spend a couple of hours slowly going through your notes on your own, working out which ones you want to give and how you want to give them. In the notes session make sure you give space for the actors to discuss their notes. Set aside the first half hour to hear their feedback – encouraging them to be brief and concrete about any problems they experienced.

Giving notes after a show is very different to giving notes in a rehearsal room. In the rehearsal room the actor has the time and space to rehearse their notes and to run the relevant scene three or four times. It is much harder to play a note for the first time in a public performance, so your notes have to be very simple and specific. It is better to give one clear note than six blurred notes. Remember, too, that if you give five notes and four of them are clear and one of them isn't clear, that one unclear note can destroy all the clear notes. If you are not certain about how to solve a problem, do not mention it to the actors. Instead, go and watch the show again and see if you can isolate the cause or the remedy. Also remember that an actor cannot hold a huge number of notes in their head for one performance – try to give a maximum of about ten for each actor. Some can take more and some less: it will take you time to learn who can do what.

Notice as part of the development of your own craft how much we depend on physical accuracy from the actors to communicate what is going on to the audience. If, for example, the place where a character is standing is cold, this information will register most clearly in what they do physically: they will keep moving all the time, flap their arms to keep warm or involuntarily shiver. If the coldness is a fixed feature of a scene, you will have to constantly remind the actor to keep playing its affect in their entire body. I am always surprised about how uneven actors can be when it comes to playing time or a temperature that affects them physically. Sometimes these ingredients are played fully and sometimes not at all; often the actor is not aware of how wildly varied the way they play these ingredients is from rehearsal to rehearsal, or performance to performance. In some instances, certain actors are simply unaware that they have stopped playing these physical ingredients altogether. Building up the physical manifestations of the situation in which the characters find themselves is essential to the actors' work. However, be warned that too much feedback about the physical life of the actors can also lead to awkward self-consciousness; if this happens, stop giving feedback on this area for a while.

If a note does not work, then apologise and suggest that the actor returns to the original choice. If you give a note and the actor says 'But I was playing that', then you have different options depending on the intensity of their feeling. If the feeling is very strong then retract the note and look again at the moment the following night to see if you were right or not, or to see if you can think of a different way of approaching the problem. If their feeling is less intense, ask them to play the note a second time and then tell them you will watch it once more.

If an actor starts talking in a group note session about general feelings of anxiety about the overall process or production, then suggest that you have a separate conversation with that actor once the group note session is over. You do not want one person's anxiety to unsettle the confidence of the ensemble. Sometimes the actor just wants reassurance about their work and you can readily give it. At other times the actor might genuinely be conflicted about the process, or a scene, or character. If this is the case, encourage them to boil down the general concern to a specific moment or moments in the action of the play. Then ask them to address their worries by taking tiny concrete steps over time. Avoid giving false reassurance. It is not a lasting remedy to a problem.

Do not give notes immediately before the performance. If you dash around the dressing rooms just before the show giving notes, the actors will not have any time to digest them properly before they go on stage. Your note will be crudely played or it will become the focus of the actor's performance, dislodging all the other notes you gave during the note session.

Summary
Do not give notes immediately after a performance. Give them the following day after you have had time to digest your thoughts properly.

When you give notes after a performance be sensitive to the fact that the actors will have to play them live in front of an audience.

Do not give too many notes – a maximum of ten or so per actor.

If you give a note and an actor claims they were playing it, either retract the note and look at the moment again or ask them to play the note more sharply the following night.

If an actor hijacks a note session with general anxiety about the entire show or process, ask them to continue the conversation in a separate session with you.

Do not give notes immediately before the performance.

Establish the way in which you will note the show after the press night.

Rehearsals during your first few public performances

In most theatres you will be able to work with sound and lights for at least half the day on the performance days before the press night. During these rehearsals, try to combine practical technical work on the show with a note session with the actors.

Set aside the first half hour of the rehearsal so that the actors can give their feedback on the previous evening and tell you what they would like to look at just as you did after the first performance. Then spend the rest of the day working to a realistic list of practical goals. Make sure that this list includes key problems that the actors brought up in their note session. Do not rush things or try to squash an unrealistic number of things into a day. This will lead to a blurred show and will mean that you might need to rework things later on. It's better to work on one or two things properly and slowly than to slot in ten changes in a scrappy fashion. Make sure that your stage manager has a list of the things you want to look at so they can run the day efficiently for you.

Do the acting note session at the beginning or the end of the working day. Do this in the auditorium or foyer so that the stage can be used by your creative team for any technical work, such as focusing lights or testing out sound cues. This note session ensures that you keep the whole piece 'cooking', not just those moments you will have worked on during the day.

Summary
Combine practical technical work with a note session with the actors.
Do the acting note session at the beginning or end of the day away from the stage
  so that your creative team can use the stage for work.

Press night

Getting through this performance is first and foremost about fear management. Fear changes the tempo of a performance making it slower or faster depending on how the actors manage it. Fear prevents the actors from doing physical tasks – sometimes because they are literally shaking. It tightens the muscles in the throat making actors vocally less distinct and audible. These things, in turn, make actors self-conscious so that they start to feel like they are standing naked on a stage rather than being a particular character in a situation. This makes them behave in a stilted and lifeless manner. Very few actors perform on a press night without a trace of one or more of these symptoms. However, careful management of the day leading up to press night can reduce the problems and, in some cases, eradicate them.

Make the day of the press night feel like any other working day during the preview period. Keep to the same hours, perhaps starting one hour later so that the actors are rested. Work on any outstanding practical problems and give a proper note session. Reinforce the atmosphere of normality by letting them know you will be noting the show and fix a time for a note session on the following day. Your presence as a working director on the press night helps them normalise the day. Remind them that the press night is not the end of the process and inspire them with the idea that they are building the work for the audiences beyond the press night – for the one person whose life may be changed by watching a performance late on in the run.

The knowledge that critics will be present can lead to actors wanting to be 'impressive'. They therefore depart from what they have been doing and start to work independently from the rest of the group. Before press night I ask the actors to work together and to avoid solo flights. I also discourage the giving of cards, presents or flowers and ask them to defer this activity until the final performance. This will not suit every director, ensemble or theatre culture but it is worth discussing it with your actors to see if it helps them deal better with press night.

The reviews after the press night will have an effect on what the actors do – whether they read them or not. Their content always seeps out somehow and has an impact on the work, however inured to them actors may claim to be. If they are good, the actors may sit back and the work may slacken. If they are bad, the actors may lose heart and their commitment will flag. You need to respond robustly to either problem. Note them hard if they sit back, and give them a lot of reassurance if they lose heart. If the reviews are bad you will also have to see the work more often and inspire them to continue to develop what they are doing; this is especially the case if the reviews have a damaging effect on the box office.

I would advise you to take any criticism you receive about your work on the chin. If you are knocked back by it, sit down with all the reviews, read them calmly and see if there are any consistent misunderstandings of your intentions. Then see if you can direct the work a little more clearly to remove the misunderstandings. When I went through my reviews for *A Woman Killed With Kindness*, I realised that most of the critics thought that the floor was covered with sand, whereas I had intended them to think it was earth. I immediately made a change to the material we had put on the floor. I am not suggesting that you bow to the critics – rather, use the fact that they are looking at your work with 'fresh eyes' to see if they can teach you anything about how to make that work clearer for future audiences.

Make sure that you establish the way in which you will give notes after this press night. Let the actors know how often you are planning to come and discuss with them the best way of giving notes. You could give notes late afternoon in a two-hour note session or you could type the notes and leave them in the dressing room for them before the show.

Summary
Be aware that fear can distort the work you have made with the actors.
Plan a day's work on press night day that helps to alleviate this fear.
Never engage with a critic about what they have written.
Establish how you will give notes after the press night.

The run of performances from after the press night until the last night

Note your show regularly during its run so that the work remains at a high standard for all the people who will watch it. Sustaining the quality of the work is one of the hardest aspects of directing. Focus yourself on the task by remembering that audiences who see the work late in a run have paid the same money as those who saw it towards the beginning and are therefore entitled to expect the same standard of work.

After press night some part of you will want to walk away, rest and wash your hands of the work for a while – especially if it has been a difficult process or if the work has been badly received. Instead, visit the work regularly and look for the things that you can do to improve or develop the performance. See your visits as a process by which you can learn more about how to direct. The best way to do this is to watch the show that follows your note session. Study carefully the relationship between how you gave the note and how it is (or isn't) played. If the note is played clearly, remember what you said to the actor – your tone of voice and the words and images that you used. Similarly, notice if the actor played a note inaccurately and ask yourself: 'Was there anything I said which was not clear?' Improve how you note in response to your discoveries.

Remember that any show you make will become slack if you do not keep an eye on it. As a general rule watch the show once a week if it has a short run and once fortnightly if it has a longer run. The actors will often want you to stay away so that they can 'own the work'. Obviously director and actors do need some breathing space in their relationship from time to time, but balance this need with the purpose of keeping the work clear. Remember, too, that your job is not to please the actors; rather, you are ensuring the clarity of their work for the audiences.

After you have watched the show you can either call a two-hour note session on the following day or you can type your notes. If you call a note session, make sure you ask each person in turn to tell you briefly how the work has been developing or to identify any problems they are having. Then give your notes. Attending note sessions after press night can be difficult for some actors because of other work or family obligations; sometimes you have no choice except to type up your notes. Put all the actors' notes on the same document and make sure everyone has a copy. That way they can read other people's notes as well as their own and anticipate any possible changes. Let the actors know that the notes will be in their dressing room at a certain time so that they can come in to digest them well before the performance begins. Reassure them not to play any notes that are not clear and give them your number so that they can ring you to check up on the meaning of anything you have asked them to do.

Summary
Note your show regularly so that the standard of the work remains.
Sharpen your note-giving skills by watching the performance that follows a notes session.
Watch the show once a week if it is a short run and once fortnightly if it has a longer run. Accept that the actors will not always want you to watch the work regularly.
Give notes in a notes session or type them and leave them in the actors' dressing rooms before the show.

Analysing your work after the run has ended

The best way to develop as a director is to analyse your mistakes. When a production ends the first feeling you will experience will be relief that it is over. You will want to rest before anticipating the next production or looking for the next job. Before doing either, take an hour or so to reflect on what you have just done. Write down your observations and make sure you refer to them just before you embark on your next job. If you had a problem with an actor, think through the way in which that problem evolved. Look back at each stage of the process, including casting, and pinpoint anything you did which contributed to the problem. Take a mental note of this so that you avoid doing the same thing next time. If you were unhappy with the design, or lighting, or sound, track back through the steps of the process in an attempt to be specific about what you might have done differently. Consider the relationship between your preparation and the final outcome. Ask yourself whether you prepared well or not and whether you can improve aspects of your preparation for the next job.

Take note of any skill deficits and look for ways of filling in the gaps in your expertise. You could, for instance, attend workshops or master classes that cover your areas of weakness. Then recharge your batteries before the next job begins.

As you develop your skills in this way remember that there is no definitive, absolute or platonic solution to the staging of any text. Every decision a director makes about putting a play on involves an act of interpretation – to a greater or lesser degree. Some of these decisions are more 'legible' to an audience than others, such as the colour of costumes or the architectural period of a particular design element. Other decisions may be more subtle, such as choices about what the characters want at any given moment, or the temperature of the environment they are standing in. All the decisions you make add up to give the audience an impression of what the play is about. You could adhere strictly to every stage direction in the text, impose your own concept on the play, or relocate the action to the future. Whatever you do – or do not do – your signature will be there on the writer's play. It may be written faintly or boldly, but it will be legible to anyone watching. It is therefore important that all the choices you make, either with the actors or with your creative team, are carefully and finely crafted.

It will also help if you seek out productions or artists, either in your field or outside, by whom you measure yourself. I was 25 when I first saw the work of the Russian directors Lev Dodin and Anatoli Vassiliev, and yet I still find myself measuring what I do against the work I saw them make 19 years ago. And there are other artists, outside my field, such as the German dancer and choreographer Pina Bausch and the Polish avant-garde company Gardzienice, whose vision and genius set an impossibly high bar for what I do today.

The Oresteia by Aeschylus

PART FOUR

CONTEXT AND SOURCES

Endgame by Samuel Beckett

CHAPTER 14

How I learnt the skills the book describes

This part of the book describes how I came to learn the skills outlined and provides a context for the tasks covered in all the previous chapters. It will give you an idea of the artists and methodologies whose thinking and practice underpins this book. It contains four steps – landmarks in my own understanding of the craft:

> Stanislavsky
> **Lev Dodin teaches directing in Russia**
> Private directing classes in the UK
> Research into the biology of emotions

Stanislavsky

Konstantin Stanislavsky was born in Russia in 1863 and died in 1938. Although he started his career as an actor, he eventually began to direct his own productions. He set up the Moscow Art Theatre in 1897 with the playwright and producer Nemirovich-Danchenko and wrote several books about theatre-making, primarily acting. During his lifetime, Stanislavsky's work influenced theatre in his own country and abroad, most famously in America where his early work on emotional memory was built into a school of acting called 'The Method'. His later work on physical actions influenced the experiments of his contemporaries (such as Vsevolod Meyerhold) as well as the practice of avant-garde practitioners (such as Jerzy Grotowski) throughout the twentieth century. The revolution Stanislavsky led affected both mainstream Western theatre and its avant-garde. No practitioner since has had such a lasting and profound impact on the craft.

Stanislavsky's legacy has been much misunderstood ever since it first emerged in the late nineteenth century. It has also been revered in a way that deters a healthy questioning and criticism of some aspects of his practice. However, Stanislavsky's writings still outline an enormously useful and practical working process for people working in theatre now – especially directors.

When we talk about Stanislavsky in our rehearsal rooms today, we are not always talking strictly about the work he developed. His exercises and ideas have been modified, challenged and updated over time as they have been chewed over and experimented with by different practitioners from Augusto Boal in Brazil to Sam Kogan in London. Sometimes what comes down to us is based on Stanislavsky's own writings; sometimes it is, rather, Boal or Kogan's interpretation of Stanislavsky. Little attempt is made to differentiate between the two sources of our understanding of Stanislavsky – a situation that understandably leads to confusion.

As a result, many of the tools that directors use in rehearsal rooms, such as isolating the characters' intentions or building their biographies, bear little relationship, in both their description and their terminology, to Stanislavsky's work. Indeed, in some cases, what Stanislavsky taught and wrote about has been muddied or given an inaccurate tone through mistranslation. For example, we often use the word 'units' to talk about the way in which we divide a play up into small, manageable chunks. Stanislavsky himself used the Russian word '*kuski*', which translates as 'pieces', to describe these chunks. The word 'pieces' implies a consideration of a small part of a whole object, such as a china vase or marble statue. It is a simple term and easy to grasp. 'Unit' is a more scientific way of describing the same thing but it conjures up a cold and clinical picture of metal objects lying on a laboratory table. It does not give us a strong picture of the whole organism to which the 'unit' or 'piece' belongs. Its coldness and intellectualism can be off-putting for actors. Even the accents of teachers who first taught his work in the West caused confusion. You might be familiar with the Stanislavskian term 'beats', a word which has been used to describe the subdivisions of units. However, Stanislavsky himself never used this word. Instead he referred to these subdivisions as 'beads' (as in the beads a jeweller might thread together to make a necklace). Legend has it that Richard Boleslavsky, who taught Stanislavsky's system at the American Laboratory Theatre in the 1920s, had such a strong Polish accent that his students misheard the word 'bead' as 'beat'. It seems that we owe one of the most widely used terms of textual analysis in the Western theatrical tradition to an error in pronunciation.

There is not one single theory or system to Stanislavsky's work. Liberating yourself from a notion of Stanislavsky's work as a fixed, immovable system will help you to use what he has to offer more effectively. His methods were always changing because he had to develop and grow in response to concrete problems he encountered in his own working life. He constantly reinvented his working practice and, at times, contradicted himself as he rejected one way of working in favour of another. However, broadly speaking, his work divides into two parts. The first involved working 'from the inside out', using emotional memories from the actor's life to support the emotional world of the character. The second involved working 'from the outside in', using physical actions as a means of communicating emotion and character. He moved from asking the actors, 'What do you feel?' to asking 'What do you do?' I have found his later work on physical actions of more use in my own work than his earlier work on emotional memory. You will soon have noticed that the process I describe in this book emphasises 'doing' rather than 'feeling'.

Many people think that the exercises of a nineteenth-century Russian can only be used when working on a nineteenth-century Russian play. This is not the case. You can use Stanislavsky's techniques regardless of the style or genre of play or project you are working on. I have used them when working on Greek plays like *Iphigenia at Aulis*, new plays like Kevin Elyot's *Forty Winks*, abstract plays such as Martin Crimp's *Attempts on Her Life* or Samuel Beckett's *Footfalls*, and even operas. Remember that Stanislavsky did not only direct Realist plays. He also worked on Shakespeare, Jean Racine and symbolist plays like Knut Hamsun's *The Drama of Life* and Leonid Andreyev's *The Life of Man*. His work remains relevant whenever you find yourself directing a play containing characters who are members of the human race, regardless of the time period they inhabit or the style of the play they belong to.

By far the best introduction to Stanislavsky's work is Jean Benedetti's book, *Stanislavsky: An Introduction*, published by Methuen in 1982. It is only 80 pages long and lays out the tools and ideas Stanislavsky developed simply and clearly. Stanislavsky himself wrote three books: *Building a Character, Creating a Role* and *An Actor Prepares*. They are all worth reading, especially now that they were re-published in 2008 in a new translation, also by Benedetti. In this new publication by Routledge, Stanislavsky's first two volumes are conflated into a single book, called *An Actor's Work*.

Lev Dodin teaches directing in Russia

My first practical contact with Stanislavsky's legacy was in 1989 when I received a Winston Churchill Memorial Trust Fellowship to study directors' training in Eastern Europe. I spent a total of five months in Poland, Russia, Georgia and Lithuania, and I watched productions and directing classes in all the main drama schools and theatres. All the directing classes were led by practising directors. It was a first-year directing class led by Lev Dodin, the artistic director of the Maly Theatre in St Petersburg, that first introduced me to the almost scientific discipline of Stanislavsky's legacy. Lev Dodin trained with Boris Zon, who had himself studied with Stanislavsky.

Dodin was a dark, thick set, bearded man. As he entered the room all the students stood neatly in a line. They all wore black tights, black ballet pumps and figure-hugging black t-shirts. In Russia, directing students train for five years; during the first year they study acting, working their way through the basic steps of Stanislavsky's system. On this particular day, the students were showing a series of studies, or 'etudes' as they call them, based on events that could have happened to them in their everyday lives. They were allowed to use tables and chairs, but all the other objects they used were imaginary. The first student had chosen to enact an inhalation for a bad cold. Halfway through the exercise Dodin stopped him.

'What kind of flat is it?' asked Dodin

'My home,' replied the student.

'A private flat?'

'Yes.'

'Then why are you taking all the objects you need for the inhalation from the kitchen into the bedroom? Why don't you do your inhalation in the kitchen or bathroom where the necessary objects live? There is no logic in what you're doing. If you're ill what's the point in making all that movement? If you're really ill, you'd take the easiest and shortest way.'

'Now I remember why I did it in the bedroom. When I was ill there was someone in the bathroom and kitchen.'

'If that was the case then you have to show those circumstances.' Dodin paused and then asked: 'Why are you inhaling?'

'To get better.'

'What are you feeling?'

'Very hot, a bad headache and a sore throat.'

'But what kind of feeling does a man who has these symptoms have? You are unlucky because you are talking to a specialist. For days I have had a bad cold. Let's try and understand what feeling you are trying to overcome.'

'A feeling of effort.'

'Of course you have that physical sensation, but that's not the most painful and difficult thing. What is most painful and difficult is that you are almost another person. You feel you are nothing because you can't get up out of your bed and work. You are sweating, wet, taking pills. Why did you make the inhalation at all? You have to have a special kind of psychology to carry things back and forth when you are ill. If it were me I would have thought: "Shall I do this or shall I just sit in bed and take pills?" Also when you spat into the bowl, you did it as if you were on a stage. But when you spit when you're really ill, you do it differently. You did it as if you were performing for an audience, to show us you had a bad physical condition. You should, rather, be doing the action as you would in real life. Also the hot touch of the towel on your face was inaccurate. It did not seem to affect you. However when you do this your eyes water, your skin burns. We did not see this.'

The student remained silent. Then Dodin continued: 'What do you have on your feet?'

'Slippers.'

'What else are you wearing?'

The student described his clothes in detail and then Dodin began to challenge him about them: 'But you're going into a cold kitchen without putting on something warm. You're sweating. You should change your shirt because you would be wet through. In this etude you are supposed to be presenting a few minutes of real life that should occupy your entire body from the top of your head to the tip of your toes. One of the most unpleasant feelings of having a bad cold is when the tips of your hair become wet. When I say this I am not inventing something. I am trying to recall something that actually happened to me in life. This is what I want you to do. Now do the exercise again.'

The disheartened student started to do his exercise again. He sat on the bed and hugged his knees to his chest. Dodin stopped him immediately.

'You are wrong already. Think a little. You have a fever and, as you're not able to overcome the fever, the body starts to relax into it. You have a high temperature and because of this you cannot think clearly. The thoughts going from your brain to your limbs – arms, legs, feet – move more slowly. When you are healthy you do not feel your body, but when you are ill you begin to feel it. Now continue.'

At this point the student really began to suffer. I could see him blushing and trying to fight back his embarrassment as he worked. Dodin interjected: 'Don't be in a hurry. When you're ill you're not in a hurry.'

The student tried to slow down. He lay down on the bed and tried to sleep. Then he opened his eyes. At this point Dodin interrupted: 'Is it dark or light in the room?'

'It's daylight.'

'Are you feeling comfortable or not? There has to be some kind of logic in what you're doing. At the moment it is not clear if it is daylight or night time. This circumstance will affect what you do. Also remember that all the time you're thinking about something.'

The student starts the exercise again by picking up a book. Dodin stops him. 'Reading a book is the most conventional way of starting an etude.'

Again the student had to start, but again and again he was stopped and noted by Dodin. This grilling continued for about an hour.

To begin with I found it a cruel process. As it went on, I realised that it was the only way to teach the level of detail that Dodin wanted – externally and internally. The precision that he demanded from his student was awe-inspiring – not least because it required an intense level of observation and concentration from Dodin himself. I saw that he could read thoughts and actions with equal accuracy. I envied him that skill and it became something that I aimed to develop in my own work. There was something scientific about his insistence on the logic of the action, and this too has stayed with me as a way of analysing and building scenes. I also realised that his main interest was behaviour and not words. Finally, and most importantly, I noticed that nothing he said was vague – all his notes were concrete and specific. This was the essential lesson that I took from his rather chilling class, and it has provided me with a touchstone in my work with actors ever since. It is the guiding principle behind the tools and tasks that this book outlines.

Private directing classes in the UK

My contact with the way of working described in the previous section was renewed ten years later when I started private classes to improve my directing. These classes were built around my professional directing schedule. I had two teachers: Tatiana Olear and Elen Bowman. Tatiana trained as an actor with Lev Dodin at the Leningrad State Institute of Theatre, Music and Film, and then performed with his company for six years before leaving to live in Italy. Elen trained as an actress at the Royal Academy of Dramatic Art in London, then as a director for three years under the Russian émigré Sam Kogan at the School of the Science of Acting in London, before pursuing a career as a director. Sam Kogan himself had trained at GITIS in Moscow, and (like Anatoli Vassiliev) his teacher was Maria Knebel, who had been taught by Stanislavsky himself.

Both Tatiana and Elen taught a variation of the Stanislavsky system. Their over-riding aim was the search for a simple and effective language with which to talk to the actor and communicate with the audience. The main difference between the two women was the result of Sam Kogan's training. He had worked as a psychiatric nurse in Russia and, because of this, he had developed a unique strand to his work that entailed a deeper scrutiny of the mental processes going on in the actors' and characters' minds.

This book contains many of the exercises these women taught me. I owe them both a great deal as they showed me how to use Stanislavsky's work simply and clearly in a rehearsal room. They also provided me with links back to Dodin, Kogan and, through them, to Stanislavsky. It made me feel part of a chain of practitioners, each sharpening tried-and-tested tools against their culture and time.

Research into the biology of emotions

The final development in my understanding of Stanislavsky took place in 2003 when I was studying his later work on physical actions as part of a Fellowship from the National Endowment for Science, Technology and the Arts. While researching Stanislavsky, I came across a reference to a leading nineteenth-century philosopher, William James. In 1884 James had written an essay called 'What is an Emotion?' that had apparently influenced Stanislavsky's later practice. James had made a crucial observation about emotions: when we are in a life-threatening situation we react physically first and then become conscious of the meaning of that physical reaction. He used the example of a response to meeting a bear in a forest to make his point. Before James it was believed if you saw a bear, you would feel frightened and then run away. James observed something different. He noticed that we see the bear and we turn and run; only then do we realise that we are afraid.

At first glance this is a minuscule alteration. However, for theatre practitioners, whose business is the accurate embodiment and transmission of human emotions, it is potentially huge. Here is a way of looking at emotions that separates off the physical response from consciousness and the mental processes that follow this moment of consciousness. It points to a way of working on emotions through recreating their physical shape or circumstances. I could see how James's observations might have affected Stanislavsky's work on physical actions in the 1890s, but I wondered whether they would hold water today, and therefore whether it would be of concrete use in making theatre now.

These questions led me to the work of Antonio Damasio. Damasio is a Portuguese American neuroscientist who writes about consciousness. His book entitled *The Feeling of What Happens* studies emotions as a means of understanding consciousness. I discovered that the observations about human emotion made by William James over 100 years ago have not yet been discarded by neuroscience – although with modern brain-imaging techniques a fuller and more complex picture of how emotions work has emerged.

Damasio, like James, argues that an emotion consists primarily of a visible change in the body. This change is legible in our facial expressions, tone of voice, posture and even our internal bodily processes. There is a gap of about half a second between a stimulus (seeing a bear in the forest) and becoming conscious of an emotion (fear). By the time we are conscious of what is actually happening to us, we would have run several metres away from the bear. The definition of an emotion as a physical change, and the half-second delay between stimulus and consciousness of the emotion, provided me with a new way of working on emotions with actors. I started to test-run these ideas with actors in a series of workshops as part of my NESTA Fellowship.

In our exercises, James's observation of the delayed recognition of emotion stood up to our practical scrutiny. I also realised that actors tend to enact a slightly more discreet and tasteful version of emotions on stage compared with what actually happens in life. This discovery became a critical point of reference in my work with actors and radically altered how I directed emotions. I began to identify gestures and actions that were about romantic theatrical conventions and not true to life, and began to weed them out of the actors' work. It was also sobering to find out that there is part of the brain which is dedicated to recognising emotions in other people and that we gather information about other people by 'reading' their bodies. If, when representing emotions on stage, we were to miss out vital physical steps in the expression of an emotion, then the emotion might not be legible to the audience. I realised that they can only read what is happening *inside* someone by what they see on the *outside*.

As a result of these discoveries my relationship to the audience radically changed. It was no longer essential for the actors to feel the emotions; now what mattered was that the audience felt them. What was essential was that the actors replicated them precisely with their bodies. They could do this either from the inside, by recalling the emotion (by remembering a time in their own lives when they experienced the same thing), or from the outside, by an almost clinical reconstruction of what the body does when a particular emotion hits it. These discoveries crystallised my understanding of Stanislavsky's interest in physical actions. I realised that his practice had endured because he was articulating some fundamental physical truths. The physiology of emotions replaced psychology as my key point of reference for talking about – and working on – acting.

Glossary

The entries in bold type are the terms that you will first encounter as you move from the rehearsal room to the theatre.

Actuals: the props that will be used in the show as opposed to stand-ins (see below).

Affinity: the subjective connections that draw you to certain elements of a play or a particular character because they relate to your own life or how you look at the world.

Audience thinking: the thoughts that actors have about the audience that get in the way of them playing a character in a situation.

Band call: the time that the composer and/or music director spends with the sound technician checking that the sound from the music played live is well balanced – whether the band is visible or hidden in a band room (see below).

Band room or box: an acoustically sealed room in which live music is played and relayed to the theatre.

Beginners: five minutes before the show starts.

Blocking: the arrangement of actors on the stage so that the action, events and key story points are visible and focused.

The book: a copy of the script in which the stage management write down all the moves that the actors make and, when you get into the theatre, where all the lighting and sound cues are notated. The deputy stage manager cues the lighting and sound operators from this script. It is not supposed to leave the theatre.

The box: the small soundproofed room or booth or area that the deputy stage manager sits in to cue the show.

Call or rehearsal call: the plan for the rehearsal day. In most large theatres this plan is drawn up on an A4 sheet of paper and posted around the building the day before the rehearsals it describes. It is also called a 'call sheet'.

Changeover: the process by which one set is removed from the theatre and another one installed if two or more plays are performed in repertoire with each other.

Emotional memory: a phrase used by Stanislavsky to describe the recalling of a real emotion from an actor's life that can be used to underpin or articulate what a character feels in the action of a play.

Events: the moments in an act or scene when something changes. The change is visible because the characters alter what they are doing.

Fit-up: the period in which the set is built on the stage of the theatre.

The five: ten minutes before the show.

Flats: these are freestanding screens which you can move around the rehearsal room to create different spaces. The word could also be used to refer to screens used back-stage or to the pieces of wood which fit together to make the imaginary walls of a room or building.

Flies: the area above the stage in which screens, scenic elements or lights can be flown in and out.

Focus session: the process by which each light is hung in the correct place on the rig and pointed in the right direction for the show. The director does not need to attend this.

Genre: the style a play is written in.

Get-in: the technical time allocated to installing the set, rigging the lights and preparing the sound.

Get-out: the technical time allocated to taking the set out of the theatre and derigging the sound and lights.

Ground plan: plan of how the set design fits into the footprint of the theatre space.

The half: a stage management term used to refer to the point 35 minutes before the show begins.

The house: another name for the audience sitting in the auditorium.

Immediate circumstances: the events that happen in the 24 hours or so leading up to the action of a scene. They might include what happened a couple of minutes prior to the action or the events of the night before. They have a direct impact on the action and give the actors something concrete to play.

An impression: the information that you derive from a reading of a line or a section of a play that contains no obvious facts.

Intentions: a term used to describe what the character wants and from whom.

Lighting desk: the table or board on which the board and screen which programme and operate the lights are placed. In a technical rehearsal it normally sits on a temporary table in the auditorium. During the run it goes into a sound-sealed booth from which the lighting operator runs the show.

Mark-up: a way of notating the set design. The mark-up is a series of lines marked on the floor of the rehearsal room with plastic tape indicating the boundaries of the landscape or architecture that the set describes.

Media server: the machine that processes live or recorded images. The media server grades or treats the images so that they can appear to be brighter or darker than the input material, and is capable of turning a colour image into a sepia or black and white image.

Meet-and-greet: a gathering of the people involved in a rehearsal process with everyone else who works for the theatre where the production is being staged.

Model showing: the showing of the finished model during the rehearsal process. The main aims of the model showing are to imprint a clear picture of the places where the action of the play will occur (the set design) on the actors' imagination and to share the ideas for the production with everyone else in the theatre or company involved in putting on the play.

Paint job: the process by which the set design is painted.

Paint shop: the room where the sets are painted (not where the paints are bought).

Pallet: a sliding platform that the scenic element of the set design can be built on.

Plotting session: the process by which sound and lights are mixed to create the sounds or lighting states for the actual show. The director needs to attend these sessions. They take place in the theatre without the actors.

Practical light: the lights on the set which are visible to the audience, such as chandeliers, standard lamps or desk lights.

Press night: the night when the reviewers come to review the performance.

Previews: the first few public performances before press night.

The quarter: 20 minutes before the show.

Quiet time: the time in the theatre given over to sound or music to work on cues.

Read-through: the moment early on in rehearsals in which the play is read by the actors for the first time.

Rig: the process by which a flying scenic element is put up.

The rig: the network of bars that the lights hang on.

Set back: a term used during a technical rehearsal meaning to get everything ready to start again.

Sightline: the 'invisible' boundaries which mark the area of the stage that every member of the audience can see.

Sound check: the process by which the sound designer or technician checks that all the speakers are working. The director does not need to attend this session.

Sound desk: a table or board where the sound equipment is placed. This equipment often sits in the auditorium for a technical rehearsal and is then relocated to a booth where the sound operator sits during a performance.

Stage weights: the heavy solid metal squares, about six inches wide, which are used to prop up the legs of a freestanding screen or provide ballast for any object or scenic element that needs to be secure or freestanding.

Stand-ins: the props that are standing in for the actual things ('actuals' – see above) the actors will use in the show.

Strike: the word used to describe the process of taking down the set that is in the theatre.

Tech or techs: the shorthand terms for the technical rehearsals.

Tempo: the overall speed at which a character or person thinks and does things.

Trigger event: the event before the action of the play begins that sets that action in motion.

White balance: the process of putting white paper in front of the camera lens in order to balance the colours when using live video as part of the performance.

White card model: a sketch model of the set design that is made of white card. It is not painted and generally has very little information about colour, texture or architectural details.

The Oresteia by Aeschylus

Index

Page numbers in *italics* denotes an illustration

Phedre 90

place 20–4; facts and questions about 21–2; feedback on 148; and first scene rehearsal 175; introducing of to actors in rehearsals 147–9, 166; maps and images of circles of 22–3, 78, 134; simple exercise in 147–8

play: affinity with 3–4; analysis of action in 53–67; dividing up of by use of events 56; ideas that underpin 47–9; introducing of to actors 132; reading of 3–5, 9–10, 19–20

plotting sessions 199; lighting 205–7; music and sound 207–8

practical work 142; on character and character tempo 159–61, 167; on emotions 154–6, 167; on ideas 150–4, 167

preparation 2, 9–112; analysing action of the play 53–67; answering difficult questions about text 19–20; back history list compilation 12–15, 31, 34, 77; building relationship with production team 75–97; casting 99–103; and character biographies 24–30, 68, 70; character work 68–74; events happening between scenes/acts 36–9; and immediate circumstances 31–6, 40; investigating the big ideas of the play 44–51; and layout of your directing script 53–4; organisation of early responses to text 11–30; organising information about each scene 31–43; and place 20–4; and rehearsal environment 106–12; research 15–19; and time 40–3; workshops 103–5

press night 197, 218–19

production manager 111

production meetings 111, 189

production team *see* creative team

projection screens 92

props 107, 112; introducing to actors in rehearsals 138

proscenium configuration 80

public performances 197, 213–22; analysing your work after run has ended 221–2; early 213–15; note sessions after shows 214–17, 220; and press night 218–19; rehearsals during first few 217–18; run of from after press night until last night 220–1

'quiet time' 207–8

read-through 133–4, 136

reading of text 3–5, 9–10, 19–20

realism genre 50

rehearsal day: dividing up of 142–3; structuring of 173–4, 192

rehearsal notes 110, 111

rehearsal room 107, 108–12; and blackout facilities 138–9; establishing of communication systems 110–11; getting ready 112; and lighting 109, 138–9; managing transition to theatre from 200–3; organising culture of 107; selection of 108–10; sitting in 131–2

rehearsals 115–92; and actors *see* actors; building good stage management team 106–8; building the world of the play 141–68; during first few public performances 217–18; establishing the language of your process 125–7, 152–3, 201; first day of 133–6; first scene 174–8, 192; giving feedback to actors 119, 127–31, 176; introducing key ingredients to actors 138–9, 200–1; introducing text to actors 132; managing of fear 133, 135; managing final days 18; meet-and-greet session 135, 136; and model showing 136–7; preparing of environment 106–12; and read-through 133–4, 136; and run-throughs 185–7, 192, 201; second and third 192; second and third scene 181–5; working on the scenes of the play 169–92; *see also* dress rehearsal; technical rehearsals